THE EVERYTHING.
MAFIA BOOK
2nd Edition

Dear Reader,

Let's face it: America likes gangsters. It always has. The public fascination with the criminal element has been part of pop culture for decades. And no matter how much is written or filmed about the mob, people are intrigued. There are literally thousands of Mafia stories to be told, and each passing year brings more and more to the theater, TV screen, and bookstore.

What I tried to do in this book was to highlight some of the more notorious figures and events in the history of the Mafia in the United States. Accuracy is something that can be elusive when dealing with the Mafia. They are, after all, supposed to be a secret organization. Bringing together the latest research in a readable fashion was my goal. I also wanted to look at some of the lesser-known figures. The Mafia was far more than John Gotti and Al Capone, though their importance merits chapters dedicated to each.

So sit back, turn on some Frank Sinatra, and enjoy.

Scott Deitche

Welcome to the EVERYTHING® Series!

These handy, accessible books give you all you need to tackle a difficult project, gain a new hobby, comprehend a fascinating topic, prepare for an exam, or even brush up on something you learned back in school but have since forgotten.

You can choose to read an *Everything*® book from cover to cover or just pick out the information you want from our four useful boxes: e-questions, e-facts, e-alerts, and e-ssentials. We

give you everything you need to know on the subject, but throw in a lot of fun stuff along the way, too.

We now have more than 400 *Everything*® books in print, spanning such wide-ranging categories as weddings, pregnancy, cooking, music instruction, foreign language, crafts, pets, New Age, and so much more. When you're done reading them all, you can finally say you know *Everything*®!

QUESTIONS?
Answers to
common questions

FACTS
Important snippets
of information

ALERTS!
Urgent
warnings

ESSENTIALS
Quick
handy tips

PUBLISHER Karen Cooper

DIRECTOR OF ACQUISITIONS AND INNOVATION Paula Munier

MANAGING EDITOR, EVERYTHING SERIES Lisa Laing

COPY CHIEF Casey Ebert

ACQUISITIONS EDITOR Lisa Laing

SENIOR DEVELOPMENT EDITOR Brett Palana-Shanahan

EDITORIAL ASSISTANT Hillary Thompson

Visit the entire Everything® series at *www.everything.com*

THE EVERYTHING®
MAFIA
BOOK
2nd Edition

True-life accounts of legendary figures,
infamous crime families, and nefarious deeds

Scott M. Deitche

Avon, Massachusetts

To my family

An Everything® Series Book.
Everything® and everything.com® are registered trademarks of F+W Media, Inc.

Published by Adams Media, a division of F+W Media, Inc.
57 Littlefield Street, Avon, MA 02322 U.S.A.
www.adamsmedia.com

ISBN 10: 1-59869-779-X
ISBN 13: 978-1-59869-779-7

Printed in the United States of America.

J I H G F E D C B A

Library of Congress Cataloging-in-Publication Data
is available from the publisher.

This publication is designed to provide accurate and authoritative information with regard to the subject matter covered. It is sold with the understanding that the publisher is not engaged in rendering legal, accounting, or other professional advice. If legal advice or other expert assistance is required, the services of a competent professional person should be sought.

—From a *Declaration of Principles* jointly adopted by a Committee of the American Bar Association and a Committee of Publishers and Associations

Many of the designations used by manufacturers and sellers to distinguish their products are claimed as trademarks. Where those designations appear in this book and Adams Media was aware of a trademark claim, the designations have been printed with initial capital letters.

This book is available at quantity discounts for bulk purchases.
For information, please call 1-800-289-0963.

Contents

Acknowledgments

I want to thank UTC for setting me up with this project. I also want to thank Gina Panettieri for getting the ball rolling and making things happen. Thanks to Lisa Laing at Adams Media for all the guidance. I want to also give a blanket thanks to all the researchers, writers, law enforcement personnel, wise guys, librarians, mob historians, and Mafia forum members who have given me information and material over the years. It all came in handy on this project.

Organization of a Mafia Family

The Commission
(made up of bosses of five families)

Boss (or don)

Consigliere (adviser to don)

Underboss

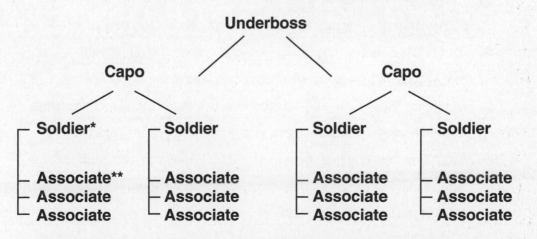

Capo

Capo

| Soldier* | Soldier | Soldier | Soldier |

Associate**	Associate	Associate	Associate
Associate	Associate	Associate	Associate
Associate	Associate	Associate	Associate

*There may be as many as ten soldiers under one capo.
**There can be any number of associates under a soldier.

Top Ten Gangsters You Will Get to Know After Reading This Book

1. Sam Giancana—the boss of the Chicago Outfit who was recruited by the CIA to help assassinate Fidel Castro.

2. Al Capone—who rose to fame as a bootlegger during Prohibition and became the most recognizable mobster ever.

3. Salvatore "Lucky" Luciano—the visionary mobster who turned the old Mustache Pete–led crime syndicate into the American Mafia.

4. Carlos Marcello—the mob boss who ruled New Orleans for decades and may have been involved in the assassination of President Kennedy.

5. John Gotti—the mob boss turned pop culture icon who ascended to the top spot after a spectacular Christmas time hit on his boss.

6. Joe Bonanno—the 1920s era don who lived longer than any of his contemporaries.

7. Henry Hill—a mob stoolie who was made famous in the movies, but still got into trouble after testifying against his old mob brethren.

8. Albert "Mad Hatter" Anastasia—a mobster who ruled his crime family with an iron fist, until a haircut and shave ended his life.

9. Benjamin "Bugsy" Siegel—a mobster who transformed Las Vegas from a small-time gambling town to a world-class high-roller paradise.

10. Carlo Caputo—the mob boss of Madison, Wisconsin. Never heard of him? You will, along with dozens of other lesser-known wise guys who lived in the shadows and stayed out of the papers.

Introduction

▶ AMERICA HAS BEEN OBSESSED with the Mafia since anti-hero gangsters first appeared onscreen during Hollywood's early years. The tales of crime and corruption were anchored by electric performances by larger-than-life actors like James Cagney and Edgar G. Robinson. From there, movies, television, and books cemented the popular iconic image of the mobster in America's collective psyche. But for all the fiction and myths that have emerged about wise guys, nothing can compare to the truth.

Much to the detriment of the overwhelming majority of Italian Americans, the Mafia dominated organized crime throughout most of the twentieth century by clawing their way up from the crowded slums of ethnic enclaves in cities across America. They fought and partnered with Jewish, Irish, Cuban, and Polish gangs. They enveloped different Italian crime groups in turn-of-the-century America. They brought in other ethnic mobsters and set up strategic alliances with global transnational crime groups at the dawn of the twenty-first century.

The gangsters got their leg up by corrupting the police, judges, and politicians. They had a ready army of lawyers for court cases, doctors who didn't ask too many questions when you brought in a bullet-riddled body for an operation, and accountants to make sure their ill-gotten gains stayed as far away form Uncle Sam's hands as possible.

The Mafia had their hands in narcotics trafficking, prostitution, loan-sharking, bookmaking, policy rackets, stolen property, chop shops, pornography, unions, construction, waste management, stocks scams, bank fraud, mail fraud, murder-for-hire, calling cards, counterfeit merchandise, securities thefts, hijacking, safe crackings, bank robberies, and about every other crime—both big and small—that you can think of.

Of course, there was the money and all the trappings that came with it—power, glory, women, and excess. Some mobsters flaunted their wealth, being chauffeured around in fancy new cars, wearing $3,000 suits with Rolex watches. Others took a different route, driving beat-up clunkers and wearing T-shirts to weddings. But all the money and power brought threats. Murder was a way to keep soldiers in line, settle personal vendettas, clean house, rise through the ranks, deflect blame, get rid of witnesses, and settle intragang wars.

The Mafia's dominance of organized crime also brought increased scrutiny from law enforcement. In the beginning few cops looked at the Mafia as an enterprise. It wasn't until after the infamous Apalachin incident that the FBI finally started viewing the mob as a national-level syndicate with outposts in over twenty-five cities across the country. The 1960s brought about a sea of change in law enforcement's efforts against the Mafia. And the general population was tiring of the increased crime, political corruption, theft of their tax dollars, and the mob wars that left many innocent bystanders the victims of violence. Wiretapping came into vogue, as did the increased use of informants and turncoats. The Racketeer Influenced and Corrupt Organizations (RICO) Act gave officials new power to prosecute the mob at a federal level.

But even with forty-plus years of intense law enforcement pressure the Mafia still exists. The smaller families in cities like Dallas, Denver, and St. Louis have for the most part died out. Midlevel gangs like those in Philly, Pittsburgh, and Kansas City still have active crews, though much smaller now than during their heydays. The big families like the five families in New York City and the Chicago Outfit are on weaker legs, but still exert influence over a variety of criminal enterprises.

In this book you'll learn more about some of the biggest names in mob history as well as the names of some of the lesser-known characters—every bit as dangerous, but not fodder for the evening news. You'll also get a peak inside the structure of a Mafia family, its arcane rules, and its colorful colloquialisms. You'll read about the Mafia's alleged role in the Kennedy assassination and learn about emerging crime groups around the world. Many of the old Mafia myths are shattered and new truths are revealed.

CHAPTER 1

A Beginner's Guide

Crime has been around since the dawn of humankind, and organized crime has been around almost as long. Ever since humans, social animals by nature, banded together in primitive tribal associations, there have always been rogue elements that banded together in the shadows to prey on the rest of the pack. From these primal bands of men rose the Mafia, known throughout the world due not just for its criminal prowess but also for its role in popular culture.

The Culture of Crime

As long as there have been societies there have been secret societies within them. Many of these had a criminal element that thought it was a better arrangement to steal from the hard-working members of the culture than to work for a living. For much of ancient history, the predominant criminal was the bandit. Gangs of bandits terrorized the countryside of every land, stopping weary travelers and merchants transporting their wares. The organization of these crime families was for the most part fairly simple. One alpha male ruled the roost. The less macho types followed him, and occasionally an up-and-coming bandit challenged and defeated the leader. If he bested the bandit leader, he was then the top dog.

FACT

Organized crime needs collaborators to thrive. As long as there has been political and governmental structure, there has been corruption. The underworld needs, and always finds, help from the "overworld" to pursue its illegal endeavors. In the early years criminals bribed kings, feudal lords, and knights.

Roving Gangs

The bandit gangs did not live by a code. Fear and control were the only methods employed by the bandit leaders. It was essential for the leader to instill fear in the rest of the bandit gang. Through fear the leader maintained control. Intimidation and the threat of bodily harm and/or death were the ways that a bandit leader stayed in power. Of course, the communities the bandits preyed upon lived in a constant state of fear.

One Man's Bandit . . .

There is a popular argument that has been made over the years that "one man's bandit is another man's freedom fighter." It is true that there have been many tyrannical governments over the millennia and that people have taken up arms against their oppressors many times in the history of the world. Legends like Robin Hood and the movie and television adventures of Zorro always capture the imagination of people. These are archetypes of the crusading hero against social injustices.

The Mafia's PR Campaign

The Mafia has tried to use this argument as a public relations tool on occasion. The Sicilian Mafia is said to have begun as a ragtag band of freedom fighters who took refuge in the rocky hills, often swooping down to attack the many conquerors in that island's long history. Al Capone tried to paint himself as a maverick rebel who was providing a service that an oppressive government tried to deny the people (a drink during Prohibition). He said he was simply giving the people what they wanted. John Gotti took the dashing rebel against society to the extreme, becoming a pop culture icon in the process.

ALERT!

Some things never change. The alleged efforts of the Russian Mafia to influence the judges at the 2002 Winter Olympics is nothing new. Similar corruption occurred at the ancient Greek Olympics. In those days it was considered "impiety," a crime against the gods, and punishable by death.

Mafia . . . What's in a Word

The Mafia has its origins on the island of Sicily, which is off the coast of Italy in the Mediterranean Sea. The island has had a tumultuous and turbulent history that proved to be fertile soil for an underworld crime structure to take root. From small towns and villages rose one of the most powerful criminal organizations in the history of the world.

Al Capone

Courtesy of AP Images

▲ Al Capone photographed at a football game in Chicago on January 19, 1931. Capone always wore a loud tie, a bent-brim fedora hat, and a camel hair polo coat and always had an entourage of bodyguards.

Where the Word Mafia Comes From

The exact origins of the word Mafia are not clear. There are some historians who claim the name derives from ancient Arabic word, *mu afyiah*, meaning "swagger." This may be a result of the Moorish occupation of Sicily.

Other noted experts claim the word comes from popular culture and plays about criminality in Sicily. By the mid-1870s police were using the term to describe criminal bandits based out of Sicily. Although the term *Mafia* is Sicilian in origin, it now denotes any type of criminal organization. The term is rather loosely defined, hence Elvis Presley and his "Memphis Mafia."

There is a school of thought that places the origin of the name Mafia as being an acronym of the phrase *Morte Alla Francia, Italia Anela*, meaning "Death to the French is Italy's Cry." It was a popular rallying cry during the French occupation of the island.

The Old Country

Sicily's history is one of occupation. The native inhabitants were called *Siculi*, and it is believed that they came over to the island from southern Italy. This was in the mists of prehistory, before the time when written records were chiseled into stone or scratched onto papyrus. These Siculi, sometimes called the *Sicani*, were subject to an almost nonstop parade of invading armies and rulers for over 1,000 years.

Ripe for Invasion

The first known new residents of the island were the Greeks and Phoenicians who took up residence on the island, from approximately 734 to 580 B.C. Next came the Carthaginians, who arrived on the island and waged war with the Greeks for supremacy. They battled it out for many decades, and control changed hands more than once.

The mighty Romans conquered Sicily. The Roman reign was the longest, lasting several hundred years until their empire fell. Then came the Vandals. These invaders killed many citizens and enslaved the rest. Afterward the Saracens, a group of Arabs who practiced the newly established religion of Islam, attacked and occupied the island. In the late Middle Ages and the Renaissance, the Spanish and French were in control of the island for various periods of time.

The native Sicilians, who came over from Italy before recorded history, never had control of their island homeland. This constant subjugation made the people insular, clannish, and suspicious. This climate allowed the secret society that became the Mafia to germinate and grow.

As an island nation, Sicily did much more than give birth to the Mafia. Celebrities like Sonny Bono, Martin Scorcese, Frank Sinatra, Al Pacino, Rachael Ray, Frank Zappa, Joe Montana, Joe DiMaggio, and Tony Danza all trace their roots back to Sicily.

Vive La France

The French were in control of the island when the Mafia as we know it came to be. It is natural for oppressed peoples to form secret societies. In Sicily, the native men banded together in groups to discuss their situation and their plans to fight their oppressors. In all tyrannies, freedom of assembly is forbidden and punishable by imprisonment or worse. The oppressors know that, as the old saying goes, "in unity there is strength," and therefore they cannot safely allow the oppressed to join together for fear of losing their power over them. But the oppressed population often does manage to come together in a clandestine manner.

The Sicilian dialect, while basically an offshoot of Italian, also has strong Greek and Arabic influences, since these cultures occupied Sicily for a time, usually as unwelcome guests.

The secret societies that formed against the oppressive invaders also battled pirates, bandits, and assorted outlaws that plagued the peasants. Some of these men were brave and patriotic and became heroes of the people.

The legend is that they became real-life Robin Hoods, battling the French invaders and instilling a national pride in a conquered people. They had gained power by fighting for the oppressed peoples of the island against a common enemy—the French.

You Need Some Protection

The Mafia's first foray into moneymaking was when it began to extort money from the very people it purported to protect. People would receive courtly and politely written letters "requesting" money for protection. The gimmick was that the money was protection from the group that sent the letter. If the recipients did not pay up, they could expect a violent response. Family members might be kidnapped and held for ransom. Their house could be set ablaze and destroyed. They might even be killed. People lived in terror that one of these notes would be slipped under their door.

The "Black Hand" was an early group of Italian criminals. It was called that for the gang's penchant for slipping a politely written note under people's doors asking them in a nice way to pay a fee to avoid being killed. The note was not signed, but instead was stamped with an inked image of the caller's hand.

Political Power

The Sicilian Mafia continued to gain power, prestige, and influence in all aspects of the island's culture and political establishment. By 1876 the Mafia chieftain Don Raffaele Palizzolo was elected to the Sicilian Parliament. He arranged for his handpicked men to become prime minister and director of the National Bank. This commingling of Mafia and politics is a tradition that has never stopped. As you will see in later chapters, the American Mafia has been a behind-the-scenes player in American politics, allegedly influencing at least one presidential election.

The Omerta Code

Omerta was the tradition in which young men were initiated into the secret society of the Mafia. It evolved into the modern Mafia tradition of Mafiosi being "made," that is, when they are allowed into the inner sanctum of the Mafia family. One of the requirements for membership in the modern Mafia family is to have killed someone or to have participated in a murder, even if the initiate isn't the one who pulls the trigger.

Ancient Wisdom

The code of the modern Mafia harks back to the Old-World traditions of the ancient Sicilian culture. In addition to the vow of Omerta, a second element of the Mafia code is a vow of total devotion and loyalty to the head of the family, or don. This comes from the ancient traditions of royalty and the divine right of kings. Among royalty, the clever kings determined that there could be no dissent or challenge of the monarch, because it was God's will that the king was on the throne.

FACT

The Sicilians go by the name Mafia, but there are actually three other crime groups on the mainland of Italy: the Calabrian *'ndrangheta*, the Neapolitan *Camorra*, and the Pugliese *Sacra Corona Unita*.

Another source of the Mafia tradition of total obedience to the don was the feudal system. This medieval social structure had a feudal lord in his castle lording over the peasant class. Serfs, as the peasants were called, worked the land and delivered the majority of the produce to the castle while they kept just enough for themselves to eat. This medieval tradition is carried on in the modern Mafia, where the people on the lower rungs of the hierarchy work for the good of those above them.

A third code of the Sicilian Mafia was the duty to offer help to anyone "in the family" that was in need and any person or group with close ties to the Mafia that needs assistance. The fierce loyalty to friends and equally fierce hostility to any outsiders is a cornerstone of both the Old-World and New-World Mafia.

The fourth code followed by the Mafia is the obligation to seek vengeance against anyone who attacks a member of the family. In its very insular unity, the Sicilian Mafia took an assault on one member of the family as an attack on the family as a whole. The Old-World term for this is vendetta. The Sicilians took it to an extreme that the American Mafia did not. The Sicilian Mafia would slaughter the entire families of anyone who offended them.

This is something the American Mafia did not do. In fact, they prided themselves for "only killing their own," and anyone who violated that rule would be killed. The Sicilian Mafia of the nineteenth century are akin to the vicious Colombian drug cartels of the later twentieth century who routinely and ruthlessly wiped out the entire families, including the small children and babies, of their enemies.

The fifth code of the Sicilian Mafia is that its members must avoid interaction with the authorities. They could bribe corrupt policemen and crooked politicians, even intimidate and kill them, but they were not allowed to socialize with them.

CHAPTER 2

Mafia . . . The Prequel

Organized crime's rise in America can be traced to the large influx of immigrants at the turn of the twentieth century. While 99 percent of all immigrants were law-abiding, there was a small but influential group that chose a life of crime. They came from the slums and teeming streets of poverty. While others rose through hard work, the early gangsters rose through crime, oftentimes at the expense of their own neighbors and friends. From these early gangs, the Mafia rose, bribing and killing its way to the top of the crime heap.

The Immigrant Experience

In the 1860s there was a wave of immigration to America from Italy and Sicily, and an even larger one in the 1890s. While some immigrants came through cities like New Orleans and Los Angeles, an overwhelming majority of them took their first look at America by gazing up at the Statue of Liberty and the neighboring Ellis Island. It was through the immigration office at Ellis that millions of Italian Americans' ancestors came through processing and on their way to Cleveland, Pittsburgh, Tampa, or Newark. There they settled into tight-knit ethnic enclaves. "Little Italys" sprang up across the country, letting the newcomers enjoy the comforts of their birthplace while making their way in their adopted homeland.

The Gangs of New York

The Five Points slum was a bad place. Not only was it a vermin-infested den of squalor, but it was also the breeding ground for thousands of thieves, pickpockets, prostitutes, con men, extortionists, and murderers. But even though the area was notorious, it was home to teeming masses of new immigrants and those not wealthy enough to move further "uptown" to more affluent neighborhoods. It was a place where bloodlines were forged as gangs battled each other for control—and it produced some of the most infamous gangsters in American history.

The Gangs in Film

Martin Scorsese's movie *The Gangs of New York* was actually based on a 1928 book by Herbert Asbury. The sensationalist book detailed the lives and crimes of the early gangsters who lived among the crowded masses. Primarily Irish immigrants, the gangs boasted colorful, even goofy, names like the Dead Rabbits and the Roach Boys. They were part extortionists, part political muscle. They operated under the protection of political bigwigs like the notorious Boss Tweed and his Tammany Hall cronies.

The Five Points Gang

One of the earliest Mafia incubators was the Five Points Gang. It was an incubator in the literal sense. Most of the members were young kids! But from these inauspicious beginnings, some of the earliest Mafia figures emerged—products of their new homeland. Paul Kelly (whose real name was Paolo Vaccareli) led the Five Points Gang, whose roster included such mob all-stars as Johnny Torrio and Al Capone.

Tong Wars

One of the earliest organized crime groups originated in China. The contemporary Chinese criminal groups, called *triads*, all trace their roots back to this old tradition. As Chinese immigration to America increased in the late nineteenth century, a new organization emerged. Called *tongs*, these groups were formed to provide assistance and support to the new immigrant experience. But the tongs soon became powerhouses in the criminal underworld.

Chinatowns are known for their vibrant, touristy atmospheres, with lots of restaurants and trinket shops. But at one time the darker specter of criminal gangs dominated, which became worrisome to community leaders. After the tong wars, the gangs decided to keep the fighting to a minimum to keep the area a place where they could make money off tourism. Capitalism at its finest!

Rumble on Canal Street

Two of New York City's most powerful tongs, the Hop Sing Tong and the On Leong Tong, had a bitter rivalry in the early part of the twentieth century that reached across to Chinatowns in other parts of the country.

Disagreements over gambling, opium dens, and liquor dealings brought dozens of killings in the narrow, crowded streets below Canal. But by the time the Mafia was on the rise, things had settled into a quiet storm. The warring tongs had made peace in 1911, cutting off their ponytails to symbolize the new relationship. But, as you'll see in Chapter 21, gangs were still a problem in Chinatown, and a far more sophisticated Chinese crime group would eventually gain control of the Asian underworld.

The Irish

The first criminal bands that emerged from the gritty slums of areas like Five Points were the Irish. Although many Irish became civil servants, there were a few who chose the underworld road to success. While the Sicilians were going by the moniker Black Hand, the Irish were using White Hand. Based out of the Brooklyn docks, these groups made most of their money by extorting the longshoremen, hijacking loads of merchandise off the boats, and running gambling operations open to the dockworkers.

FACT

Philadelphia had its own Irish mob group. The K&A Gang, headquartered in northeast Philly, were a loose-knit gang of Irish-American mobsters who dealt drugs and ran sophisticated burglary rings through the 1990s.

Wild Bill

The leader of the White Hand gang was a young, wide-eyed upstart who rose to the top in the usual gangland way, by murdering his former boss. Wild Bill Lovett saw the Italian gangs across the river as his biggest challenge, rather than other Irish mobsters. But his reign over the underworld scene on the docks was short-lived. Less than five years after becoming the boss of the White Hand he was shot and had a meat cleaver sunk into his skull. Needless to say that took care of Wild Bill, and the White Hand soon followed.

The Killer Irishman

The most successful and ruthless of the New York Irish gangsters in the 1930s was a tough mug called Owney "the Killer" Madden. He was a dapper man who partied in the high society of the day. He had interests in the bootleg racket and was the owner of the legendary Harlem nightclub called the Cotton Club. Lucky Luciano treated him with respect, and they did business amicably.

Madden did a year in the slammer and then retired to Hot Springs, Arkansas. This was a Mafia resort town discovered by Al Capone, and it is famed for its natural and restorative mineral baths. Gangsters put it on the map, and now ordinary citizens still flock there to "take in the waters" and gamble at the world-famous racetrack, Oaklawn Park.

The Westies rarely ventured from their tight-knit neighborhood, preferring to run their operations out of Irish pubs and back alley clubs. Coonan, however, led the suburban life in New Jersey, commuting into New York City each morning.

The Westies

The Irish mob's last stand in New York took place in Hell's Kitchen, a working-class neighborhood on the West Side of Manhattan. The longtime boss Mickey Spillane (no relation to the writer) was killed on March 13, 1977. Jimmy Coonan replaced him. Jimmy's tenure as head of the Westies was one of violence and brutality. He lacked the finesse of his elders. His gang was more like a crew of out-of-control street punks than a sophisticated organized crime family. They drank too much and also indulged in the drugs they pushed.

Coonan and his cronies had a penchant for chopping the hands off those they murdered. There were no fingerprints to identify the body that way. One assumes he was too brazen to consider that the cops might use dental records to get the deceased's identity. He was certainly on the right track, however.

Owney
Madden

Courtesy of AP Images

▲ Owney Madden, left, suspected but unconvicted racketeering boss, is escorted by detective Thomas Horan shortly after Madden was ordered on Febuary 13, 1932, to report to Sing Sing as a possible parole violator. He was en route to the Tombs Prison in New York pending a hearing two days later.

There were more than thirty unsolved murders in Hell's Kitchen in the 1970s through the mid-1980s that had the mark of the Westies. Coonan was ultimately convicted under the RICO Act and sentenced to seventy-five years.

Climbing the Ladder

The early slum gangs gave rise to homegrown crime groups, while immigrant mobsters joined in the noxious mix. Throw in Jewish and Irish racketeers in New York, Polish and black racketeers in Chicago, Cuban and Anglo racketeers in Tampa, and the early underworld scene was a multiethnic jumble. The power quickly shifted to the Italian crime gangs, the Camorra, and the Mafia. But after a bloody war for control, the Mafia became the main Italian crime group in the poor ethnic slums. But they would not stay there for long.

FACT

During the infamous Mafia-Camorra wars that ran from 1914 to 1918, the Mafia was headquartered in Manhattan, while the Camorra had their largest operations in Brooklyn. There was a series of tit-for-tat retaliatory hits, leading up to the execution of one of the Camorra hit men by the State of New York, one of the few mobsters ever executed for murder.

The Mafia in Sicily

The Mafia continued to be a powerful and dangerous force in Sicily after it branched off to set up shop in America. The Sicilian and American Mafia families formed alliances, had feuds, and did business together. While the Mafia in Sicily was distinctly separate from its cohorts in crime, the American melting pot brought them together. While poverty brought many hardworking immigrants from Italy to America, some of the criminals came by way of force.

Il Duce

Benito Mussolini was the fascist dictator of Italy from 1922 until his assassination during World War II. It was to be expected that a totalitarian dictator and an organized crime family would not get along together. Like rivals in a Wild West town, the island of Sicily was not big enough for both of them.

During one of Mussolini's many parades, this one through a Sicilian town, the local don, who felt this dictator was unworthy of respect, ordered the townspeople not to come out and line the parade route in tribute. To add to the flagrant disrespect, he had several bedraggled homeless men amble into the square to hear the dictator's bombastic and bellicose ranting. The bullet-headed Mussolini was furious and launched a crackdown on the Mafia. When he was done, many were dead and most of the major dons were behind bars. Ultimately, however, the Mafia would have the last laugh, with a little help from Uncle Sam.

Mussolini did not have a chance to fully rid Sicily of the Mafia. His alliance with Adolf Hitler and Nazi Germany launched Italy into World War II. The feud between the Sicilian Mafia and the dictator Mussolini inspired the Americans to side with the Mafia. Sicilian Mafiosi spied for the Americans during the Allied invasion of Sicily, and after they kicked the Germans off the island, they allowed the Mafiosi to come into positions of authority.

CHAPTER 3

The First Family of the American Mafia

People usually associate the beginning of the Mafia with the Roaring Twenties and the rat-a-tat-tat of Tommy guns in Chicago or New York. But the word *Mafia* came into national consciousness in 1891 in the Deep South. New Orleans may be the birthplace of the American Mafia. The land of jambalaya and crayfish was a sweltering melting pot of various ethnic groups, including Sicilians. And on the docks emerged the first vestiges of the Mafia in America.

Coming to New Orleans

Italian immigrants came to America in great numbers in the last decades of the nineteenth century. From 1860 to 1890 thousands of Sicilians came to New Orleans, Louisiana. Both criminals and noncriminals alike encountered racism from the locals; the city was not used to the darker-skinned Sicilians. But there was a Mafia element that fed on the fear. The Mafia element went into the shadows, functioning in the nooks and crannies of the culture. This was their comfort zone. In the periphery they banded together and made plans.

FACT

The mayor of New Orleans, Joseph Shakespeare, did not like the wave of Sicilian immigration and spoke against them in no uncertain terms. He called them "vicious and worthless," adding, "They are without courage, honor, truth, pride, religion, or any quality that goes to make good citizens." He even made the threat, "I intend to put an end to these infernal Dago disturbances, even if it proves necessary to wipe out every one of you from the face of the earth."

Emergence

New Orleans was the first foothold of the Mafia in America. The families that formed later in New York, Chicago, and other big and small cities have become very well known, and the Mafia is usually associated with Northern urban types, but the Southern Mafia family was here first. The port city of New Orleans was an ideal place to begin its crooked business dealings. A port city was ideal for the Mafia's penchant for muscling in on trade and commerce, and demanding "protection money."

The Black Hand Revisited

The Mafia gangs used the "Black Hand" technique to extort money from their own kinsmen. A politely written note would be left for the merchant or businessman stating that money was expected at a certain date/time or he would be brutally killed. The bizarre Old-World gentility of the letter's wording contrasted with the threats of violence. This was no bluff. People were beaten, businesses trashed, and families killed if they did not make a prompt payment to the sender. The signature of the letter was a black palm print, hence the name "Black Hand."

The New Orleans Mafia family was never very large. At its height it had only a couple dozen made guys with a few hundred associates. But they were powerful, controlling vast swaths of the Gulf Coast with strategic alliances in Tampa and Dallas.

Blood on the Docks

From their earliest efforts Italian gangsters had a penchant for the waterfront. In 1890 the earliest Mafiosi in America quickly muscled in on the docks. New Orleans has been an active port city since its inception. Ships from all over the world docked on its waterfront.

In addition to having a climate similar to their homeland, one of the reasons Sicilians found New Orleans appealing was the fact that it had a Catholic culture. In the North and elsewhere, Catholics were in the minority and often subject to discrimination.

Two enterprising brothers, Tony and Charles Matranga (born Antonio and Carlo Matranga), formerly of Palermo, Sicily, were making a nice living shaking down and intimidating skippers and ship owners, who were obliged to pay extortion money or else end up shot, stabbed, or beaten to a pulp and tossed into one of the many canals. It was a reign of terror that the chief of police was determined to stop.

Common Killings

A rival group of brothers was vying for control of the New Orleans waterfronts. The underworld was well aware of such delineations and distinctions, while to the untrained eye they were all just thugs. Savage hits were commonplace. One gangster's head was stuck into a burning stove, many were shot, some hits were near misses that only succeeded in grisly mutilation and the amputation of various body parts. The escalating violence was played out against the reality of postwar Reconstruction, making life even tougher for the immigrant communities of the South.

Joseph Macheca—The First American Don

The name Joseph Macheca is not well-known to the general public. Even in Mafia historian circles, he is an enigmatic figure. But this unknown may have been the first Mafia don in America. He led an enterprising crew of gangland figures in the years following the Civil War, decades before organized crime is generally thought to have originated. By absorbing hoodlums into his group, Macheca avoided much violence. But as always, violence came to the mob.

New Orleans served as a port of entry for many Sicilians, and many of the early mobsters got their start there before moving on to cities like Chicago and New York. New Orleans–born mobsters also moved to Rockford, Illinois, and Tampa, Florida, cementing ties between the respective Mafia organizations.

Macheca welcomed an exiled Sicilian Mafia leader into his "family" after Macheca led his team to victory in a war against rival gangsters in 1869. When this exiled leader was deported back to Italy by New Orleans authorities, the Macheca hold on the local mob started to splinter. Two distinct factions emerged. And as is the case with every mob family where factions emerge, the blood began to run. The two factions were the

Macheca-Matranga group, briefly mentioned in the previous section, and another, led by the Provenzanos. War erupted between the factions around 1888.

Crusading Cop

New Orleans Police Chief David C. Hennessy was determined to put an end to the ongoing violence of the Macheca-Matranga/Provenzano war. He spoke to some of the Sicilian immigrants and learned that even the non-gangsters were inclined to be insular and clannish. They had the Old-World innate distrust of authority. Most would not talk to him, but those who did whispered an alien phrase not uttered before on American soil—La Mafia. That was when Hennessy discovered the existence of a secret organized collective of criminals. He was dealing with something deeper and more menacing than mere street hoodlums.

Police chief David Hennessy had a hard time getting anyone on his staff to work with him in his crusade against the Mafia. They had all received threats, and they didn't doubt that the Mafia would follow through on those threats.

Dead Man Walking

Desperate to break the cycle of violence, Hennessy took sides. He supported the Provenzano brothers over the Macheca-Matranga factions. Hennessy had members of his police force vouch for the Provenzano gang after a vicious attack on the Matranga clan. Hennessy was planning on testifying on behalf of the Provenzanos. Although he had a previously friendly relationship with Joseph Macheca, that friendship had spoiled. Hennessy was now a marked man. The Mafia was following him and his routine was being noted. A hit was in the works, though Hennessy probably felt safe and in no danger.

Hennessy was brave but foolish. He could not be bribed and he was not alarmed by the many death threats he received. He meticulously built a case against the Matranga brothers. He was ready to present his airtight case to a grand jury when four men surrounded him on a darkened street. All four men brandished shotguns and fired at close range.

Even though he was badly injured, Hennessy fired in vain at his murderers and then dragged himself back to the police station. His friend Captain Billy O'Connor and another policeman discovered him. He was asked if he knew who shot him and he uttered a sentence that unleashed a wave of violence and retribution that achieved national attention: "The Dagos did it." The next day complications from his wounds set in and Hennessy took a turn for the worse and died.

National Scandal

New Orleans was outraged at the police captain's murder at the hands of these foreign hoodlums. As a result of Hennessy's murder, anti-Italian sentiment swept through New Orleans and the nation. Demonstrations were held in all the major cities that had large Italian populations. Mayor Shakespeare ordered a crackdown on the Mafia. More than 100 men were arrested, many simply because they were Italian. The media made things worse with sensational and racist editorials. The word *Mafia* became nationally known, and it automatically became associated with poor Italian immigrants.

Dividing the City

Among the men rounded up in the dragnet were the actual culprits in addition to innocent parties. An informant in the jail got cozy with one of the accused, who spilled the beans about the conspiracy against Hennessy. The loose-lipped prisoner implicated high-level members of the Matranga clan, including Charles Matranga, Joe Macheca, and numerous others. The trial divided the country along racial lines. The Mafia exploited ethnic pride to collect money for a defense fund for the accused.

Nineteen Sicilian men were brought to trial for the murder of Police Chief Hennessy, but using an old Mafia trick, the local gangsters bribed and intimidated the witnesses and the jury. The frightened jurors found sixteen of the accused not guilty, and couldn't come to a verdict on the other three, including the two kingpins, Matranga and Macheca, who would have to stand trial again.

Although it is highly likely that the Mafia murdered Police Chief Hennessy, the fiasco of the trial and subsequent chaos and carnage overshadowed the quest for justice. The case is still officially listed as unsolved.

Lynch Mob

The jury verdicts created an uproar in the city of New Orleans. The aftermath of the verdict coincided with an Italian holiday. The leader of Italy, King Umberto the First, was a hero who had unified the country. The Italians in New Orleans flew flags and were engaged in a festive celebration. Whether the non-Italians in the city thought the party atmosphere was a celebration of the verdict or they simply did not like the pomp and parades immediately after their police chief's killers did not meet the justice they felt was their due, they were incensed, and protests broke out.

Did the New Orleans family run Dallas?
Yes, they did. Though considered a separate family, Dallas crime boss Joe Civello was a native of Baton Rouge, Louisiana, and a close ally of Carlos Marcello, as was his successor Joe Campisi. The New Orleans family also held sway over Galveston through the Maceo brothers.

Thousands of people assembled at City Hall. They listened to a lot of inflammatory rhetoric from several notable citizens, one of whom flat out exhorted the throng to take the law into their own hands. The crowd raided the city armory and proceeded to the prison where the Mafiosi were being held. The prison warden let the Italians out of their cells so the rioters could get to them.

Bastille Day Redux

The angry mob barreled into the prison looking for the Mafiosi. Top man Joseph Macheca was shot dead. Six other men were also rounded up and shot. Manuel Polizzi was dragged from the prison and lynched. Several members of the lynch mob shot him as he writhed at the end of the rope. A total of sixteen men were killed that day. Two of them had no mob connections at all. They were executed simply for being Sicilian. In a stroke of luck for the Mafia, its leader, Charles Matranga, the man who had orchestrated the murder of the police chief, survived the mob's bloodlust. He had been able to successfully hide during the carnage.

We will never be sure whether it was a less-than-airtight case by the prosecution or Mafia intimidation that resulted in the charges against the accused being dismissed or mistrials declared and defendants found not guilty. No matter which side you take in these tragic events, justice was not served.

Aftermath to the Slaughter

The newspapers ran editorials in support of the vigilante murders. One paper lauded the crazed mob for its self-control in that only the Mafiosi were killed, which was not true. The episode became an international incident, drawing rebukes from several European leaders. The Italian ambassador lodged a complaint with the president, as did the Italian government. Rumors of a potential war between the United States and Italy filled the newspapers, though that was more idle speculation than a real, concrete threat. The president of the United States, Benjamin Harrison, denounced the incident, and the government paid settlements to the families of the murder victims. None of the vigilante mob or the men who incited them were brought to trial.

Matranga's Legacy

Charles Matranga ultimately had all charges dismissed, and he laid low after that. The lion's share of the $25,000 sent to the families of the victims ended up in the Mafia's coffers. After the massacre, the newspapers announced that the Mafia was dead and buried. But the press was dead wrong. Matranga was able to hold onto his power base, as he watched the Provenzanos lose theirs. The New Orleans Mafia continued to do quite well in its illegal enterprises. The man who guided the New Orleans crime family through most of the twentieth century, Carlos Marcello, will be discussed at length in later chapters.

CHAPTER 4

The Roaring Twenties

In January of 1919 the Eighteenth Amendment, better known as Prohibition, was ratified. America's experiment with Prohibition opened the door for the Mafia to make a bundle in the trafficking of illegal booze. This was the catalyst for the mob to move up the ladder on the American crime scene. Gangsters were everywhere, keeping the illegal speakeasies open and stocking Americans with illegal alcohol, much of which was not fit for human consumption! In addition to making their own, gangsters were bringing booze across the border from Canada and up to Florida from Cuba. And one stocky Neapolitan wise guy from Brooklyn set up shop in Chicago and changed history.

Prohibition

There have been many attempts to deal with the problem of alcoholism in America since the 1800s. These were called *temperance movements*, an antiquated phrase meaning moderation in one's indulgence in the so-called vices. Most temperance movements in history have been initiated by religious folks who felt that only a spiritual conversion could combat the deleterious effects of "demon rum." And there were many who wanted to ban all alcoholic beverages from the American landscape.

FACT

Temperance firebrand Carrie Nation was one early leader of the movement against alcohol. Standing six feet tall, Nation led militant crusades against the scourge of alcohol and the damage it caused families and society as a whole when it was abused. She regularly brandished a hatchet to personally smash casks and kegs of whiskey and beer and go after barkeeps who served alcohol.

In the late nineteenth century, the temperance movement in America became increasingly popular and influential. It was sometimes called the "Women's War," since most of its members were women who were fed up with their drunken fathers, husbands, and sons. The Anti-Saloon League (ASL) gained popularity in many states. The ASL endorsed candidates and tried to influence state and local governments, and its dream was to have an impact at the national level.

Prohibition Passes

The movement was gaining momentum, and twenty-three states had prohibition laws by 1916. There was enough support for an amendment to the Constitution. An amendment requires two-thirds of the states to vote in favor of it, and in 1919 the Eighteenth Amendment to the Constitution was ratified, outlawing the manufacture, sale, or exportation of alcohol by anyone in the United States.

It became the law of the land in 1920. It was called Prohibition for short, and it lasted until the early 1930s. Ironically, the 1920s was, for many Americans, one big party that preceded the Great Depression of the 1930s. The booze never stopped flowing during Prohibition, thanks to the friendly neighborhood Mafia.

Bootlegging was not exclusively an enterprise of the Mafia. Many immigrant families, who saw nothing immoral about drinking alcohol, made their own wine and beer for their personal consumption. In the American South and Midwest, rural stills made moonshine, a practice that continues to this day.

Getting Around It

The National Prohibition Act was passed to enforce the Eighteenth Amendment. It was also known as the Volstead Act, named for the congressman who introduced the law. There were some exceptions to the rule. Alcohol could be used for medicinal purposes, and priests could perform Mass with sacramental wine. It was generally accepted that it would be difficult to enforce, and that law enforcement officials were not necessarily going to aggressively enforce the law. Many of them liked to drink and were not eager to deny themselves the pleasure.

The demand for alcohol was there, and someone who could supply the demand was more than welcome. At first it was the Irish saloon owners who had brothers and cousins on "the force." But soon the Italian and the Jewish mobsters muscled in on their turf. Prohibition was counterproductive. It spurred the increase of organized crime.

The Jazz Age

When saloons became illegal, they went underground and became "speakeasies." Now there was an illicit element that made drinking more attractive. People did not stop drinking during Prohibition. They just had to pay more money (a shot of booze went up from ten cents to $3 in some places) for substandard booze, and they had to do it in secret. In these underground clubs you didn't hear classical music or the stiff, high-pitched whines of male pop vocalists of the day. The down and dirty atmosphere of the speakeasies was the perfect match to the quintessential American music . . . jazz.

Many performers who went on to great fame got their start in the Mafia-owned nightclubs. Harlem's famous Cotton Club was owned by Irishman Owney "the Killer" Madden and regularly featured the likes of Duke Ellington and Cab Calloway. Louis Armstrong was another regular. Although the clubs rarely let in black patrons, in some ways the mob gave the jazz musicians exposure they weren't getting anywhere else.

The Irish Players

The first bootleggers were Irish. They constituted most of the saloon owners, and after Prohibition was enacted they immediately became criminals if they continued to do business. Two Irishmen were the big-time bootleggers in the Northeast. Owney "the Killer" Madden was New York's main bootlegger until the Mafia demolished the Irish mob. And Boston's premier rumrunner was a man named Joseph P. Kennedy. Yes, the patriarch of the Kennedy clan was considered to be a major-league player in the illegal booze trade and an associate of many an overt gangster. (See Chapter 12 for more about him.) In 1922 Kennedy provided the booze that was served at the tenth anniversary reunion of his Harvard graduating class.

One of the biggest smuggling gangs operated out of Detroit. The Purple Gang, as it was known, was primarily a Jewish gang, and they were responsible for bringing booze across the Great Lakes from Canada. After Prohibition ended, the gang broke apart, and the Detroit Mafia family took over the Gang's nonbootlegging rackets.

Irish Versus Italian

Irish gangs controlled the Brooklyn waterfront after World War I. They took protection money for keeping the ships and the merchandise therein safe and sound. The Irish were unable to outgun the Italians and were relegated to secondhand status. One of the upcoming young Italian gangsters was a bouncer and bartender in the speakeasies. This outspoken, chubby tough guy once told a female patron of a speakeasy, "You got a beautiful ass." This prompted her brother to try to cut the bouncer's throat. The man missed and sliced the bouncer's cheek. And that is how the bouncer, destined to become the most famous Mafioso ever, got the name Al "Scarface" Capone.

Scarface Al

Alfonse Capone was one of the first American-born Italian gangsters. His parents came from Italy like so many other immigrants seeking the American Dream. His father was a barber who wanted to open his own shop. They settled in Brooklyn near the Navy Yard. The family later moved to a more ethnically diverse neighborhood. He mingled with kids who were Irish, German, Jewish, and Asian. This exposed young Al to the American "melting pot" experience, making him less insular than his Old-World relatives. He fell in line with the way of thinking that Lucky Luciano would later use to forge a new Mafia.

Al left school at the age of fourteen after hitting a teacher who had struck him. He was expelled and never looked back. There were bigger things on the horizon for young Al Capone. He would soon take his first adolescent steps into the underworld. And there was no better place to be brought into "that life" than Brooklyn.

Johnny Torrio

The Capone family moved to another neighborhood, and their new residence was a few blocks away from the headquarters of Mafioso Johnny Torrio, who was one of the first of the modern hoodlums. Capone began running errands for Torrio, who took a liking to the pugnacious street urchin and gave him more and more responsibilities. Capone watched the older men conduct business, and they served as role models to the impressionable boy.

Capone also became involved in the teenage street gangs of the day. They were usually divided along ethnic lines and were territorial about their "turf." At various times in his misspent youth, Capone belonged to the South Brooklyn Rippers, Forty Thieves Juniors, and the Five Point Juniors.

FACT

After he retired Johnny Torrio moved to St. Petersburg, Florida, where he owned numerous homes, rentals, and parcels of real estate on the beaches. He was also in close contact with members of the Tampa Mafia, including Angelo Bedami Sr. and Salvatore "Red" Italiano. St. Petersburg was also a favorite vacation spot for Al Capone.

Yale Grad

The next mentor Al Capone had in the life of crime was Frankie Yale (born Francesco Ioele). Yale owned a bar ironically called the Harvard Inn, and he hired the eighteen-year-old Capone as a bartender and bouncer. It is in this gin mill that he made the inappropriate remark that resulted in the scar on his face.

Capone learned about business finesse from his first mentor, Johnny Torrio; Yale schooled him in the more brutal arts of the Mafia. Capone became proficient at both in his notorious career. During this time Capone met and married (after their first child was born) an Irish-American girl named Mae Coughlin.

Shortly after his wedding, Capone flirted with respectability by taking a regular job, but this phase did not last long. His former boss, Johnny Torrio, called Brooklyn for his former protégé. Torrio had gone out to the Midwest and the emerging metropolis of Chicago. With its organized crime anything but organized, Torrio saw it as an opportunity to make something big. And he knew Al would fit right in.

Chi-Town

The Windy City was already known for vice and corruption when Capone got off the train in 1920. It was known as a slaughterhouse in more than one respect. Neighbors could hear the feral squeals from the meatpacking district, and the pitter-patter of Tommy guns punctuated the night.

The "Mr. Big" at the time was a man named "Big Jim" Colosimo. His wife was also Chicago's most celebrated madam, Victoria Moresco. At that time the fledgling crime gang had a large-scale prostitution empire. When Johnny Torrio arrived in Chicago, he became Colosimo's right-hand man. Together the two men opened a brothel, and Torrio had Al Capone work there when he arrived from New York.

Torrio was a stable gangster who did not indulge in the vices from which he profited. The same could not be said of Colosimo, who was spiraling out of control. He became wrapped around the little finger of a singer named Dale Winter. The call of the siren distracted him from more important matters, such as business. When Prohibition started Torrio suggested that Big Jim start making big money from booze. Jim was more into his women, so Torrio had him taken out of the picture.

Now that Johnny was top dog, Al rose to be his second in command. Capone started out managing the many brothels in Chicago, but he was not very comfortable in the role of pimp. When Prohibition roared into the 1920s, he got into the speakeasy end of the business.

Equal-Opportunity Mafioso

Capone, being American-born and exposed to many other ethnic groups growing up, was not as clannish as other Mafiosi. He married an Irish girl and met his new best friend in Chicago, an Orthodox Jewish family man named Jake "Greasy Thumb" Guzik. Capone put on the façade of a mild-mannered used-furniture dealer for his neighbors while he let it loose when engaged in his other life. Like many Mafiosi, he strived for respectability while making a living in illegal enterprises and using terror and murder as tools of his trade.

For many years Capone had a free ride in Chicago. The politicians and police were shamelessly corrupt. The people wanted their vices, and Capone was more than happy to provide them. Cries of outrage and calls for reform from the political machine were nothing more than lip service. It was a wide-open town where the mob ruled. Mayor "Big Bill" Thompson was considered to be one of the most corrupt men in a long line of corrupt politicians.

However, real reform was slowly making inroads into the Windy City. A man named William E. Dever succeeded Thompson as mayor, and he promised to crack down on the vice and corruption on his town. The Mafia took it in stride. A reformer at the top was a minor inconvenience when the rest of the team was more than eager to play ball.

Capone and Torrio were not the only Italian bosses operating in the Windy City. The Genna brothers, Angelo, Tony, Mike, Sam, Peter, and Vincenzo, controlled the South Side of Chicago. They were bitter rivals with the North Side gang, led by Dion O'Bannion. But after three of the brothers were killed in shootouts, the survivors left the racket business for good.

Al's Private Fiefdom

When the heat in Chicago proper got too hot, Al left for the nearby suburb of Cicero. Located just outside the city, Cicero was a perfect place to open a new headquarters. They simply bought the town with the smoking barrels of their machine guns, using bribery as needed. In short order Capone controlled all the prostitution, gambling, and bootlegging in the town. He even took over the racetrack. Capone's brother Frank acted as liaison with the corrupt local government.

Freedom of the Press

A maverick journalist named Robert St. John openly opposed the Capone invasion in his newspaper. It looked like Capone's handpicked politicos might lose the election of 1924. Capone used muscle to try to sway the voting public. His goons loomed around polling places making it clear which candidate would be the "healthiest" choice. The cops were called in response, and Frank Capone was gunned down. He allegedly pulled his revolver when he found himself surrounded. (A dumb move, if indeed it's true.) It was deemed that the police acted in self-defense when they killed him. At the end of the day, Al Capone owned Cicero, but at a terrible price, a brother's blood.

Capone vented his frustration by shooting a small-time hood who dared to call the little big man an ethnic slur. He was brought to trial for the first time in his life, but he beat the murder rap. Witnesses were hard to come by, as was always the case with Mafia trials. The highly public trial made him something most mobsters did not want to be—famous.

King of Chicagoland

Few twenty-five-year-olds achieve the power and wealth that Al Capone had at that young age. And few people have to deal with murderous rivals and regular assassination attempts. Such is the price one pays for being King of the Underworld. Capone knocked off opponents, and they in turn were out to get him. One attempt on his partner Johnny Torrio was almost successful. The volatile hoodlum Bugs Moran pumped several shots into Torrio as he was entering his apartment building, but Torrio survived. Capone stayed with him at the hospital, even sleeping on a cot at the bedside of his friend and mentor.

Torrio got out of the business after being shot. He decided to retire and head for warmer climates, and he turned over his share of the massive empire to Capone. Success spoiled Capone. He moved into the palatial Metropole Hotel and lived a very public life of a media darling and national celebrity. He was a showman gangster, attempting to cultivate a Robin Hood image. He was a regular Joe who provided a service that the public wanted, a man who was misunderstood and being harassed by the authorities. Capone provided meals for the jobless, even serving up meals at makeshift soup kitchens. He regularly made public appearances, craving the spotlight. After all, he was just a businessman trying to live a good life. Or so he wanted people to believe.

Death of the Party

Capone continued to cement his position as über-thug when he orchestrated a flamboyant hit on an old rival. He was back in New York attending a Christmas party and got wind that an old enemy, Richard "Peg-Leg" Lonergan, was going to crash the bash with some of his boys.

The boisterous blowhards did not get very far before the Capone mob wished them a very bloody Christmas.

McSwiggin's Curse

Capone faced another legal dilemma when his men machine-gunned a gang of Irish bootleggers. He did not know that partying with the Irishmen was Billy McSwiggin, the prosecutor who had unsuccessfully tried Capone for murder. Capone had not intended to hit McSwiggin, but

"Bugs" Moran

Courtesy of AP Images

▲ George "Bugs" Moran, a prominent figure in Chicago's underworld, poses in this circa 1932 photo.

nevertheless he took the heat from the otherwise indifferent police force. Cops, like the Mafia, look out for their own, and Capone had inadvertently broken the Mafia's "we only kill our own" code. His gambling joints and bordellos began to be raided. Capone went into hiding. He surrendered after three months on the lam, but faced no charges. There was not enough evidence for an indictment. The frustrated authorities could not get this slippery gangster.

Al Capone was not averse to being a true "hands-on" murderer. He personally killed many men in his time, and ordered the hits of many more. The notorious scene in the movie *The Untouchables* when Capone bashes the man to death with a baseball bat is based on a true story. In reality, however, Capone cracked the skulls of three men in the same session.

Peacemaker?

Capone fancied himself a peacemaker. Since he did not skulk in the shadows and everyone knew who and what he was, he called a public peace conference asking his fellow gangsters to put an end to the violence. Many felt his calls for peace were insincere. While he spoke publicly for an end to violence, he ordered the murder of dozens of rivals. He sent his armed hoods after Irish, Italian, and Polish competitors, and muscled in on the traditional black neighborhood numbers rackets.

Happy Valentine's Day

To modern society, the scene of a mass murder has unfortunately become an all-too-common event. But back in the 1920s, even through the height of the bootlegging wars, no one was prepared for what has become the most famous "hit" in American Mafia history. Al Capone was still fuming over Bugs Moran's attempt on Johnny Torrio's life. In addition to almost whacking Torrio, Moran had twice tried to hit another Capone pal with the colorful name "Machine Gun" McGurn. Since Scarface was ruthless and not prone to forgiveness, he set a plan in motion to topple once and for all the pesky Bugs Moran and his gang of irksome rivals.

Capone had bought a lavish estate on Palm Beach in Florida and spent the winters there. He took off for Florida after setting the plan in motion to give himself an airtight alibi. He knew he would be the first suspect when the job was done. He left the details to Machine Gun McGurn. McGurn hired out-of-town talent and planned to lure Moran to a garage on the morning of February 14. The bait was a stash of quality booze at a good price. The hit team would be dressed as cops. Moran and company would think it was a raid, not an assassination. The phony cops burst into the garage simulating a police bust, made the hoods line up against the wall, and mowed them down. There was good news and bad news. The good news was that the hit went off without a hitch. The bad news was that Bugs Moran did not show up that day. The target of the hit had a guardian angel on his shoulder that Valentine's Day.

Jack McGurn, whose real name was Vincenzo Gebardi, became known as one of the most feared gangsters in Chicago. Though not a major threat to the new leadership of the Chicago mob, McGurn was killed almost seven years to the day after the Valentine's Day Massacre.

Capone was out of town, and McGurn had checked into a hotel across town with his girlfriend, so he had witnesses who could place him at the hotel and not at the scene of the crime. Everyone knew who ordered the hit but no one could prove it. The murders captured the fascination of the nation and have become one of the most recognizable events in crime history.

Hoover Takes Notice

In addition to the sensational media attention, the powers-that-be in Washington began to take a closer look at the shenanigans taking place in Chicago. President Herbert Hoover announced that he wanted to see Capone behind bars. He got the U.S. Treasury to set up a task force to go after the crime boss. Though Capone was the master of a multimillion-dollar empire of vice, graft, and murder, he was taken down by the innocuous-sounding charge of tax evasion. But this seemingly small charge was big trouble for Al. He was convicted and sentenced to eleven years in prison.

The Last Years

Capone was first sent to a federal prison in Atlanta, where he lived in relative comfort and used his influence to enjoy special privileges. Unfortunately for Al, he was transferred to the infamous island prison of Alcatraz. Here Capone enjoyed no creature comforts. On Alcatraz he was just

NYC Prohibition is replealed

Courtesy of AP Images

▲ A crowd gathers as kegs of beer are unloaded in front of a restaurant on Broadway in New York City, the morning of April 7, 1933, when low-alcohol beer is legalized again.

another number. He had minimal contact with the outside. All letters were censored, and he was not allowed to read the daily newspapers.

Capone's health deteriorated during his prison stretch. The syphilis he had contracted in his youth grew progressively worse. He only served six and a half years of his sentence. He retired to his Florida estate and continued a slow but steady mental and physical decline until his death in 1947.

Capone's Successors

The city of Chicago was too rich in racket revenue for the mob to simply give up after Capone's conviction on tax evasion. He had left a sizable territory for gambling, vice, corruption, and murder. The Chicago Outfit's empire extended across Illinois into Wisconsin and Indiana, not to mention the pull they exerted over Milwaukee, St. Louis, Kansas City, and Rockford. After he died in 1947, the Chicago mob, or the Outfit, was already becoming a more streamlined, efficient moneymaking machine, one that would rule Chicago through to the twenty-first century.

Nitti

Capone's right-hand man Frank Nitti was the obvious successor. With his underboss Paul "the Waiter" Ricca and a cohort of Italian, Irish, Polish, and even Welsh gangsters under his command, Nitti expanded the Outfit's lucrative rackets all the way out to Hollywood, where the Chicago boys were shaking down movie studios and infiltrating the labor unions. Nitti ran into some trouble with the cops, and he was not well respected by his underlings. When the movie studio extortion ring was indicted, Nitti decided to make a grand exit. He shot himself on the railroad tracks; he was one of the few bosses to take his own life.

The Big Tuna

Tony "Big Tuna"/"Joe Batters" Accardo was a Capone henchman whose uncanny intellect and cagey ability to evade law enforcement put him in a good position to lead the Outfit in the post-Capone era. While Paul Ricca took over after Nitti's death, Accardo became boss, and though he only officially served for a few years, he was considered by many to be the actual boss behind the scenes, putting figurehead bosses (most notably Sam Giancana) out front to take the heat from the feds. The Big Tuna retired to Palm Springs in his later years. When he died in 1992 at the ripe old age of eighty-six, he outlasted most of his mob cohorts, and spent little time in jail.

Mob hit man Frank Calabrese obviously had some serious family issues. When he went to trial in 2007 for racketeering and murder, his own brother and son both testified against the aging South Side crime figure. Calabrese kept a big smile on his face throughout the testimony. But in the end his brother and son got the last laugh when Frank was found guilty.

Family Secrets

The Outfit expanded its hold not only over the Chicagoland area, but down into Indiana, west to Rockford, north into Wisconsin, and way out west to San Diego. They skimmed cash from casinos in Vegas and stole millions from union pension funds. And although the Tommy-gun happy days of the 1920s were over, the Outfit still used murder as a way to keep the troops in line.

In 2005 the feds announced the biggest indictment ever against the Outfit's bigwigs. Dubbed Operation Family Secrets, the parade of senior citizen mobsters was the culmination of decades of law enforcement activities. They were charged with a host of murders and criminal acts dating back over thirty years. Some of the names like Joey "The Clown" Lombardo were familiar to mob watchers. Then there were guys like Frank Calabrese. Frank grew up on the South Side of Chicago, along with many of the Outfit's other soldiers. Calabrese became known as a hit man, loanshark, and all around tough guy. In the end, Calabrese, Lombardo, and the current reputed head of the Chicag Outfit, Jimmy Marcello, were all found guilty. But despite the outcome of the Family Secrets trial there are plenty of Windy City mobsters waiting in the wings to continue Scarface Al Capone's legacy.

CHAPTER 5

The Real Untouchables

The Mafia felt they were above the law in part because corruption of local police and judiciary were one way the gangsters were able to keep their operations running smoothly. In some cities public corruption became so rampant that the police and public officials were actually part of the mob's illegal enterprises. But public outcry at a local level eventually worked its way up the line. There was no shortage of crime fighters eager to put a stop to the illegal activities that were going on. In this chapter you will learn about some of the famous crime busters who battled the Mafia.

Federal Case

We have all heard the expression "Don't make a federal case out of it." This originated in Al Capone's Chicago. The Mafia did not want to tangle with the federal government. It shined too much light on them, and the power of federal law enforcement was formidable. Local cops were more easily bribed and intimidated.

Capone's growing celebrity status and his increasing willingness to revel in the attention put the spotlight on his organization and activities. But the FBI was still a fledgling organization and the Mafia was not yet under their radar.

In Capone's case, the orders came from Washington to get Scarface. Federal agents formed teams to try and take down the seemingly untouchable mob boss. Television and the movies later made Eliot Ness and his story part of the fabric of American folklore.

FACT

Eliot Ness's post-Treasury career failed to live up to his expectations and he spiraled into alcoholism. Eliot Ness died before his memoir *The Untouchables* was sold to television and became a hit series starring Robert Stack. Kevin Costner played Ness in the award-winning 1987 feature film that costarred Sean Connery and Robert De Niro.

Ness assembled a handpicked team of agents. He wanted his agents to be under thirty and unmarried. It was a dangerous business, and he did not want to be a widow-maker. After extensive interviews, he settled on nine men. For the record, the real "Untouchables" were Marty Lahart, Sam Seager, Barney Cloonan, Lyle Chapman, Tom Friel, Joe Leeson, Paul Robsky, Mike King, and Bill Gardner.

The Taxman Cometh

It may seem like a strange strategy to prosecute a murderer for not paying his taxes. Capone was always able to slip out of any murder indictment against him. Taxation was another matter altogether. Compliance and/or noncompliance with tax laws is kept on record. Back then gangsters didn't think enough to make sure all their flaunted ill-gotten gains were kept on record. In later years they came up with creative ways, including no-show jobs on construction sites, and nonexistent sales positions. But Capone did not have any backup documentation for his extravagant lifestyle.

Elmer Irey

Most people have heard of Eliot Ness, but fewer folks probably know the name of Elmer Irey. While Ness went to Chicago to try to nail Capone on Prohibition violations, it was Irey who did the paper shuffling and bean counting to catch Capone on income tax fraud. Ness had recruited a team of intrepid fellow agents who could not be intimidated or bribed. They could not be swayed or stopped by the seductive nature of sin or the potential violence against them.

The word *untouchable* when applied to Eliot Ness and his crime fighters has nothing to do with its more familiar usage, the lowest rung in India's rigid caste system. To be an untouchable in Al Capone's Chicago meant that you could not be bribed or intimidated out of performing your duty.

When the Rat's Away

Al Capone was arrested in Philadelphia for carrying a concealed weapon. He did a little time behind bars. In his absence he left the business in the hands of his brother Ralph and one of his henchmen, Frank Nitti. Nitti took over the administrative duties while Capone was in jail, and he eventually ran things after Capone was sent away for good. Ralph Capone did not have the intelligence, caginess, or business acumen of his brother. He found himself charged with tax evasion. The dogged Elmer Irey had been trying to nail Ralph for a long time. And Eliot Ness had been listening in on Ralph's business dealings courtesy of hidden wiretaps. Ralph was not adept at covering his financial tracks and he was an easier target for the feds than his brother Al.

Hidden in Plain Sight

Ness did more than simply listen in to private conversations. He began to raid Capone's breweries, which were often "hidden" in plain sight. Distilleries were also raided, but most of the hard liquor consumed in Chicago was imported from elsewhere. The Capone mob made its own beer, and there were hundreds of breweries in the greater Chicagoland area. As Sean Connery's character tells Kevin Costner's Eliot Ness in the 1987 movie *The Untouchables*, "Everybody knows where the booze is. The problem isn't finding it. The problem is, who wants to cross Capone?" Ness was willing to cross Capone. It is estimated that Ness cost Capone over $1 million in spilled beer by seizing and destroying illegal breweries run by Capone. Capone's first response was to try to bribe Ness and the Untouchables; later he tried to kill them.

FACT

Eliot Ness's legacy of fighting organized crime in Chicago continued through the activities of William Roemer, a venerable FBI agent who was among the first to use wiretapping against mob bigwigs in the Windy City. Roemer was well known to mob bosses like Sam Giancana and Anthony Accardo. He later recounted his exploits in a series of books about the Chicago Outfit.

America's Most Wanted

When Capone got out of jail (he was released early for good behavior) he was surprised to learn that he and several of his underlings were now on FBI boss J. Edgar Hoover's Most Wanted list. It seemed that he was in denial about his invulnerability and the bad publicity that his criminal activities inspired. He was popular with the populace but not quite beloved.

The feds decided they needed an agent in place within the enemy camp in order to get a better handle on Capone's strengths and weaknesses. An Irishman named Malone passed himself off as a Brooklyn hoodlum eager to join the Capone organization. Malone was what is called "black Irish." He had a Mediterranean look that could pass for Italian. He was also an accomplished actor and good with dialects. He earned the trust of Capone's henchmen, even met the Big Boy himself, and got a job in one of the many gambling joints.

Malone and another undercover agent provided valuable intelligence. Their information thwarted an attempted hit on a federal agent, and they found out the names of a couple of accountants who had cooked Capone's books.

Deal with the Devil

Capone, stone-cold killer that he was, preferred to reason with Ness rather than kill him. Bumping off Ness would make it a "federal case" and create myriad problems. Instead, Capone offered Ness $2,000 a week to look the other way. Ness turned down the bribe. Ness was making about $2,800 a year at the time. Ness, never shy of publicity and often accused of egomania, held a press conference to announce that he had turned down the bribe. It was one of the newspapermen who covered the press conference who coined the term "the Untouchables."

Eventually there were attempts on Ness's life. He discovered a bomb under the hood of his car at one point. On another occasion gunshots were fired at him as he escorted a date back to her home, and he was almost the victim of a hit-and-run. However, none of these attempts was successful.

ALERT!

Chicago was a dangerous place to be during the wild days of Al Capone. Authorities estimated over 1,200 people were killed as a result of the gangland violence. While most were underworld figures, innocent bystanders and lawmen were also among the victims.

The Feds

Eliot Ness wanted to up the ante with his nemesis after the murder of one of Ness's associates. Ness figured if Capone got really riled he would act impulsively and slip up. So Ness led a parade of the various trucks and other vehicles that had been used in raids on Capone's bootleg operations down the street outside of Capone's office, in an attempt to mock Capone. Ness even called Capone and told him to look out the window. Capone went ballistic and trashed his own office in a rage. The trucks were also a painful reminder of the millions of dollars Capone lost in Ness's relentless raids.

What ultimately brought the big man down, however, was his long history as a tax scofflaw. An investigation that was years in the making culminated with an indictment against Capone in 1931. He faced twenty-two counts of tax evasion, on top of the evidence Ness had gathered of several thousand violations of the Prohibition law. The tax case was judged the easiest to win, and Capone went to trial.

Twelve Not-so Crooked Men

Capone had a couple of months before his trial began, but the jury had already been selected. His henchmen took the time to locate and bribe the jurors-to-be. Big Al walked into the courtroom quite confident. He got the shock of his life when the judge switched juries, bringing in twelve men from another trial. Capone was found guilty, fined $50,000, and sentenced to eleven years. The reign of Al Capone was over.

QUESTIONS

Who were the Secret Six?
This crime-fighting team was so secretive, it's not exactly known to this day who they were. The Six were a group of Chicago businessmen dedicated to ferreting out mob influence in the city. They funded investigations, lobbied influential politicians, and helped businesses deal with extortion attempts.

Eliot Ness and the feds brought down Al Capone, but the Chicago Outfit (as the mob in the Windy City came to be known) continued on. Frank Nitti took over after Capone's demise, but "offed" himself. Evidently it was too stressful being the big cheese. Anthony "Joe Batters" Accardo, Tony Aiuppa, and Sam Giancana were a few of the successors to the legacy of Capone.

Hoover and the Mafia

Hoover became director of the FBI and remained there for almost fifty years. In that time he amassed detailed files on thousands of politicians, entertainers, and ordinary citizens. It is believed that the dirt he had on the revolving-door residents of the White House was sometimes used as blackmail, and was one of the ways he maintained job security. He was a larger-than-life figure whose image still echoes in the halls of every FBI field office across the country.

Hoover worked for the Library of Congress and later the Justice Department. He tracked down illegal aliens on the home front during World War I. There was a fear that many Germans were potential spies and saboteurs. After the war it was a fear of the communists.

The FBI Story

Hoover was placed in charge of the newly formed General Intelligence Division of the Justice Department, and his career as a lawman had begun. It was here that Hoover began his lifetime obsession of amassing files on people. In these early days it was mostly files on suspected "radical" groups. A necessary endeavor, but over the decades Hoover fancied himself the final arbiter of what was considered radical and "anti-American." The Hoover Files eventually included people like Bing Crosby and Rock Hudson, hardly rabid anarchists bent on toppling the government.

Hoover rose within the ranks of the Justice Department, seeking out and destroying communists and other radicals both real and imagined. His eyes were on his prize, his personal Holy Grail—directorship of the Bureau of Investigation, later called the Federal Bureau of Investigation. He achieved that goal in 1924 and remained in the position until his death in 1972.

Hoover dressed in white linen suits and had an avid interest in collectibles. He was never seen in the company of women and had a longtime male companion, fellow FBI agent Clyde Tolson. They worked together and lived together. Naturally, rumors about Hoover's sexual tastes were dished for decades. One mobster claimed to have seen a photograph of Hoover in women's clothing, dressed as a 1920s "flapper." The photo has never surfaced.

J. Edgar
Hoover

Courtesy of AP Images

▲ This photo shows FBI director J. Edgar Hoover speaking to the Senate Crime Investigating Committee, urging them to continue its exposure of organized crime in Washington, D.C., on March 26,1951.

FACT

There have been many movies glorifying the Federal Bureau of Investigation. James Cagney starred in the 1935 movie *G-Men*, and James Stewart put on the badge in the 1959 movie *The FBI Story*. These were done in Hoover's lifetime and with his approval, as was the long-running television show from the 1960s called *The FBI*. An updated version of that show, *Today's FBI*, ran in the early 1980s.

Melvin and Hoover

Hoover was a man full of righteous indignation and by all accounts not blessed with a sense of humor or healthy self-deprecation. He was outraged by the romanticization of gangsters in the Roaring Twenties. He achieved national attention in the Depression-ravaged 1930s when a different breed of gangster terrorized America's heartland. These were not the slick and well-oiled cogs of elaborate La Cosa Nostra machinery. These were oddballs and outcasts and misfits with colorful names like Machine Gun Kelly, Pretty Boy Floyd, Baby Face Nelson, Ma Barker, and Bonnie and Clyde.

As with the Mafia, the media often treated these cold-blooded killers as romantic modern-day Robin Hoods. Hoover was indignant and set the FBI on their trail. The spectacular shoot-'em-ups that ensued made the FBI the Wyatt Earps of the day. James Cagney took a break from his usual gangster roles to star in a movie called *G-Men* (gangster-ese for the FBI, the *G* stands for government).

The FBI has been venerated, but also criticized for their focus on the Mafia at the expense of other organized crime groups from both law enforcement and civil rights groups. In recent years the agency has formed task forces to combat emerging crime syndicates, coming a long way from the days when people joked that FBI stood for Forever Bothering Italians.

One of Hoover's star agents in the bureau was the flamboyant Melvin Purvis. He is the agent who hunted down and killed the ruthless bank robber John Dillinger, with a little help from a shady dame who has gone down in history as the "Lady in Red."

Purvis went on to corner and kill Pretty Boy Floyd and Baby Face Nelson shortly after that. He was outshining Hoover, and J. Edgar deeply resented it. Hoover made life in the FBI so miserable for Purvis that he finally resigned. Not satisfied with that, Hoover followed Purvis's career with malevolent interest, often using his influence to prevent him from getting jobs in law enforcement. In 1960 Purvis shot himself with the same gun he had used to shoot down John Dillinger. He was a victim of the egotism and hubris of J. Edgar Hoover.

Denier of the Mafia

Hoover, the intrepid lawman, keeper of the national dish and dirt, did not have an exemplary record as an antagonist of the Mafia. In fact, he repeatedly denied that an organized crime network existed in the United States. His reason for this stubborn denial could have been his titanic ego. Conspiracy theorists may find more sinister reasons for his refusal to acknowledge the mob's existence. Whatever the reasons for his belief, it made Hoover either a willing or unintentional accomplice in the Mafia's rapid growth and increased influence on the American landscape.

FACT

The FBI originated in 1908. Called the Special Agents of the Department of Justice, the group was created by President Theodore Roosevelt and Attorney General Charles Bonaparte. Initially they investigated mainly financial crimes, but the list grew exponentially. After a few more name changes the agency officially became the Federal Bureau of Investigation in 1935.

It's All Politics

The theory that gives J. Edgar Hoover the benefit of the doubt is that he was afraid that corruption would spread through the bureau if his agents had close contact with the Mafia. The Mafia would not have become as powerful as it did if not for the greed of law enforcement officials at the local and state levels. Hoover's rationale may have been to steer clear of the Mafia's seductive allure and concentrate on his favorite pursuit, tracking down real and suspected communists. Skeptics suggest that Hoover focused on the easy targets to increase his crime-busting statistics, which would enhance his personal quest for acclaim and his ability to go to Congress to make the case for higher and higher funding for his bureau.

Kindred Spirits

Some of the critics of Hoover's lack of conviction in going after the Mafia suggest that Hoover viewed the gangsters as ideological soul mates. The Mafia did not advocate the overthrow of the government and the American way of life. They were no threat to the status quo—in fact they thrived in the status quo. In some twisted way this could have mirrored Hoover's patriotic, anti-Communist stance.

It has been alleged that Hoover mingled with the Mafia. Supposedly, they were often at the same parties and social functions. Hoover loved gambling, especially on the horses, and this was a main source of the Mafia's income. Hoover was often at the racetrack with his pal Clyde Tolson. He was publicly seen betting at the $2 window, a seemingly innocuous pastime. But he had agents placing bets for him at the $100 window. It would have ruined his reputation as Mr. Law and Order if the public found out he was a high-stakes gambler.

While his track record on dealing with the Mafia is lackluster at best, Hoover was aggressive in his war against communism, called the "Red Menace" in those days. The FBI even published a pamphlet called Red Channels, which listed prominent men and women suspected of having communist affiliations.

Or were the stakes really that high? Hoover got his betting "tips" from the notorious syndicated columnist Walter Winchell, who in turn got them from Mafia boss Frank Costello. In other words, Hoover was, whether he knew it or not, betting on fixed races. Hence he was a big winner. If he did not know it then, he was being manipulated by the Mafia. If he did know about it then, Mr. FBI was engaging in behavior punishable by imprisonment.

Local Cops

For all the notoriety that the FBI has received over the years in regards to working against the Mafia, there have been scores of local and state police who had been on the front lines of the war on the rackets. The street-level cops were usually the ones who the mob tried to bribe first, but they were also the ones who usually knew what was going on in the neighborhood and where the gangsters' operations were.

Irish Joe

Joe Coffey is one of the most recognizable mob busters, due to his book and numerous TV appearances on cable news shows. The one-time head of the Organized Crime Control Bureau for the NYPD, Sergeant Joe was on the front lines, going toe-to-toe with the bad guys until he himself was put under a cloud of suspicion. He retired from the police force, became a state investigator, and cemented his reputation as a respected authority on the subject. It was Joe who first heard about the murderous Irish gangsters, the Westies, and started investigating the group. Coffey also dealt with other criminals, including serial killer David "Son of Sam" Berkowitz. Joe's sharp New York accent and stereotypical Irish cop appearance made him a natural for the news cameras. He's now a consultant for numerous news channels.

QUESTIONS

Who promoted Joe Petrosino through the ranks?
That would be our twenty-sixth president, Theodore Roosevelt. Teddy was the police commissioner from 1895 to 1897. Petrosino was promoted to the head of the homicide division under Roosevelt's tutelage.

The Original Mob Buster

Joe Petrosino was the original mob buster. An immigrant from Campania, land of the Camorra, Joe was dedicated to ridding his ethnic community of the scourge of the Black Hand. It was unusual at that time for an Italian to enter the police force. The NYPD, though, had a need for new immigrants to tackle the emerging gangster menace.

Joe was moved to a new division, the Italian Squad, dedicated to working the Italian community to root out Mafia influence. Joe hated the mob, and saw it as a stain on the character of his community. One of his targets was an elusive mob power, Vito Cascio Ferro. The mob boss fled New York to avoid prosecution. Petrosino made a bold move—he sailed to Italy to bring the criminal to justice. Unfortunately Ferro's tentacles reached far. After an evening dinner in Palermo, Sicily, Petrosino was waiting for a trolley when he had to relieve himself. With the dearth of proper public restrooms, he took to the bushes. Two gunmen took that opportunity to shoot Joe in the back, killing him instantly.

CHAPTER 6

Meanwhile Back in the Big Apple

New York City was the breeding ground for thousands of mobsters over the years, as well as a place where many of them died. Some of the early formative wars that took place in New York shaped the modern mob. The blood was spilled on crowded streets and deserted back alleys. Some bodies were found, while others simply vanished, never to be seen again. The rivalries were ages-old, the young upstarts looking to wrest control from the older, lazy bosses. The young usurped the old, and the modern Mafia was born.

Old-School Dons

The term *Mustache Pete* was an old slang expression for a conservative and cautious fellow, but it became a derisive comment used for stodgy (and stingy) bosses. It had nothing to do with facial hair and everything to do with attitude. The earliest American mobsters were given this moniker by their rivals and the young turks who sought to seize power from the old guard. The old boys were believed to be too traditional and Old World to make the Mafia a viable enterprise in the New World. Static was their ways; tending to their olives and tomatoes or leisurely sipping a cappuccino or some vintage wine while business got done at a leisurely clip was their style. The younger breed of mobster was lean and hungry, and very dangerous. They had the eye on the prize, always looking to get into new schemes and team up with mobsters across ethnic boundaries.

Boss of Bosses

In the 1930s, the most powerful and influential of the Mustache Petes were Joe "the Boss" Masseria and Salvatore Maranzano. Salvatore Maranzano originally studied for the priesthood in his native Sicily, but by the time he came to the United States in 1918, he already took the path to the underworld. But his experience in crime was not enough. He was not inclined to think outside the criminal box, and that made him a target for the up-and-coming next generation.

From Sicily

Maranzano's hometown was Castellammare del Golfo, so when he came to America, he hooked up with some people from the old neighborhood. Joseph Bonanno, Joseph Profaci, and Stefano Magaddino were all ruthless Mafiosi in their own right and future bigwigs in the new underworld order. Maranzano's mandate was to solidify power for his Sicilian master. This compelled him to butt heads with the Mafia "mainlanders," as they were called. His main nemesis among the mainlanders was Joe "the Boss" Masseria.

Who's the Boss?

Joe "the Boss" was New York's answer to Al Capone during the 1920s. He left his native Sicily, first seeing Lady Liberty in New York Harbor in 1903. Masseria did not come to America as a law-abiding transplant. A murder charge hung over his head in Sicily. Upon arriving in New York, he went to work for the Morello gang on Manhattan's Lower East Side, where his singular talents as an enforcer were in great demand. It was the same story as so many immigrants before him.

Future Mafia dons are nothing if not ambitious. It was not long before he grew tired of being somebody else's leg breaker. The Mustache Pete syndrome got its first kick in the pants when Masseria and a few loyal confederates attacked the Morello gang's headquarters and killed several loyalists. He carried out additional hits until the hoods decided it was better to switch than fight and consolidated under his leadership. Masseria was then one of the stronger bosses in New York City. If he could make it there, he could make it anywhere.

A rival gangster ambushed Masseria in 1922. The rival opened fire on Joe and his bodyguards, hitting them but missing Joe, who ran into a nearby shop to avoid the onslaught. The rival mobster followed Masseria into the shop firing away. Joe ducked behind merchandise and managed to run out of the store without being hit.

Unbreakable

Masseria gained a reputation as something of a super-gangster by his ability to survive multiple assassination attempts during his reign. One of the first hits was ordered by a certain Signor Morello, the guy who had his gang shot out from under him. In this legendary near hit, Masseria's two bodyguards were shot dead as they flanked him on the sidewalks of New York, but hit man Umberto Valenti missed Mr. Big. He chased him into a shop, firing ten shots that the boss successfully dodged. This earned Masseria a reputation as being "bulletproof." No bad deed went unpunished, and Valenti was later whacked on the orders of Masseria. A pragmatic hood, Masseria accepted the olive branch from Morello and even made him one of his lieutenants.

Desegregating Crime

One of Masseria's protégés was the man who went on to become known by the moniker "Lucky Luciano." Lucky was not averse to mingling with the Jewish and even Irish criminal element in New York City. Masseria, an insular Mustache Pete, did not approve. He wanted to keep things among the Italians.

Masseria was, for the most part, unopposed until 1928, when Maranzano ascended to the throne of another Mafia family in New York. The rivalry between the two Mafia dons would be the first big mob war on American soil. There would be much "going to the mattresses" as they prepared for a long battle. Maranzano set out hijacking shipments of Masseria's swag and bootlegged liquor. Masseria fought back. The bodies started to pile up.

Salvatore Maranzano's killers, who shot and stabbed him to death in his New York City office, were never found. It is believed that Meyer Lansky recruited them, and two of them were named Sammy Levine and Abe Weinberg.

The Castellammarese War

The feature bout of Maranzano versus Masseria was a brutal free-for-all that went the distance and left fifty known dead, though that number is probably much higher, since the Mafia is not known for reporting its homicide statistics to the public at large. Masseria thought it was going to be a breeze. He had more men and means than the younger upstart and his Sicilian sidekicks. But the ruthless and determined Sicilian underdogs gradually wrested more and more power in the violent struggle.

Rivalries Run Deep

The two Mustache Petes battled it out for supremacy of New York City, but the real machinations were going on among the ambitious young hoods who were coming to the conclusion that they did not want to serve the winner of the war, no matter which one it may be. And the leader of the pack of wolves in waiting was a young Charlie Luciano, who would prove to be very "lucky" indeed when the dust settled and the Tommy guns were silenced.

One of the four gunmen who shot Joe "the Boss" Masseria in a Coney Island restaurant was allegedly Albert Anastasia, the man who would later make a name for himself as the head of Murder Incorporated. The driver of the getaway car for the gunmen was Ciro Terranova, nicknamed "the Artichoke King." He was so nervous he almost botched the getaway.

Lucky Luciano was, in a twisted sort of way, an insightful man of vision. He believed that Masseria and the other Mustache Petes were squandering great opportunities out of Old-World prejudices and their reticence to adapt to changing times. He wanted to do business with the other ethnic crime organizations, and Masseria would have none of it. Masseria, though slow to act, was not stupid. When he learned of Luciano's grumblings, he knew the younger man was a threat, and he took decisive action.

Lower Manhattan was full of other ethnic mobsters. There were Jewish gangsters like Sam Weiss, Abe "Kid Twist" Reles, Harry "Happy" Maione, and Charles "Charlie the Bug" Workman. The Irish had men like Big Bill Dwyer and Jack "Legs" Diamond. And Chinatown was home to warring criminal gangs affiliated with the tongs.

Luciano was kidnapped at gunpoint by three goons and hustled into the back of a limousine, where he was bound, gagged, beaten, and stabbed. Luciano regained consciousness on a desolate beach. He was surprised to find himself still alive. He wandered off the beach and walked for about a mile before offering a policeman $50 to call him a cab. The cop took him to the hospital instead, and Luciano was subjected to interrogation from law enforcement officials. He kept mum. The code of Omerta forbids squealing upon threat of a painful demise. Luciano assured the police that he would take care of the problem himself.

It was Luciano's pal Meyer Lansky who offered the theory that it was Masseria who orchestrated the hit. They could only assume that the bumbling thugs had intended to kill him, leaving him for dead without making sure he was indeed deceased. Together, Lansky and Luciano devised the plan that would end the reign of the Mustache Petes and bring the Mafia into the twentieth century.

The Last in Line

Luciano took a look at the warring factions and decided to play the two sides against each other to his own advantage. Luciano dreamed of establishing a "commission" of crime syndicates on a national level by bringing together the brightest minds in crime regardless of ethnic background, though the Italians would dominate. This was something unimaginable to the narrow-minded Mustache Petes.

Luciano met with Maranzano and some of his agents at the Bronx Zoo. Luciano agreed to take out Masseria in exchange for taking control of his rackets. Lucky set a plan in motion. He invited Masseria for a lunchtime meeting at Scarpato's Restaurant in Coney Island, a section of Brooklyn. Masseria felt safe there. He knew the owner and he knew the turf. When Luciano went to the bathroom, four men entered and blasted Masseria away. The cops questioned Luciano, but he feigned innocence. One Mustache Pete down, one more to go.

Lucky's Power Play

Lucky Luciano had made a secret deal with Maranzano to whack Masseria, but he also had plans to take care of the other Mustache Petes. The death of Masseria was only half of Luciano's business plan. Maranzano was now *Capo di tutti Capi* (the Boss of all Bosses). He summoned mobsters from all over the country for a convention. They decked the halls with religious iconography to fool the feds and any other law enforcement officials who might want to crash the party.

Meeting of the Minds

It was at this meeting that the Mafia flow chart that became "the five families" was hashed out. Maranzano was the CEO, and he appointed five VPs who would each head a "family." The heads of the criminal households would be Joseph Bonanno, Phil and Vincent Mangano, Charlie Luciano, Joseph Profaci, and Tom Gagliano.

Despite the Mafia's constant claims of honor, the old adage that there is no honor among thieves is a universal truth. Soon after this arrangement was made, Maranzano created a hit list that included most of his top lieutenants, including Lucky Luciano. He knew that one or more of these Young Turks would already be plotting to usurp him. The shooter was to be a particularly nasty killer aptly named Vincent "Mad Dog" Coll. Luciano was as lucky as ever. He got wind of the conspiracy and took preemptive measures.

QUESTIONS

What mobsters were on what sides during the war?
The Maranzanos had among their ranks future bosses Joseph Bonanno, Joseph Profaci, Thomas Lucchese, Joseph Magliocco, and Gaetano "Tom" Gagliano. The Masseria team had Lucky Luciano, Frank Costello, Joe Adonis, Vito Genovese, Albert Anastasia, and Carlo Gambino.

Luciano learned that he and Vito Genovese were to be summoned to Maranzano's office, where Coll would be waiting to off them. He also learned that the long arm of the Internal Revenue Service had its sights on Maranzano. His organization was to be the subject of an IRS audit.

The New Old-Fashioned Mob

The elder Maranzano assured his younger lieutenants that there would be room at the table for everyone and enough money to wet the beaks of all the mobsters in New York City. He envisioned control of all the rackets across the country, a worldview that eluded his neighborhood-centric predecessors. But his scheming nature was too much for Luciano. Lucky knew his days were numbered.

The End of the Petes

Once Luciano knew of the plot against him, he decided to take swift action to head off the threat. He hired four hit men to go to Maranzano's place of business, in midtown Manhattan, and take him out. The gangsters posed as IRS agents to gain entry in to the building. They disarmed Maranzano's security guard and stabbed the elder don. The era of the Mustache Petes was over, and Luciano was now the Boss of all Bosses.

The Dream

Luciano, perhaps having been influenced by American democracy and corporate structure, rejected the title. He resolved that the five families would remain intact and, along with Meyer Lansky, formed the National Crime Syndicate, also known as "the Commission." But Luciano's vision of a multiethnic Mafia did not last that long. Pretty soon it was apparent that the Italians would take center stage in the ruling commission, leaving little room for anyone else. But other forces were working. Jewish immigrants were moving out of the teeming ethnic slums at a steady clip, leaving few recruits for the ranks. The Irish were moving uptown and splintering into smaller criminal gangs, while many were taking the opposite route and becoming police officers and municipal employees. But they were never totally out of the scene. While the Mafia remained strictly Italian, there was plenty of room for other ethnic groups to work, and profit, with them.

CHAPTER 7

Charlie "Lucky" Luciano

Lucky Luciano is credited with being the architect of the American Mafia. He took the old Sicilian organization, expunged the Old-World thinking, and created the modern Mafia. He envisioned an organization run more along the lines of a business than its Sicilian counterpart was at that time. Had he been a businessman he would have made millions—legitimately. He rose to prominence during the Castellammare War. Luciano survived the bullets and lived a long life as one of the most ruthless and successful gangsters of the twentieth century.

Luciano—The Early Years

Lucky Luciano was born Salvatore Luciana in Sicily in 1897. Like so many other millions of Europeans in the nineteenth century, who heard tales of a promised land where the streets were paved with gold, his family set sail for America only to learn that the hype did not match the reality. Nevertheless, it was a land of opportunity for those on both sides of the law.

Charlie got his first arrest when he was ten. It was for shoplifting. Not a particularly glamorous start. He also ran a juvenile "protection agency," offering to protect the weaker boys for a few pennies. It was a no-win scenario for the boys—if they did not pay Charlie for protection, he promptly pummeled them.

The immigrant Mafiosi that came to America as boys and adolescents were raised in this atmosphere and were more willing to interact with other ethnic groups. In some ways this breaking down of the barriers enabled law-abiding immigrants to better assimilate into American culture, while it helped the criminals gain a stronger foothold in the existing American underworld.

While his protection racket was expanding, Luciano was getting involved in more serious crimes. While still a teen, he was on the New York Police Department's short list as the suspect in several gangland murders. He was well known to the local beat cops. And he was a member of the infamous Five Points Gang.

Getting All the Boys Together

While Luciano was shaking down kids on the street corners for protection, one of the kids refused to pay up. This kind of bravery was one way for anonymous kids to get noticed, and also a way for them to make sure they didn't remain a victim. This particular kid was another immigrant child, a Jewish kid from Poland named Meyer Lansky. Meyer stood up to Luciano, and they became fast friends and lifelong partners in crime. From this fateful meeting sprang the most successful crime outfit in American history.

Drugs and Booze

Lucky Luciano did time in a reform school for dealing heroin and morphine in 1915. This early foray into the business would expand in the coming years. In addition to drugs, booze was another profitable commodity. Every gangster was in the bootleg business during the 1920s, including Luciano. He mingled with other young hoodlums who formed a virtual Who's Who of gangland: Meyer Lansky, Bugsy Siegel, Joe Adonis, Vito Genovese, Frank Costello, Dutch Schultz, Arnold Rothstein, and an assortment of Irish gangsters. Luciano had no prejudices about mingling with hoods of all stripes. His fraternization with Irish and Jewish gangsters was unique for the time.

In Charge

After the Castellammarese War, Lucky Luciano was the top Mafia don. He did not get the nickname from surviving the near-fatal beating that left him with a fashionable scar on his cheek, an emblem befitting his status as a tough guy. He was called Lucky because of his handicapping acumen. He could pick winners at the racetrack with uncanny accuracy. And most of the time the races weren't even fixed.

FACT

Lucky Luciano had the posthumous distinction of being named by *Time* magazine as one of the 100 "Builders and Titans" of the twentieth century. He was placed in the same company as Walt Disney and Bill Gates.

Mafia bosses do not have a wide circle of trusted friends; most of the time they are keeping an eye out for underlings with a little too much ambition. Luciano maintained business and personal relations with the tough little kid who steadfastly refused his shakedown intimidation. His business and personal relationship with Meyer Lansky was one of the key factors in helping him stay at the top of the Mafia heap.

Meyer Lansky, the role model for the character of Hymn Roth in *The Godfather II*, was a shrewd and savvy businessman. But instead of choosing a career in the corporate world, Lansky stayed true to his criminal roots and became a legendary mastermind of criminal activities, probably best illustrated by the lack of time he spent behind bars.

He was born in Poland, and his real name was Majer Suchowlinski. Gambling was his true passion, and his involvement in pre-Castro Cuban casinos, racetracks, wire services, and Las Vegas brought tens of millions of dollars into the wallets of wise guys from New York to Chicago. This cohesion of mob control over mob rackets was helped along by the Commission. Now that there was a gangland "syndicate" that spanned the country and united organized crime families across America, there needed to be a governing board.

The Mob Board of Directors

Luciano and Lansky maintained the basic structure of Maranzano's Commission. The other East Coast boys were Joseph Bonanno, Vincent Mangano, Joseph Profaci, Tom Gagliano, and Stefano Magaddino of Buffalo. While the bigwigs were from New York's five families, there were also representatives from Philadelphia and Chicago. The families in larger cities controlled families in smaller cities. For example, the Chicago boys controlled all the Midwest families in Kansas City, St. Louis, Milwaukee, and Detroit (though some say that Motor City boss Joe Zerilli was a Commission member for a time).

FACT

The last known meeting of the Commission took place in 2000 and was led by Bonanno boss Joe Massino as well as representatives from the other New York families. Although that was the last one that the feds know about, there may have been some since then. It's supposed to be a secret after all.

Also there were various side meeting, like the La Stella meeting in Queens in the 1960s that featured Tampa boss Santo Trafficante Jr., New Orleans boss Carlos Marcello and his underlings, and some of the New York Commission members.

In the early years, the Commission was made up of mostly Italian and Jewish gangsters. The "Big Six" included Frank Costello, Joe Adonis, Meyer Lansky, Tony Accardo, Jake Guzik, and Longy Zwillman. However, the Jewish influence faded over time as the sons of the Jewish gangsters, for the most part, did not follow in the family business. The next generation went into legitimate careers. Lansky even saw one of his sons go to West Point. The sociocultural phenomenon of Jewish gangsterism lasted just a single generation in America, although there are still some active Jewish associates of the Mafia.

There is a supposed tell-all book by Luciano. Entitled *The Last Testament of Lucky Luciano*, by Martin A. Gosch and Richard Hammer, it is an account of the legendary gangster's exploits he relayed to the authors before his death. Be forewarned, however, that many experts on the Mafia doubt the truthfulness of many of the authors' claims that this information was all from Luciano's mouth.

One of the reasons that the Commission was a long-lasting success was because it was structured as a board of directors, each with equal power and no one man in charge. There were men who came to be regarded as the "Boss of Bosses" from time to time, but all major decisions were voted on, and no one man had veto power. This also made is easier to try and smooth over differences before they erupted into all out war. This, of course, did not always happen.

Mediation and Murder

Much of the role of the Commission was to mediate and settle disputes between rival families in the United States, and to keep things running smoothly with the Sicilian Mafia in the old country. When things could not be worked out over a discussion, the problem was taken care of with a gun or garrote. At its height, the Commission represented about 1,700 made Mafia members in over two dozen families nationwide, not to mention all the associates that were under the made members.

The Dream Is Over

The legacy Lucky Luciano and Meyer Lansky had left behind suffered an irrevocable blow in 1986 when the heads of the five families were successfully prosecuted and convicted for their crimes by U.S. attorney Rudy Giuliani. Of course, that wasn't the deathblow to the Mafia, but it was finally official proof that the Commission existed and made decisions regarding the Mafia's activities.

ALERT!

Lucky Luciano, at the end of life, had this to say about his legacy: "I learned too late that you need just as good a brain to make a crooked million as an honest million. These days you apply for a license to steal from the public."

Dewey Defeats Lucky

Lucky Luciano was a high-profile gangster. Unlike the low-key Meyer Lansky, Mr. Lucky was often seen at the trendiest nightclubs hobnobbing with the glitterati of the day. The high life took its toll. Prostitution was one of his many rackets, and his familiarity with the prostitutes gave him multiple bouts of gonorrhea and syphilis. When the Mafia ventured into the drug business, Lucky Luciano made sure that he got as many of the prostitutes hooked on heroin as he could, to better control them. This also made them turn their profits right back to him to feed their addiction. But the law was growing impatient with the mob run amok. The government went after Lucky Luciano in the form of Special Prosecutor Thomas Dewey.

The Prosecutor

Thomas Dewey aggressively went after the prostitution racket in New York. And while his attention to the vice was admirable, he also had certain political aspirations that a well-publicized campaign could help bring about. During the early part of his campaign, forty brothels were raided and 100 or so women were arrested. Many of them told sad tales of their lives and their many abuses at the hands of the syndicate. Soon Luciano had a large group of women spilling the beans to the law. Dewey saw this as an opportunity to take down the biggest mobster in town, but more importantly, get him the publicity he was craving. He started compiling an airtight indictment.

Feeling the heat, Luciano decided to take in the waters at Hot Springs, Arkansas. Just before Lucky went there, famed English gangster Owney "the Killer" Madden left New York and opened up a hotel. Over the years it became a de facto hideout for gangsters on the lam, as well as those looking to get some relaxation at one of the many spas. Not soon after Luciano arrived, he was arrested. They shipped him back to New York and he was put on trial. The sensational news media covered it all breathlessly, eagerly awaiting each day's testimony. In the end, he was convicted and sentenced to thirty to fifty years in prison.

FACT

Dewey's political career soared after his prosecution of Luciano. He was elected as governor of New York State three times and ran for president three times, albeit unsuccessfully. After his last term as governor, he started a private law practice. He died in 1971.

In the Big House

Luciano was sent to the Clinton State Prison in upstate New York. The prison is also referred to as Dannemora, and was not considered to be as "comfortable" as Ossining, known in the vernacular as "Sing-Sing," just a few miles north of Manhattan. Lucky was assigned number 92169 and put to work in the laundry room. In short order he went from laundering ill-gotten booty to washing other convict's clothes.

Dannemora was not a model modern rehabilitation facility. It was positively medieval, with none of the amenities to which Mr. Big had grown accustomed. However, his influential pals on the outside saw to it that he had certain privileges.

Uncle Sam Wants Lucky

Lucky Luciano was locked up from 1936 to 1942. He was allowed as many visitors as he liked, and no record was made of who came to see him. Thus he continued to pull the strings and run the syndicate from his prison cell. And when America entered World War II after the Japanese attack on Pearl Harbor, the godfather found a surprising ally in his bid to win freedom—the very government that sent him there in the first place.

Benito Mussolini, Italy's fascist dictator, had made many enemies among the Sicilian Mafia. The old political adage "the enemy of my enemy is my friend" suddenly applied to relations between the United States government and the Mafia. Luciano used the *Normandie* incident to make a case that he could guarantee the safety of the American ports. He dispatched Meyer Lansky to let the mob's political contacts know that Luciano would be of valuable assistance in the war effort. Lansky pointed out that in addition to the port safety issue, Luciano could help with espionage in Sicily. Sabotage was a serious threat, and who better than the gangsters who ruled the docks to "police" them for the government?

FACT

The ocean liner *Normandie*, renamed USS *Lafayette*, was being overhauled into a troopship for American soldiers. It caught fire on Pier 88 in Manhattan, capsizing in the Hudson River. Authorities suspected arson, though other sources say it was an accident. Whatever the cause, this event spooked military officials and made them give the threat of sabotage on American soil more credence.

Luciano was moved to Great Meadows Prison in Comstock, New York. This was a Club Med compared to the dank Dannemora. From this new base of operations he continued to run his underworld enterprises and help the Office of Naval Intelligence by providing information about German military activity on the island of Sicily. Military intelligence agents made numerous clandestine trips to Luciano's prison cell to secure his assistance.

"Lucky" Luciano

Courtesy of AP Images/Remo Nassi

▲ Reputed mobster Charles "Lucky" Luciano sips a drink during a news conference he called in the bar of Rome's Excelsior Hotel, June 11, 1948. Luciano said he wanted "to set the record straight." At extreme left is AP writer Johnny McKnight.

The Mafia was happy to oblige. Mussolini's government had waged a war against the Mafia in Sicily, sending hundreds to prisons while killing many more. Ironically, when the American and British forces liberated Sicily, they also released hundreds of Mafiosi from Sicilian prisons, thinking they were political prisoners of the fascist government.

Room Service

Lucky Luciano was granted gourmet meals, plenty of booze, and even the pleasure of female companionship while incarcerated in Great Meadows. He also expected an early release from prison as a reward for his contribution to the war effort. It is ironic that the man who had him locked up, Thomas Dewey, was also the man who commuted Luciano's sentence. Now governor of New York, Dewey was asked by the federal government to set Luciano free. But both the feds and Dewey were not too keen on letting Luciano back onto the streets of New York City. Since Luciano never bothered to become an American citizen, he was deported to Italy.

The Later Years

Luciano left America in 1946, never to return. He settled in Naples under the watchful eye of the Italian authorities. He could not travel more than a few miles out of town, and all foreign visitors had to be reported to authorities. But those restrictions did not last long. Luciano traveled to Cuba to hold a major conference with representatives from all the Mafia families, as well as Corsican, Italian, and Canadian crime figures.

FACT

Lucky Luciano was not publicity-shy at the end of his life. In fact, he suffered a fatal heart attack while waiting at the Naples airport for a visitor—not one of his Mafia buddies but a Hollywood producer who was interested in making a movie about the famous gangster's violent life.

Luciano's absence from the American scene kept him out of touch with the day-to-day activities of the mob. Luciano was still the de facto head of the Commission, but since he was deported, his influence naturally faded, and Lansky assumed more power. This did not go over too well with Luciano, who was expanding his drug empire in Italy, but there was little he could do.

While Luciano's role in an international heroin smuggling ring with ties to the Trafficante family in Tampa and the Canadian mob was under investigation, he beat the law once more. In 1962 he suffered a fatal heart attack in Naples. It was the end of the violent life and times of a man who made a nice living through nasty means and helped create a modern criminal empire.

CHAPTER 8

Essentials of the Modern Mafia

The Mafia has a structure and chain of command like any other corporation. There are CEOs who run things, boards to answer to, midlevel managers climbing their way up, and even accountants. And while some people may joke that there's little difference between a corporate board and the Mafia, the fact is the Mafia's structure is one of the reasons the mob has been able to succeed in the business of crime. But like the business world, jealousy, people striving to get ahead, and office politics cause friction. But unlike the corporate world, in the mob when such upsets happen, people get killed.

The Commission

The Mustache Petes, the conservative Old-World dons, established the Commission. But while the old system had a supreme leader who called the shots over the rest of the representatives, Lucky Luciano envisioned a more representative body that could work out disputes and territorial differences. The Commission was originally made up of the five New York Mafia families as well as the Buffalo family.

FACT

Before he became mayor of New York City, Rudy Giuliani made a name for himself as the U.S. attorney general for southern New York. In 1986 he succeeded in getting convictions against the five New York mafia heads in the "Commission Case."

Corporate America

The Commission was one of the most successful and long-running "corporate" entities in the history of American "business." For the most part it ran smoothly. Decisions were made and disputes were settled with a minimum of hard feelings. And when it came time to whack someone, a vote was taken. Hotheads who took it upon themselves to kill someone were often killed, especially if their target was someone outside the Mafia. The Commission met many times over the years in Chicago, Havana, and New York City. Police started getting a handle on the meetings and actually survalenced one in New York City. It is believed by law enforcement that the Commission is now a shadow of its former self; the last known meeting was in New York City at the turn of the new century.

The Administration

At the head of every Mafia family, there is one man who calls the shots. He is called the boss, the don, or sometimes the godfather. As the boss, he has the ultimate say in how the family operates, what rackets it gets into, and settles disputes not only among its members but with other criminal organizations. As a result, the boss has a target on his back from both upstarts in the mob and law enforcement. It's a stress-filled job, but there always seems to be candidates willing to fill it. Directly below the boss is the aptly named underboss. He is the second most powerful member of the crime family. He deals with the day-to-day operations of the family and has a more hands-on approach than the don. There are occasions when the boss and/or the underboss are in prison and they may assign an acting boss or acting underboss to take their place. Usually the acting boss or underboss serves as a conduit, relaying messages from prison.

Sometimes families have a *consigliere*, or counselor. This person is the chief adviser to the don in all matters of policy. In many cases the consigliere is an older member of the mob family, usually semiretired. He's used to give advice on all family matters and is relied on as an objective voice. In some cases, like Tampa, there is an advisory council, or group of consiglieres who advise the boss on mob matters.

Middle Management

At the middle-management levels of the Mafia, there is the *caporegime*. He is the equivalent of a lieutenant in the crime family. Usually called *capo* for short, he controls a crew of about ten or so underlings. Capo is also sometimes the diminutive of *capodecina*, which literally means "captain of ten." These crews commit the crimes and report the results and surrender the lion's share of the loot to the capo. He sees that it flows upward to the boss.

Button Men

Below the capos are the soldiers. These are the grunts who get their hands dirty. The crews carry out the heists, hijackings, and hits that make up the day-to-day workings of a typical Mafia family. The soldiers are all "made" men, meaning they have been officially indoctrinated into the family, taken the vow of Omerta, and have committed at least one murder, though the last requirement seems to be more folklore than fact.

There have been relatively few father-to-son transfers of power in the Mafia. One of the earliest was the ascension of Santo Trafficante Jr., who took over for his father in 1954. Some transfers were not so successful. John Gotti Jr. was appointed to run the Gambino family by his imprisoned father, but he was arrested only a few years later.

Rising Through the Ranks

Unlike in legitimate businesses, men often rise in the Mafia through murderous means. Albert Anastasia killed his don to become the boss. So did John Gotti. This is why a don can never truly be at peace. The vice president of sales may be concerned about an aggressive young salesman who is out to get his job, but it is unlikely that he will be whacked by the junior man. The mob is full of stories off bosses being whacked, especially during the '20s and '30s, when the mob was in its infancy.

People often run into difficulty when they hire friends and relatives. But some Mafia families, like the Detroit family, are a collection of intertwining relationships, both through blood and through marriage. There are also cross-family marriages that link together powerful Mafia families.

On the lower rungs of the Mafia ladder, promotions can come more peacefully. A soldier can make capo without necessarily having to whack his superior; though, this does happen. Transfers of power naturally happen based on merit, but just like any other business, it is not always what you know but who you know. A favored underling can rise within the ranks and surpass more deserving mobsters.

Associates—The Vital Link

Next down on the Mafia food chain are the associates. They are not made guys, but they are the most important part of a successful Mafia family. They work with the crews, some with hopes of one day being made, others knowing they can't because of their ethnic background. Some associates, like Chicago gangsters Murray "the Camel" Humphries and Gus Alex, were probably more powerful and influential than many of the made guys in the Mafia.

Associates are usually the closest to the street and are the bookmakers, loan sharks, drug runners, as well as the errand boys and messengers for the made mobsters. Some associates are corrupt cops, accountants, politicians, business partners, and financial consultants who help the mobsters in a variety of ways—all illegal.

Associates are the main group of criminals in a mobster's crew. They are often used for the dirty work, and that includes murder and beatings. If a leg needs to be broken, a made guy will often send an associate. They report directly to their soldier or in some cases, the capo. They are ambitious young hoods who desperately want to be made. Though valuable (they are more than willing to hit, whack, ice, or burn any target, since this is a prerequisite to being made), they are also regarded with a wary eye by the elder gangsters, since they may be a threat sometime down the line.

For a look at street-level gangster life, a great movie to see is the criminally underrated *Friends of Eddie Coyle* about low-level Irish gangsters in the Boston underworld. It gives an overview off the less-than-glamorous aspect of mob life.

What It Means to Be Made

As important as an associate may be, he is still thought of as a simple errand boy or enforcer. He may run a huge, sophisticated betting operation, or he may visit regular customers, take the bets, and collect the money and return it to the "office." Either way, he is still not a made guy and does not get to enjoy some of the privileges of being an official member of the Mafia.

To be made, a prospect must be sponsored by a made guy. The gangster vouches for the prospect (which can cause a problem if the prospect is an undercover cop). Then a ceremony is held to officially induct the prospect into the Mafia. From then on they are considered made guys, or "friends of ours." To be made means they can control and demand money from associates, they cannot sleep with the girlfriend or wife of another made guy, and cannot hit another made guy. Being made also means a bigger set of responsibilities and respect from others in the underworld. Of course, being a made guy puts you out in front as a target for the law.

CHAPTER 9

The Five Families of New York

The Mafia gained its greatest presence in New York City. From the turn of the twentieth century, the organized crime outfits that have become known as "the five families" of New York have had their share of family ties, family feuds, and family affairs. Together they carved up the biggest city in the nation into their own personal fiefdoms. A slogan that appeared on T-shirts a few years ago in Greenwich Village summed it up best: "New York City, Family Owned and Operated Since 1920." This chapter will look at the history and the cast of characters of these infamous crime families.

Epicenter of the Mafia

New York gained a lot from the immigrants that streamed into the country at the turn of the twentieth century—future business leaders, politicians, doctors, and so on. As discussed in previous chapters, there was also the dark underside of the Mafia. New York was the breeding ground for thousands of mobsters over the years. It was a natural place for the mob to work their trade. As an economic powerhouse, New York also had a strong union presence, easy pickings for the mob. With two of the busiest airports in America, coupled with an extensive port facility, the mob had a ready supply of goods to hijack and sell. And with various ethnic neighborhoods spread across all five boroughs, it was easy for the gangsters to recruit young talent.

Manhattan

The heart of New York City was the first major home of organized crime. Along Mulberry Street in Little Italy, among the street vendors and restaurants, were social clubs where mobsters gathered to discuss schemes over drinks and cards. Just across Canal the Asian gangs ruled, but the two groups didn't intermingle often. Just east from Little Italy was the Lower East Side, the once predominantly Jewish neighborhood that gave rise to some of the infamous early Jewish gangsters. The last place where the gangsters grew up was East Harlem. Now dominated by Latinos, it was once a large, thriving Italian neighborhood and home to large-scale narcotics dealers. It was also the headquarters of Genovese boss Fat Tony Salerno, the stereotypical gangster with a permanent scowl and a half-lit cheap cigar hanging from his mouth.

The Outer Boroughs

Brooklyn was home to some of the largest mobbed-up neighborhoods in New York. The Brooklyn accent is the one most people associate with the stereotypical mobster. The necklace of neighborhoods of South Brooklyn, including Bensonhurst, Bay Ridge, Gravesend, and Canarsie, were fertile grounds for the mob. Not only did they recruit from there and run their rackets, but they also lived in the neighborhoods.

Queens was home to mob boss John Gotti, who lived in the close-knit neighborhood of Howard Beach, located near Kennedy Airport. Queens was also the home to influential members of the Lucchese families. Continuing eastward, out into suburban Long Island, all five families had representatives who chose the life of middle-class suburbia over the crowded rat race of "the Volcano," a term Joe Bonanno used to describe New York City.

The Bronx, traditionally a symbol of urban decay, actually had a significant mob population. The area around Arthur Avenue was a mobbed-up neighborhood. And currently there is a significant mob presence in the Pelham Bay/Throgg's Neck section of the borough.

Staten Island has always been the forgotten borough, but some wise guys chose to live there. It was an easy commute into the city. Mob boss Paul Castellano lived in a garish white mansion on the Island. Staten Island also had a lot of young wise guys operating there over the years.

Of course, the mob was an extremely small portion of the population of these neighborhoods. And while some people viewed them as Robin Hood–type protectors of the local populace, the fact was these neighborhoods were as much the victims of Mafia crime as other areas of the city.

Bensonhurst was home to dozens of mobsters, including Sammy "the Bull" Gravano. During the 1970s Bensonhurst and nearby Bay Ridge were the centers of the disco scene popularized in *Saturday Night Fever*.

The Bonanno Family

Joseph Bonanno, also known as Joe Bananas, died in 2002 at the ripe old age of ninety-seven in the dry sunny climes of Arizona. He was the first Mafia don to violate the sacred code of Omerta. The way he did it was a little different than the so-called "rats" who sang for the feds. He never testified to any grand jury or prosecutors. Rather, he wrote a memoir, detailing his life as a mob boss. But since he wasn't that active after his move to Tucson, much of what he wrote about was ancient history. But his recollections of Commission meetings gave the then U.S. attorney Rudy Giuliani the idea to use Joe Bananas's memoirs to try and get the aging don to talk under oath. Joe refused and spent a year in jail for contempt. Sometimes "wise guys" are not very smart. Ego has been the downfall of more than one Mafia don.

Joe Bonanno leaves a courtroom in San Jose, Calif. in this Jan. 13, 1981, file photo. When Bonanno, then eighty, retired and living in Arizona, was summoned in 1985 to testify at a federal prosecution, his lawyer William Kunstler said his client was definitely too ill to take the witness stand. The stress of testifying, Kunstler insisted, was too much for the octogenarian mobster. Bonanno died at the ripe old age of ninety-seven. Kunstler had died seven years earlier at seventy-six. ▶

Joe Bonanno

Courtesy of AP Images

Leading the Family

It was a small family, but Bonanno ran a tight ship. His was a presence that commanded respect. He was a natural leader of men, one of many Mafiosi who could probably have done much good in the world with their people skills had they been inclined toward the straight and narrow.

FACT

Though a long-respected Mafia family, the Bonannos were actually dropped from the Mafia Commission for a time due to their drug activities. Ironically, when the Commission met in the late 1990s, the Bonannos were the only ones with a boss who was not imprisoned.

Joe Bonanno ascended to power in 1931. The twenty-six-year-old Bonanno, handpicked by Lucky Luciano himself, was the youngest man ever to become head of a family. Bonanno made alliances with more powerful dons. He made his family's fortune through gambling, loansharking, and eventually drugs.

Though he kept a low profile and tried to steer clear of the troubles that plagued the other mob families, in the 1960s, Joe Bananas was fed up with the Gambino and Lucchese families. He plotted, with mob boss Joe Magliocco, to have the leaders of the other two families, as well as Joe's cousin, Buffalo boss Stefano Magaddino, taken out.

ALERT!

Gay Talese's book *Honor Thy Father* is an insider's look at the Bonanno family in the 1960s. It was written in cooperation with the Bonannos themselves, so the other four families had a beef with the way they were depicted in the book.

But to Bonanno's chagrin, one of the hit men assigned to the task, Joe Colombo, switched allegiances and spilled the beans to the opposition. The Commission summoned Bonanno and Magliocco to appear, but Bonanno refused and went into hiding. Magliocco was let off with a fine, but Bonanno was dethroned by the Commission and replaced by Gaspar DiGregorio.

After the Commission basically took control of his family, Bonanno vanished. After his surprise reappearance a number of months later, he said he was kidnapped by the Buffalo family, but skeptics thought that he was just avoiding a subpoena to appear before a grand jury, as well as any attempts on his life.

Going Bananas

Joe Bonanno emerged from his mysterious disappearance after nineteen months. He declined to say where he had been. Some believe he had been a prisoner of the Commission. It is thought likely that he was set free on the condition he would leave the crime scene quietly and permanently. He did no such thing. The Banana War, as the local news media liked to call it, was on. The Commission had replaced Gaspar DiGregorio with a hood named Paul Sciacca after DiGregorio botched a hit on young Bill Bonanno, son of Joseph Bonanno, and his boys. Sciacca's team was no match for the Bonannos. Nevertheless, the war went on for years during the 1960s. Bonanno suffered a heart attack and headed for Arizona and retirement. The Banana War ground to a halt, and Sciacca took control of Bonanno's Brooklyn rackets.

Carmine

Brutal narcotics trafficker Carmine Galante took the reins of the Bonanno family. Galante was tough and fearless and more than a little sadistic. He was universally unpopular with the mobsters from all five families. The Commission had wanted Bonanno out of power so they could better control the unruly family, and in Carmine Galante they had a far worse and more reckless and violent loose cannon. There was a meeting of the Commission as well as Galante associates like Tampa boss Santo Trafficante Jr. They decided that Galante had to go. Carmine was gunned down at Joe and Mary's Italian Restaurant in Brooklyn. Though he fell to the ground after being shot, his cigar never even fell out of his mouth.

Galante was replaced by Rusty Rastelli, who returned to the role after an absence of many years. He brought the family into the video pornography business and an expanded role in drug trafficking that pushed the family to the brink of oblivion. Rastelli went to prison, where he died in 1991. He was replaced by Joseph Massino, who rebuilt the family to the third most powerful in New York. But after a series of successful prosecutions and the turning of Massino himself, the family was battered—but not totally down.

Under the don-ship of Rusty Rastelli, the events that formed the basis for the Mafia movie *Donnie Brasco* occurred. FBI agent Joseph D. Pistone infiltrated the family, lived the lifestyle, became friends with Dominick "Sonny Black" Napolitano and Benjamin "Lefty Guns" Ruggiero, and then betrayed them, sending several family members to jail and prompting the "disappearance" of Napolitano in the 1970s.

The Colombo Family

Like Joe Bonanno, Joe Profaci took over a crime family when the Castellammarese War ended. He had a reputation as a cheapskate Mafioso. He charged members of his family the equivalent of union dues. Each soldier and capo (literally "captain" in Italian, meaning a Mafioso who supervises the soldiers) had to fork over $25 a month for the privilege of being in the family.

He was so unpopular that there was a mutiny in his ranks. Three brothers—Joey, Larry, and Albert Gallo—and others were dissatisfied with Profaci's reign and were making plans to oust him. This came to be known as "the Gallo Wars." The Gallos were making some strides against Profaci until Joe was sent to prison in 1961 for ten years.

The Don Is Dead

Joe Profaci died in 1962 and was replaced by his underboss, Joe Magliocco. After the failed Bonanno/Magliocco attempt on the Lucchese and Gambinos, Magliocco started a downhill slide, and he died of natural causes a few months later. He was succeeded by Joe Colombo, the very turncoat who ratted out Magliocco and Bonanno to the Commission.

Italian Civil Rights

When Joe Colombo took over the family, it became known from then on as the Colombo family. While the other mob bosses took pains to keep themselves as low profile as possible, Colombo swaggered around with a flamboyant air, drawing not only the watchful eye of law enforcement but the ire of the other dons as well. He was told on numerous occasions to downplay his role.

ALERT!

New York's five families were forever fighting one another, but the Colombo family earns the distinction of the most fights within its own ranks. Three brutal internal wars were fought in its bloody history.

Civil Rights Crusader

With various groups campaigning for civil rights, Joe Colombo thought it would be a good idea to exploit the ethnic pride of Italian Americans by staging a series of public rallies that would equate anti-Mafia sentiment with anti-Italian racism. He accused the feds of being anti-Italian in their prosecution of the Mafia, even going so far as to picket FBI headquarters in New York City. Joe took it one step further, forming the Italian-American Civil Rights League and holding a unity rally. The first Italian Unity Day rally was a huge success, even drawing the participation of politicians. But Carlo Gambino was fed up with the man he recommended as don. Gambino told Colombo to stop—or else—and Colombo refused.

At the second Italian Unity Day rally, Joe Colombo was shot in the head. The perpetrator was an African American who was killed at the scene by a police officer. Though portrayed as a lone gunman, he was likely sent by Gambino. Colombo did not die immediately, however. He lingered in a vegetative coma for seven years before finally dying.

The Snake

Vincent Aloi took over briefly as acting boss of the Colombo family after Joe Colombo's shooting. He was an old-timer who had served in the lower levels of the Mafia since its glory days. After only a short reign, he transferred power to Carmine "the Snake" Persico, who was in prison when Colombo was shot. The Snake was the official underboss at the time.

Joseph Anthony Colombo Sr.

Courtesy of AP Images

▲ Organized crime boss Joseph Anthony Colombo Sr. is shown in 1971.

Persico was sent to prison in the 1980s, but he pulled the strings from behind bars, setting in motion a vicious internal war in the early 1990s that virtually wiped out the family's active membership from both killings and the increased pressure from law enforcement. Since Persico's imprisonment, the family has gone through over ten acting and official bosses. The family is now the smallest of the five families.

FACT

Colombo family member "Crazy Joe" Gallo had many celebrity friends. He was married in the home of actor Jerry Orbach. Gallo was also the subject of the classic Bob Dylan song "Joey."

The Genovese Family

The celebrated and infamous Lucky Luciano was the first head of this crime family. When Luciano was sent to prison in 1936, his henchman Frank Costello took over.

Costello was a different breed of don. He was not a micromanager, nor was he into the sensational aspects of being a gangster. He was more like quiet Meyer Lansky, who pulled strings and made bundles of money and stayed out of the headlines. Costello was a "big picture" guy who looked beyond New York City to expand his family's interests as far west as Las Vegas and as far south as Cuba. Costello was affectionately called "the Prime Minister" because of his diplomatic skills, and his ability to delegate leadership made his family a lot of money.

Vito and Costello

Vito Genovese, the namesake of the crime family, had served as Luciano's underboss, and by all rights he should have succeeded Mr. Lucky as boss. Genovese, however, left the country to avoid a murder charge and was languishing in Italy. After World War II, Genovese came back to America, where he was expected to stand trial for the murder. As often happens in

Mafia murder trials, key witnesses were themselves mysteriously murdered. As a result, Genovese remained a free man.

Vito Genovese and Frank Costello vied for control of the crime family for many years. Genovese chipped away at Costello's power with a series of small but significant moves. A series of hits eliminated many of the top guns in Costello's corner. But Costello was able to keep control by exerting his influence over other families. This kept the balance of power in Costello's favor for a few more years.

Frank Costello, born as Francesco Castiglia, preferred negotiation to assassination and was a shrewd and skilled leader of men. (And a lucky one, too.) He survived a shot to the head, which only grazed him, by a hit man who could not shoot straight; Costello lived to tell the tale.

In 1957, Vito Genovese staged an unsuccessful hit on Costello. Costello was shot and wounded in the lobby of his luxury apartment building on Manhattan's Central Park West. The hit man who missed was Vincent "Chin" Gigante, who went on to be one of the Mafia's most colorful characters.

But Genovese was able to get rid of one of Costello's closest allies, Albert Anastasia, boss of the soon-to-be Gambino family. In the sensational barbershop chair hit, Genovese was helped by an Anastasia associate, Carlo Gambino, who then assumed control of the family. Gambino then switched sides and joined an alliance with Costello and Meyer Lansky to take out the ambitious Genovese.

Frank Costello decided to retire. Genovese was now the top dog. However, Genovese dabbled in narcotics, which led to his downfall. He was sent to prison after assuming control of the family.

Successors

Genovese continued to control his empire from his jail cell. Mafiosi have often had special privileges while in prison. Through bribery of guards and prison officials, mobsters had access to better food, drugs, phone calls, meeting rooms, and plenty of conjugal visits. This freedom behind bars enabled many of the big kingpins to continue to oversee and run their crime families from the slammer.

Genovese was monitoring his gangland operations and even ordering hits during his sentence. Nevertheless, he could not be a completely hands-on don from the little cell he shared with informant-to-be Joe Valachi. The men on the outside whom Genovese relied on were not the brightest bulbs lighting the underworld, and they could not compete with the machinations of the savvy Carlo Gambino and usurpation in his own family.

The Genovese family leadership went to great lengths to avoid being watched by the feds. They would hide in the backs of cars while traveling to meetings, hold sit-downs in the early mornings, and rotate their hang-outs across New York City.

Vito Genovese died in prison on Valentine's Day 1969. While he was in prison the Genovese family was ruled by a threesome—Thomas Eboli, Gerardo "Jerry" Catena, and Philip "Benny Squint" Lombardo (also known as "Cockeyed Phil"). While Eboli was out front, many in the know thought that Lombardo was the real boss. The wily Genovese wise guys were known to have false front-bosses in order to hide who was really running things.

Gerardo Catena was one of the most influential Genovese bosses in New Jersey, but he remained above any internal family politics and below law enforcement's radar. After his release from prison in 1972, Catena moved to Florida. He died of natural causes at age ninety-eight in 2000.

Eboli was not respected by his own men or the Mafia community at large. And if you're not a man of respect in the Mafia, your lifespan is often a short one. After a botched drug deal with the Gambino family, Eboli was whacked while leaving his girlfriend's apartment. Lombardo and Catena sank back into the shadows and Gambino cleared the way for Frank "Funzi" Tieri to fill the slot. "Funzi," though not a household name like Gotti or Capone, was an effective don who brought the Genovese family back to prominence. He also never forgot that it was Gambino who put him there.

When Tieri died in 1981, it is believed that "Fat Tony" Salerno took over, though other sources maintain that it was "Cockeyed Phil" Lombardo. The Genovese crime family became the second most powerful of the five families, second only to the Gambinos.

Taking It on the Chin

When Salerno was sent away for 100 years, the colorful and eccentric Vincent "Chin" Gigante took over. The Chin had a unique way to keep the law off his case. And it almost worked. Gigante was often seen wandering around his Greenwich Village neighborhood in a bathrobe and talking to himself. This behavior caused wags to give him the moniker "the Oddfather." It was generally accepted that he was faking it in an effort to avoid prosecution for his many crimes via an insanity plea. The feds were not fooled. Secret wiretapped conversations revealed a sane and lucid criminal mind at work. In 1996 he was charged with murder and racketeering and was sentenced to twelve years in prison. He died in December 2005.

The Gambino Family

The Gambino family became the most famous and successful family in America under the leadership of Carlo Gambino and later the "Dapper Don," John Gotti. From 1957 until his death in 1976, Gambino made the family more powerful than the formidable empires of Lucky Luciano and Al Capone. It also suffered its greatest setbacks under the egotistical Gotti's flamboyant stewardship. Most recently the family let in an undercover FBI agent, Jack Garcia, known on the street as Jack Falcone. Garcia so ingrained himself into the family's structure that capo Greg DePalma was going to propose him for membership. But before that could happen the feds closed the operation and took down a sizable chunk of the upper echelon.

The Beginnings

The earliest incarnation of what was to become the Gambino family began in New York in the 1920s during the days of the Castellammarese War. Alfred Mineo and Steve Ferrigno were bosses of the Brooklyn crime outfit. They were taken out of the picture in 1930, more victims of the mob war. Frank Scalise took over briefly, before Vincent Mangano took control. Along with his brother Phil they ruled the roost until they were killed by their ambitious and psychotic henchman Albert Anastasia, who remained boss until his famous barbershop murder in 1957.

Under Anastasia's watch, which in turn was under the watchful eye of Frank Costello, the crime family grew in power and stature. But Anastasia was not nicknamed the "Mad Hatter" for nothing. Being a don required more subtlety and diplomacy, things Anastasia did not have in abundance. He was a loose cannon who brought unwanted publicity to the Mafia, not to mention his penchant for stepping on other mobster's shoes, especially in trying to muscle in on the Cuban rackets.

Anastasia's henchman Carlo Gambino was a collaborator in Anastasia's murder, and Gambino assumed control of the family as a reward for a job well done.

Changing Leadership

With Vito Genovese in jail and Frank Costello in retirement, Carlo Gambino became the unofficial Boss of Bosses. It was unofficial because the structure of the Commission was just that, a committee with no one boss. But Gambino's family was the strongest; he ran a tight ship. Their reach extended across the Northeast and south into Florida and Louisiana.

When Carlo Gambino became ill in the 1970s, his underlings were jockeying for position as his heir apparent. Gambino did not choose his underboss, Aniello Dellacroce, who would have been next in the chain of command. Instead he made a rare strategic mistake and chose his brother-in-law Paul Castellano. He gave Dellacroce the consolation prize of control of the family's Manhattan rackets. Carlo Gambino died in 1976, immortalized by the *Daily News* headline, "Carlo Gambino Dies in Bed."

Carlo
Gambino

Courtesy of AP Images

▲ Carlo Gambino, Cosa Nostra organized crime leader, is shown circa 1930s.

Young Punks

The Castellano-Dellacroce leadership was uninspired, and the Young Turk John Gotti was plotting and planning as he waited in the wings. The young soldiers and capos respected Dellacroce; they did not respect Castellano. When they learned that Dellacroce was dying of cancer, they waited. In the most famous modern mob murder, Paul Castellano was killed in front of Sparks Steak House during rush hour in December of 1985.

The Lucchese Family

The Lucchese family is the smallest of the big five crime families. It does not have the name recognition factor that the Bonannos or Gambinos have. It has always had smaller membership and has kept a low profile compared to the other families. It does, however, have the distinction of being the family whose activities are the source for one of the best Mafia movies, *Goodfellas*.

FACT

Lucchese family member Peter Chiodo was shot twelve times in an attempt by the Lucchese family leadership to kill him, but he survived. They suspected he was an informant. In fact he wasn't an informant, but after being shot gave the government enough evidence to convict the Lucchese hierarchy.

The first don of the Lucchese family was Gaetano Reina. He controlled bootlegging in the Bronx under Joe Masseria. He switched sides and supported Masseria's rival Maranzano. When Masseria learned of his treachery, he was rewarded with a shotgun blast to the head administered by future crime family boss Vito Genovese. He was followed by a Mafioso with the same first name, Gaetano Gagliano. The next boss too had the first name, but he Americanized his to Tommy. He was Tommy "Three Fingers Brown" Lucchese.

Tommy Lucchese's area of expertise was corruption in the garment industry. For decades the Lucchese family was a controlling force in New York City's garment industry, and by default the rest of the country's garment business. They were involved in all aspects, from shaking down garment companies to controlling the truckers that shipped the merchandise. It was an easy way to keep their coffers full of cash and keep the gangsters in plenty of new suits.

The family was also heavily into gambling, loansharking, hijacking, and drugs. The drug trade was done on the sly. This was the era when the Mafia was becoming increasingly involved in narcotics trafficking despite its outspoken "just say no" stance. The underlings dealt drugs but coyly declined to tell their bosses where the money came from when they handed over the bosses' take of the profits. The old Mafiosi turned a blind eye to the drug dealing because it was making them a lot of money. The Luccheses even stooped so low as to sell crack cocaine in their own neighborhoods in Brooklyn.

The Lucchese family had a strong New Jersey presence, but with a large number of informants, snitches, and stoolies, their leadership in the Garden State has been decimated. Most recently in late 2007, the leadership was indicted for running a multimillion-dollar gambling operation and partnering with the Bloods in criminal endeavors.

Real Goodfellas

Paul Vario was a powerful capo in the Lucchese family. He controlled a crew in East Brooklyn that specialized in hijacking trucks and selling stolen property. In his circle was Jimmy "the Gent" Burke, a legendary Queens-based Irish gangster. Henry Hill was a punk kid who became enthralled by the neighborhood Mafiosi and fell under the influence of these two older wise guys who schooled him in the ways of gangsterism. Henry Hill's turncoat testimony, covered in a later chapter, eventually sent both Vario and Burke to prison, where they both died.

Decline and Fall

Tommy Lucchese died in 1967. He was followed by Carmine Tramunti, who served as don until he was jailed for life. His replacement was a man with the nickname "Tony Ducks." Anthony Corallo was called that because of the many times he successfully beat the rap and ducked prison. He oversaw the Lucchese family's continued involvement in corrupt labor unions, the private garbage removal business, and construction projects.

Corallo's downfall was that his car was bugged, and Ducks liked to talk a lot. In 1986, after twelve years as don, his ducking skills failed him, and he was finally imprisoned. He was sentenced to 100 years and died in prison in 2000. His successor, Vittorio Amuso, was not amused when he himself was sentenced to life imprisonment in 1992. Taking over after him was "Little Al" D'Arco. But by then the boss of the Lucchese family was not a good job to aspire to. D'Arco and his successors have all been taken out by the feds.

A Rat Problem

Henry Hill is the most famous rat in the Lucchese family, but this family has had more of a vermin infestation than any other. Hill squealed in 1980 and went into the Witness Protection Program. "Little Al" D'Arco sang for the feds during the Amuso years. So did two badfellas named Anthony "Gaspipe" Casso and "Fat Pete" Chiodo. Even with all these turncoats the family is still active, albeit severely weakened and only a shell of its former self.

CHAPTER 10

The War Years

The beginning of the Mafia's long reign at the top of the crime heap in the United States began in the years immediately following World War II. Although killings were still common, the gangland landscape began to calm for a time as the crime families took shape, weeding out the competition and solidifying ties with unions, politicians, and foreign governments. It was also the emergence of the next generation of Mafiosi. Some of the older underworld figures were aging, leaving room for the young upstarts to push their way to the front of the line. And as usual money was being made hand over fist.

Murder Incorporated—Myth or Reality?

One of the most murderous elements of the Commission merits a closer look. These gangsters decided it would be beneficial to have an elite corps of killers permanently on the payroll, just as any business will routinely contract the services of an exterminator. These guns for hire were known collectively as Murder Incorporated. Although this group's very existence has been disputed, there definitely was a group of violent criminals operating in New York at the time. The very name Murder Inc. was invented by, you guessed it, a newspaper reporter.

The Killer Elite

The mythical history of Murder Inc. gives its origins as a group of hit men for hire. Some say they were under the thumb of Lucky Luciano, as his own private army. Murder Incorporated was an internal execution squad. It did not go after law enforcement officials, journalists, or politicians. But other mobsters were fair game. The old saying that the Mafia "only kills its own" was attributed to Bugsy Siegel, a friend of both Luciano and Lansky.

Going Dutch

The man who proved that the Mafia expected the mandate of Murder Inc. to be obeyed was Dutch Schultz. Dutch Schultz was born Arthur Simon Flegenheimer in the Bronx in 1902 to Jewish parents. He was something of a mama's boy and remained close to her until his untimely demise. In a perverse way, he remained true to his mother's deep faith.

FACT

Similar to the plot of the movie *A Bronx Tale*, young Dutch Schultz grew up on the mean streets of the Bronx and became starstruck by local mob boss Marcel Poffo. He began to work for Poffo and never looked back to the straight and narrow road.

Schultz was a man on a spiritual quest. Sometimes he would claim he was practicing Judaism, other times he considered himself Catholic. He was a gangster who gave a lot of thought to the afterlife. He considered himself a religious hood.

Dutch Schultz

Courtesy of AP Images

▲ An undated photo of Arthur "Dutch Schultz" Flegenheimer.

He began his criminal career in the Bronx. Sent to prison at the age of seventeen, he was a problem inmate and was transferred to a harsher prison from which he promptly escaped, only to be soon recaptured. Committing the crime was a badge of honor among his Bronx buddies, who gave him the snappy tough guy moniker "Dutch Schultz."

Like every other gangster at the time, he was involved in the bootlegging racket during the '20s. His area of expertise was beer, and he and his cronies controlled the beer distribution in the Bronx and Upper Manhattan. His gang was comprised mostly of Jewish and Irish hooligans. But Schultz stepped on too many toes and became one of the most famous victims of Murder Inc.

Dutch Schultz lies wounded

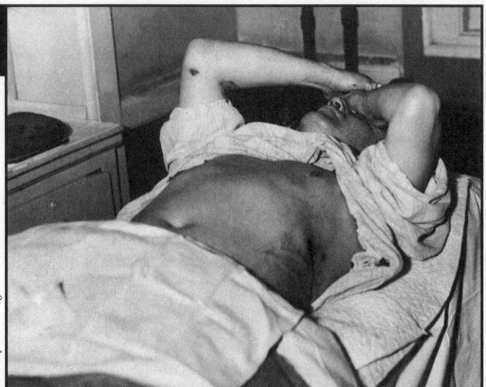

Courtesy of AP Images

▲ Mobster Dutch Schultz holds his head in agony as he lies on a hospital cot, his arm and chest wounds exposed, in Newark, N.J., on Oct. 23, 1935. Schultz and his bodyguards were shot by rival gangsters and he died later the same night from his gunshot wounds.

On October 23, 1935, in the Palace Chop House in Newark, New Jersey, Dutch Schultz and three of his associates found themselves in a pitched gunfight with Murder Incorporated. Schultz died in a nearby hospital days later. He converted to Catholicism on his deathbed, and his delirious dying ramblings are a legendary stream of consciousness mobspeak rant that inspired beatnik author William S. Burroughs to fashion a work called *The Last Words of Dutch Schultz: A Fiction in the Form of a Film Script.*

Dutch Schultz was known as "the Beer Baron of the Bronx." He made his name muscling in on the bootleg business of Irish saloonkeepers who did not shut down operations during Prohibition.

The End of the Gang

Most of the members of Murder Incorporated were Jewish gangsters. They were methodical hit men. They operated out of a Brooklyn candy store. They did not operate without orders, and their hits were well thought out and for the most part dispassionate. Hits had to have the unanimous approval of the Commission. The operated nationally, so they got to see America as they plied their trade. A simple shooting was the common form of execution, but staged accidents, faked suicides, and the occasional garroting were also accepted practices. Often the law had to write off the murders as missing-persons cases when the bodies were never found. Most hits remain unsolved, except for those revealed by the rats that squealed, and until Anastasia took power, they remained insular in their targets.

Murder Incorporated came to an end when several low-level members were arrested and began to "sing" to the authorities. The most famous was a man named Abe Reles, who was called the "Canary." He gave the police information on about 200 murders in which he was directly or indirectly involved. He was in police custody when he decided to "take a dive" out of a hotel window. It is unlikely that he took his own life out of guilt over turning traitor. It is generally assumed that he was given a gentle nudge.

What is a "policy racket"?
This was a numbers game that was popular long before state governments made it legitimate and legal in the many lottery games of today. Policy rackets thrived in poor neighborhoods, where people dreamed of making a big score and improving their lot in life.

Lepke and Sparky

One of the two top members of Murder Incorporated was Louis Lepke, born Louis Buchalter. His first mob antics involved breaking strikes by the garment workers' unions through threats and intimidation (and worse) during the 1920s. He paired with Lucky Luciano in the bootlegging racket and later became the main hit man for Murder Incorporated, carrying out hundreds of hits. He was eventually convicted of a narcotics charge, but while in jail some informants ratted him out, and he ended up convicted on a murder rap. In 1944 he and two other Murder Incorporated alumni, Mendy Weiss and Louis Capone (no relation to Al), met their maker courtesy of Old Sparky (a slang expression for the electric chair) in Sing-Sing.

Louis Lepke was betrayed by a boyhood friend with the curious name of Moey Dimples. While Lepke waited to meet his maker on death row, Moey had a few more dimples impressed upon his person in the proverbial hail of bullets. For more information on the vicious gangster Louis Lepke, look for the 1975 movie *Lepke*, starring Tony Curtis.

Wartime

The American government formed an alliance with the Mafia during World War II. They prevailed upon the jailed American gangster Lucky Luciano to use his connections with the Sicilian Mafia to monitor German troop movements as the Allied forces prepared for the invasion of Sicily. Other mobsters joined in to help, namely Vito Genovese. The Allies took control of the island, and this led to the fall of Italy and the end of Benito Mussolini's reign. Italy switched sides and joined the Allies, and Mussolini was assassinated.

Sicilian Allies

The American forces released the Mafiosi from the prisons and put them in charge of reorganizing the social and political structure of the country. To give the United States the benefit of the doubt, one can say that the military was not aware of the criminal tendencies of these men. If they were looking at the situation in straightforward terms of black and white, they may have assumed that anyone who was clearly not a "common" criminal that was imprisoned by Mussolini must be there because he was a political prisoner and part of an organized opposition of freedom fighters.

QUESTIONS

Did any mobsters fight in World War II?
There were a few mobsters who fought for their country in the war. Tampa mobster Henry Trafficante served in 1943. Tampa mob associate Jimmy Donofrio also served, as did the "Cracker Mob" boss Harlan Blackburn, who used his wartime experience to deal in stolen ration stamps and run gambling operations behind the lines.

Given the fact that the Americans helped Nazi scientists escape from the clutches of the Russians in the days right before the end of and immediately after World War II, one could make the case that the American leadership may have known that these prisoners were Mafiosi. The Nazi scientists helped America in the Cold War and during the space race to the moon in the 1960s, so it is not out of character for the American government to work with unsavory characters to further its goals. In either case, the Mafia benefited from the Allied liberation of Sicily and returned to prominence in Sicilian society.

One hoodlum who benefited from Allied assistance was Calogero Vizzini. The Allies made him the mayor of his community. He and other

Mafia men were given political offices because they were known in the communities and clearly commanded respect. But this was actually more fear than respect. The citizenry knew them well as Mafiosi and would not dare oppose them. Vizzini ultimately became the "Boss of Bosses" of the Sicilian Mafia. The whole Mafia made out like Sicilian bandits during the post–World War II era. They became more powerful than ever and solidified their stranglehold on the island.

When Vizzini died in 1954, the Mafia went through a metamorphosis. Gone were even the pretensions of Old-World civility and honor. The younger generation were called "gangsters," a common and generic term in America. In Sicily, however, the dignified, albeit deadly, Mafia had disdain for this low-class criminal element and its coarse manners and tactics.

Unholy Alliance

It was during the 1950s that fences were mended and relations re-established between the Sicilian Mafia and its American brethren. Lucky Luciano was the hoodlum who extended the olive branch. The American Mafia's "Commission" (an organization of the bosses of the biggest crime families) and the Sicilian "Cupola" joined forces in the lucrative drug trade. Both factions claimed they regretted having to get into the drug business. As enterprising gangsters, they would have been remiss not to become involved in the narcotics industry. Other criminal forces were entrenched in the trade, and the Mafia wanted a piece of the action.

The Sicilians Grow Violent

The Sicilians were even more bloodthirsty than the Americans when it came to their business practices. They committed more murders, including the brazen assassinations of judges, police, and politicians, than did their American counterparts. The Sicilians were more intertwined with the political sphere than the American Mafia. Business, politics, and even the Catholic Church interact seamlessly in Sicily, working together to achieve their goals. The Archbishop of Palermo issued a press release saying that an organized crime group called the Mafia did not exist. But of course we know this to be untrue now, and many believe that the people knew it wasn't true at the time, either. It is indicative of how deeply entrenched the Mafia was in every aspect of Sicilian culture.

Moving on the Unions

Back in the States the Mafia was finding ways to infiltrate legitimate businesses. One of the most effective and long-standing cash cows for the mob was raiding labor union pension funds and getting loads of no-show jobs for lazy gangsters who needed a real paycheck to report on their taxes. But their influence in the unions did greater damage than almost any of their other illicit ventures. They cost citizens millions of tax dollars, they beat opponents, they killed others who stood in their way, and they irrevocably wrecked the reputations of many of the unions that were trying to do good for their members.

The American and Sicilian Mafia supposedly had a four-day summit at the Grand Hotel des Palmes in 1957. Lucky Luciano arranged a meeting between prominent Sicilian bosses and Joe Bonanno. Although no one is sure of the meeting's particulars, it was allegedly to cement the relationship between the two groups in the heroin trade.

The Mad Hatter

Anastasia got his start on the Brooklyn docks, rising in the ranks of the mob-controlled longshoreman's union. Known as the Mad Hatter, Anastasia was a larger-than-life mob boss. The Sicilian-born criminal brought his brother Anthony along for a ride through the world of crime. The Mad Hatter was a hot-tempered hood who killed another longshoreman early in his career. This faux pas landed him a reserved room on death row. He was granted a second trial when four of the witnesses who had testified in the first trial suddenly reversed their statements. When four key witnesses suddenly went missing before the second trial could be held, Anastasia walked.

King Hood

In other trials over the years, witnesses had a tendency to turn up dead, guaranteeing acquittals for Anastasia. One man and his wife vanished, never to be heard from again. The fact that blood stains splattered their home was a clear indication of foul play. Another man was found in the trunk of a car in the Bronx, and yet another was dumped in the Passaic River in New Jersey.

The Hatter served Lucky Luciano with gleeful enthusiasm during the violent power struggle. He was allegedly one of the four-man hit team that whacked Masseria. And given that publicity would have been bad for his particular line of work outside of Mafia circles, we will never really know how many people met their end at the Mad Hatter's hands.

Coming Up

Luciano and fellow mobster Frank Costello could keep Anastasia on a reasonably short leash. Anastasia was a loose cannon, and cooler heads in the Mafia kept a watchful eye on him. He was loyal to these two bosses. Though they knew he was loyal, they felt that he was unstable. Anastasia was promoted despite his apparent incompetence. His two benefactors made him boss of the Mangano crime family, much to the indignation of Vince Mangano. This created an enmity that ended when Mangano's brother was murdered and Vince joined the ranks of the mysteriously missing folks who got in the way of Anastasia's ambition.

His benefactors backed up Anastasia's claim that he had uncovered a plot against him and his actions were in self-defense. As a result, the Commission deemed the hit justified and Anastasia was free from reprisals. For a little while at least.

Anastasia enjoyed his new position, but his handlers had their own reasons for promoting him. Frank Costello was in the midst of a rivalry with Vito Genovese as the two crime lords vied for control of the interests and rackets of the recently deported Lucky Luciano.

Anastasia was more interested in killing than making lucrative business deals. His lack of subtlety and finesse made him a liability rather than an asset in the long run. He even ordered the hit of a man he saw on television. The man had testified as a witness against celebrated bank robber

Willie Sutton. Sutton was the man who, when asked why he robbed banks, offered the now-famous reply, "That's where the money is." Anastasia was outraged at the witness's attitude and had him murdered. This of course violated the mob's unwritten rule not to mess with outsiders. It shines too much light on them and creates too many problems. The fact that a high-level Mafioso would so casually order a hit raised the red flag for the other members of the Commission. Anastasia's explanation was an offhanded, "I hate stoolies."

Just a Little off the Top

In 1957, Tampa mob boss and Havana casino magnate Santo Trafficante Jr. wrote Anastasia a letter filled with lavish promises of Anastasia's chances of getting in on the operation of the Havana Hilton. Santo was flying to New York with two Cuban investors and told Anthony "Cappy" Coppola, Anastasia's trusted bodyguard and a frequent visitor to Trafficante's casinos in Cuba, to take care of his buddies.

The first night the group was in town, they got a surprise visitor at their suite. Joe DiMaggio, who was reportedly friendly with Anastasia, came up to say hello to Trafficante and his boys. Speculation was that DiMaggio was going to be one of the investors and faces of the Havana Hilton if Anastasia was let in on the deal. This was Anastasia's last shot. His brash attitude and the typical churning of underworld waves had brought some storm clouds on his rosy future as boss of the Mangano family.

The character of Johnny Friendly, played by Lee J. Cobb in the legendary film *On the Waterfront*, was reportedly inspired by Albert's brother Anthony, know on the streets as "Tough Tony."

On October 25, 1957, Anastasia went to the barbershop of the Park Sheraton Hotel in New York City. Two masked men entered and the Lord High Executioner was himself offed in a hail of bullets. The fact that his bodyguard did not quickly join his boss in the barbershop after parking the car indicates that there was a conspiracy in his own family, no doubt led by the man who succeeded him, Carlo Gambino. Coincidentally Trafficante was staying at the Park Sheraton and left only hours before.

Albert Anastasia's murder

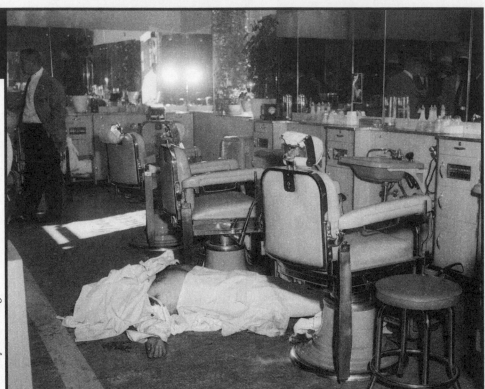

Courtesy of AP Images

▲ The body of Mafia boss Albert Anastasia lies on the floor of the barbershop at New York's Park Sheraton Hotel after his murder in October 1957. Anastasia's crime family was taken over by Carlo Gambino.

Apalachin

One of the most famous, infamous, and embarrassing moments in Mafia legend, involving all five major families and most of the smaller families, was the conference held in Apalachin, New York, in 1957. They revealed themselves as the gangs that couldn't think straight in this fiasco that put the

Mafia squarely in the national spotlight, a place that most Mafiosi were prudent to avoid.

Meeting of the Minds

The Commission met regularly to resolve disputes and doom any unlucky mobster who crossed them. But occasionally large-scale meetings were needed to make major policy changes, much like a meeting of all the office managers in a multinational corporation. In 1957 the meeting was held at the upstate New York estate of Pennsylvania mobster Joseph Barbara.

Law enforcement officials had been trying for years to identify the heads of the big Mafia families. They wanted to get a handle on the secret society's power structure and chain of command. The Mafia obliged them by gathering every major don under one roof. There is no existing agenda or itinerary of what was to be discussed at the meeting. Maybe it was the controversial drug-dealing dilemma. Perhaps it was the recent murder of Albert Anastasia and the bungled hit on Frank Costello. None of the gentlemen in attendance deigned to discuss the affair. They probably did not have a chance to discuss much, since it ended rather abruptly.

Trouble Afoot

Joe Barbara did not know that he was under surveillance and had been for some time. He had received visits in the past from Joe Bonanno and others who the cops suspected were criminals. He also booked most of the hotel rooms in the small town of Apalachin. This raised a red flag for the state police.

Dons and assorted bodyguards and wise guys descended upon the sleepy little community. Goombahs in pinstriped suits flooding the area must have looked a little conspicuous in a land of cows and cornfields. The local police sensed something was afoot, and they alerted higher authorities. On November 14, 1957, four law enforcement officers pulled up to the house in two cars. The dons assumed it was a raid and scampered into the woods, $2,000 suits and all. Those who escaped by car were nabbed at roadblocks and became overnight guests of the New York State Police. All of them maintained that they were paying a call on their sick friend Joe

Barbara. Barbara himself told the law that it was a convention of salesmen from the Canada Dry soft drink company.

Joe Bonanno always maintained that he was not at the Apalachin meeting, but rather in a nearby town meeting with Buffalo mob boss Stefano Magaddino. When two of Joe's men were driving near Barbara's estate they were caught in the state trooper roadblock. Joe stated that one of his men had Joe's driver's license, and that's why they said Joe Bonanno was at Apalachin.

The names of those detained is a Who's Who of hoodlums: Carlo Gambino, Paul Castellano, Tommy Lucchese, Joe Profaci, Joe Colombo, Vito Genovese, Frank Costello, Tony Accardo, Santo Trafficante Jr., Carlos Marcello, and Sam Giancana. There were also numerous representatives from lesser families, like James "Black Jim" Colletti from Pueblo and Russell Bufalino from northeast Pennsylvania.

Believe it or not, none of the approximately sixty gangsters were arrested; they were only detained for questioning. So little was known about the shadowy Mafia in 1957 that the cops had no idea that they had in one fell swoop nabbed the most vicious and successful criminal kingpins in the country. The shadow life of the Mafia was over.

Apalachin Agenda

Several sources offer different reasons for why the meeting was called in the first place. Joe Valachi said it was a coming-out party for the new dons, including Carlo Gambino. They were also there to grant clemency to Vito Genovese for his role in the Anastasia murder. The Mad Hatter was so despised and feared that no one was particularly sorry to see him go.

The brother of the late and not especially lamented Anastasia, who went by the name Anastasio, said that the objective of the meeting was to decide which misbehaving mobsters and which intrusive federal agents were to be whacked. Still another theory is that the whole thing was designed to set up and embarrass Vito Genovese, and the police were made aware of the meeting. Genovese was sent to prison on drug charges less than a year later.

Apalachin Aftermath

The Mafia was no longer a badly kept secret or a word that was only uttered in a hushed, fearful whisper. Dons were on the covers of *Life* and *Look* magazines. The media was abuzz with all things Mafia, and even J. Edgar Hoover had to admit that it existed.

The FBI under the directorship of Hoover did very little to combat organized crime. Hoover steadfastly denied that there was a structured society of criminals who acted in unison to further their villainous goals. Hoover knew many reputed gangsters and was a big-time horseplayer. There were also the allegations that the mob knew about his cross-dressing predilection and blackmailed the G-man.

Public Opinions

Hoover and his beloved bureau took a lot of heat in the court of public opinion and from the politicians in Washington, DC. They wanted to know "what he knew and when he knew it," as they say in Washington. And if Hoover did not know anything about the Mafia, Congress wanted to know why. Hoover engaged in some aggressive damage control with a program he called "the Top Hoodlum Program." The FBI were playing catch-up with the Bureau of Narcotics, but they would eventually eclipse them in all-things Mafia.

The Top Hoodlum Program included wiretapping that was not the slightest bit legal but that garnered reels and reels of Mafia chatter. These tapes were inadmissible in a court of law but provided valuable information and insight into the underworld.

After the Apalachin blunder, the Mafia entered American popular culture as a subject of fascination, outrage, and revulsion. Never again would the activities of these ruthless and brutal men remain completely in the shadows. They were now as famous as they were infamous, and their world was no longer an inner sanctum of clandestine criminality. The law turned up the heat, and the public loved to read about their exploits and see movies about them. Mafiosi would do the unthinkable and break their sacred vow of Omerta. Newspapers across the country turned up the heat, leading some crusading reporters to take the gangsters, as well as the police, to task for not going after the illegal gambling and vice in their respective cities.

In cities like Tampa, grand juries were convened that brought dozens of criminals to the courthouse, where they were eagerly photographed for the headlines in the next morning's newspaper. But for all this fleeting interest in the Mafia, little came of it in the '40s and '50s. In fact, it was another dozen years before the law began to make some inroads against the Mafia.

CHAPTER 11

Vegas, Baby, Vegas!

Las Vegas is also known as "Sin City," and the place where if things happen, "they stay in Vegas." It's a carnal playground where you can indulge your deepest, darkest fantasies and maybe even make your fortune. The Mafia was a fixture in Vegas during its glitzy glory days and transformed it from a wild and woolly honky-tonk town to the entertainment capital of the world. Along the wild way, the Mafia fell from its lofty perch and was reduced to scrapping out meager bucks from low-level rackets while corporate suits raked in the big bucks.

Oasis in the Desert

Gambling casinos existed before the Mafia got to Las Vegas. Gambling was legalized in 1931 by the state of Nevada. The early casinos were more like rowdy honky-tonks and cowboy hangouts than the modern casinos that would soon spring up in the desolate wilderness. Who would have thought that a bunch of immigrant kids from New York's Lower East Side would become the power brokers and robber barons in the Wild West? When the Mafia decided to "enter the western market" they sent an emissary to the Promised Land and, so the legend goes, he put Las Vegas on the map.

Bugsy

Benjamin "Bugsy" Siegel was a member of the New York mob. A Jewish kid from the mean streets of immigrant New York City, he was also a charismatic and good-looking guy who had ambitions to be a movie star. He was born in Williamsburg, Brooklyn, but cut his teeth running nickel-and-dime crap games and extorting pushcart operators on the Lower East Side, where he fell in with upcoming Jewish mobsters Meyer Lansky and Moe Sedway and moved into the lucrative bootlegging racket. It was all uphill from there for the young gagnster. Siegel strove to rise above the street-level thug image that was portrayed in the movies. He wanted to leave a legacy that would ensure his place in history.

Meyer Lansky is the most famous of the Jewish Mafia men and is considered one of the founding fathers of Las Vegas. Lesser-known but influential gangsters Moe Sedway and Dave Berman may not be household words, but they could also be on a Mount Rushmore of Vegas founders.

While most hoods kept a low profile, Siegel was one of the first of the celebrity gangsters. Tall, dark, and handsome, he became a darling of the Hollywood set, many of whom got a vicarious thrill from flirting with danger. Starlets who went for the "bad boy" type needed look no further than a psycho mobster murderer. Bugsy's name came from his mercurial temperament and tendency to fly off into violent rages, which in the parlance of the underworld was called "going bugs." He did not like the name but would prove its validity by pummeling the poor soul who called him "Bugsy" to his face.

"Bugsy" Siegel

Courtesy of AP Images

▲ Benjamin "Bugsy" Siegel poses after apprehension in Los Angeles on April 17, 1941, in connection with an indictment returned in New York charging him with harbouring Louis "Lepke" Buchalter.

A Change in Plans

Siegel also had a crackpot plot to personally assassinate Italian dictator Mussolini. He hated him on two counts—as a Mafioso and a Jewish man. Mussolini had jailed many Sicilian Mafiosi and adversely impacted business, and he was an ally of Adolf Hitler. Even before the concentration camps were liberated at the end of the war, there were stories about what was happening to European Jews under Hitler's tyranny.

Siegel planned to ingratiate himself with members of the Italian aristocracy, get invited to Italy for an audience with Mussolini, and whack the dictator the good-old American Mafia way. It never happened, and the rational Meyer Lansky was deeply concerned whenever his friend would ramble on about this crazy scheme.

When Dewey turned up the heat, the gang split up. Meyer Lansky went to Havana, Cuba, to open and operate casinos in conjunction with the government of the island's dictator, Batista. Bugsy Siegel went off to Las Vegas.

There were several thriving casinos in the downtown section of Las Vegas: the Apache, the Northern, the Boulder, the Las Vegas, the Golden Nugget, the El Cortez, and the Horseshoe. Siegel looked toward the outskirts of town to an area called "the Strip." The Strip only had a few casinos at that time, including the El Rancho. But these casinos were sawdust-floored hangouts for locals. Siegel was going to build his dream casino. It was to be a touch of urban sophistication in the middle of the desert. His vision became the Flamingo Hotel and Casino.

Bugsy Loses Out

The Flamingo was an opulent and expensive establishment, too costly for Bugsy's benefactors back East, including his boyhood friend Meyer Lansky. Theoretically, it should have been the best of both worlds. The Mafia could step out of the dark shadows and into the neon light of semi-respectability. They could indulge in familiar vices, but in this oasis in the desert it was all perfectly legal. Bugsy, however, spent far too much money building the

Flamingo, and some suggested that he was skimming money off the construction costs and putting it in his own pocket. There were rumblings that his mistress, Virginia Hill, was behind his spending. Siegel lived a lavish lifestyle. He had the grandiose ambition to outdo Clark Gable and Cary Grant as Hollywood's latest leading man.

FACT

Mafiosi were not above mixing business with pleasure. Mob boss Sam Giancana, in addition to being a pal of Frank Sinatra, also reportedly had a long-term relationship with Phyllis McGuire of the popular singing group the McGuire Sisters.

An Eye for an Eye

Bugsy Siegel's mismanagement and possible outright thievery earned the wrath of the boys back East, including Meyer Lansky. Their $1 million investment had ballooned to $6 million, with no sign of a profit in the foreseeable future. Mob mythos has it that Lansky stayed the inevitable execution twice, but ultimately endorsed the execution of Bugsy Siegel.

Things seemed to be headed up at the splashy opening of the Flamingo. Hundreds of patrons, including mobsters and movie stars, made it clear to Bugsy that his time and effort had paid off. But the Flamingo's rise was going to be at the expense of Bugsy's fall. No matter how successful the casino would be, Bugsy's time had run out.

ESSENTIAL

Some underworld figures in Vegas stole from the mob without them knowing. Eddie Trascher, the fastest hands in Vegas, devised numerous ways to steal chips while he was a dealer in mobbed-up casinos. He would sew a pocket in the sleeve of his jacket and flick the chips in so fast that the camera couldn't even catch him.

A Shot in the Dark

On June 20, 1947, Bugsy was in the posh Hollywood home of his mistress Virginia Hill reading the paper. He was relaxing in his suit, not aware that a gunman was perched outside the window. The calm summer night was shattered by the sounds of gunfire as Bugsy was pumped full of lead and died; he was just forty-one years old. The force of the hit was so substantial that one of Bugsy's baby blue eyes was found at the other end of the room. Bugsy was gone, but Las Vegas was just getting started.

QUESTIONS

Who was the most famous gangster 'moll' in history?
That would have to be Virginia Hill. A Georgian by birth, Hill moved up to Chicago where she became involved with a series of wise guys from Al Capone to Frank Nitti. Along the way she started dabbling in some rackets herself. When she went out to Los Angeles she hooked up with Siegel and became his constant companion, except on the night of his death. When questioned by authorities she was baffled, "I can't imagine who shot him and why."

The Rat Pack

Las Vegas has always been an almost surreal place, and as a source of pop culture entertainment it is unrivaled. Entertainers have always flocked to Vegas, and it continues to be the barometer of who's cool and "in" at the moment. The city was a popular destination; there was plenty of money to be made, there were many ways to liberally indulge vices, and many got a vicarious thrill from hobnobbing with the hoodlum element. Perhaps no entertainer was more enamored of the Mafia and its brethren than Frank Sinatra.

Jack on the Rocks

Sinatra had an association with the mob going back to his early days as a saloon singer in Hoboken. From the 1920s to the 1940s almost every singer and comic had to contend with the Mafia, since the mob has a long history of involvement in the clubs and venues where they perform. Most performers of that generation accepted this fact and for the most part got along with their employers. Sinatra, by all reports, had a schoolboy romanticism of gangsters. And when he was down on his luck and his career was in a slump, it was his mob friends who still paid him to sing in their saloons. Sinatra was nothing if not loyal to his friends, and when the Vegas party was in full swing, he was a regular fixture at the Sands and Dunes, along with his cohorts, Dean Martin, Peter Lawford, Sammy Davis Jr., and Joey Bishop. Together they created a slice of pop culture lore that continues to fascinate people everywhere.

The Chairman

Sinatra, who was given the option to purchase 9 percent of the Sands Hotel by his mob friends, performed there often, always packing the house. And a sold-out crowd of Sinatra fans inevitably wandered over to the slot machines and gambling tables. Sinatra got it in his head to make a movie in Las Vegas. This became the 1960 film *Ocean's Eleven*, more memorable as a time capsule of an epoch than as a cinematic masterpiece.

The Rat Pack filmed *Ocean's Eleven* by day and performed at the Sands by night. The show was called "the Summit," named for the Cold War conferences between the United States and the former Soviet Union.

QUESTIONS

Did Frank Sinatra ever play a mobster in a movie?
Frank played a gambler in *Guys and Dolls*, a mob boss in *Robin and the Seven Hoods,* and a satire of his "Mafia" personality in the otherwise forgettable *Cannonball Run II.* In fact, Sinatra played cops far more than he played bad guys.

Progressive Retro

One positive thing Old Blue Eyes did was help break the race barrier in Las Vegas. Black performers were not allowed to stay in rooms at the hotels in which they performed to sold-out crowds and standing ovations. Velvet-voiced crooner Nat King Cole was instructed not to make direct eye contact with the swooning fur-adorned and bejeweled ladies in the audience. Black performers had to withdraw to a shantytown on the wrong side of the tracks at the end of the show.

FACT

In the ultimate example of "strange bedfellows," many of the workers, pit bosses, and managerial types in the Mafia-owned casinos were Mormons. The faithful of the Latter-day Saints do not drink alcohol, coffee, or gamble. But they are not forbidden to work in casinos. It was a strange alliance that served the Mafia well.

One day Sinatra announced that he would not go on unless his chum Sammy could stay at the Sands and play blackjack at the tables and swim in the pool. Sinatra helped pave the way for integration in Las Vegas. The Mafia did not fret much either way. Green was the only color that truly inflamed their larcenous hearts.

The Howard Hughes Era

The Mafia's era in Vegas began to diminish when the poster boy for eccentric millionaires, Howard Hughes, decided he wanted to make the town his life-size Monopoly board. The old hoods were ready for retirement. They had gorged themselves on the sumptuous Las Vegas buffet. It was a great run for the underworld, so the big bosses decided to cash in.

Hughes was an enigmatic and megalomaniacal mega-millionaire who made his money in the aviation arena and also dabbled as a Hollywood mogul. When he arrived in secrecy, he immediately set to work acquiring a stable of properties. He bought seventeen casinos. The old hoods went back home with their loot and the young ones remained, but their power and influence were diminished. "Respectable" robber baron capitalists proved more than a match for the shady underworld.

Gone in a Flash

When Hughes bought up his cadre of properties, observers believed that Vegas was headed for a huge boom. Hughes, though, was beginning his descent into madness. He was increasingly out of touch with reality and let his business acumen fail. He lost a bundle, sold out, and left town after a few years—or rather, his handlers did. When he died several years later his corpse looked more like that of a homeless man than one of the richest men in the world. Emaciated with long hair and nails and covered in sores, he had left his handlers to rule the empire while he died an ignominious death.

Al Capone missed the boat vis-à-vis Las Vegas. In the 1930s he had interest in a gambling joint in Reno, Nevada, but did not have the foresight to see the potential millions to be made. Santo Trafficante Jr. lost his casinos in Havana, but was preoccupied with opening another Caribbean resort, thus missing the Vegas gravy train.

Skimming Their Way to the Bank

After the demise of Bugsy Siegel, less flamboyant but more efficient mobsters flooded Las Vegas. The less publicity hungry Lansky took over the Flamingo and had it running smoothly and profitably within a year. He also was the brains behind the Thunderbird casino. Other gangsters filled out the mob roster of hidden ownership of Las Vegas's biggest casinos. The Cleveland mob owned the Desert Inn. The Chicago Outfit had an interest in the Stardust resort. The Detroit Mafia had a piece of the Frontier. Sinatra's compatriot Sam Giancana had interests in the Sahara and the Riviera, along with the Fischetti brothers. The Fischettis—Joe, Rocco, and Charlie—were cousins of Al Capone and ran huge gambling operations for the Chicago Outfit. Known for their political influence as well as their talent for running successful nightclubs, the Fischettis were also close friends of Frank Sinatra.

The Last Shout

The Mafia reasserted itself in the post–Howard Hughes days, but the 1970s and 1980s saw the mob under attack from both the feds and the Wall Street crowd. FBI probes and indictments sent many a mobster packing, and legitimate businessmen and corporations filled the void. The main investigations were aimed at breaking the mob's control of skimming. (Basically the gangsters were stealing money before it was officially counted by the staff at the casino.)

ALERT!

The Teamsters Pension Fund, as administered by the notorious Jimmy Hoffa, loaned millions to the Mafia to build their casinos up and down the Las Vegas Strip. The hardworking Teamsters, however, shared in none of the booty.

When the oodles of cash and coins were collected and taken to the "counting rooms" of the big casinos, a certain percentage was "skimmed" off the top and sent as tribute to the big crime families. This was cold cash free and clear, not subject to the grasping talons of the Internal Revenue Service. In a cash business where the money was flowing, the profits made via skimming were astronomical.

It was a simple racket, and one that didn't require any violence or threats. The Mafia simply walked out of the casino with bags of cash. The lucrative operation was shared among Mafia families from Chicago, Kansas City, St. Louis, Detroit, Cleveland, and Milwaukee.

Tony the Ant

Anthony "Tony the Ant" Spilotro was the Chicago Outfit's representative in Las Vegas and one of the most powerful Vegas crime figures in the 1970s. The Ant grew up in Chicago and fell into petty crime as a juvenile. He caught the attention of some Outfit soldiers and they brought him in as an associate. Through the 1960s Spilotro grew from a leg-breaker and strong-arm man to leading his own crew of robbers and bookmakers. In the early 1970s he was sent out to Vegas. He made a name for himself, teaming with the late Lefty Rosenthal, a noted bookmaker and casino owner, and running up the city's crime stats with his crew. But as Tony the Ant's stature grew and he became more of a law enforcement target, he was beginning to be viewed as a liability by his superiors. On June 14, 1986, Spilotro and his brother were beaten to death in a suburban Chicago basement then dumped in a shallow grave in an Indiana cornfield.

Strawmen

The Mafia always had a problem with loudmouths and big shots who drew attention. Both of these mob types brought the heat, as usual. The FBI started an investigation into the skimming, and through a combination of wiretaps and turncoats, the mob's hold on Sin City quickly started to slip away. The Tropicana, the Stardust, Desert Inn, Circus-Circus, Caesar's Palace, the Fremont, the Aladdin, the Sands, the Riviera, and the Sundance all fell out of mob hands, and the Dunes and the Marina were demolished in the inexorable juggernaut of respectability. The Golden Age of Vegas had come to an end. Chieftains of the Kansas City, Cleveland, Milwaukee, and Chicago mobs felt the long arm of the law unceremoniously shove them into an eight-by-ten cell.

FACT

"Tony the Ant" often ran foul of Las Vegas police and the FBI. Criminal defense attorney Oscar Goodman represented him. Oscar was elected mayor of Las Vegas in 1999. As of this writing he is still in office.

Today, Las Vegas resembles more of a giant theme park for adults than the naughty "Sin City" of its heyday. Millions of people still flock there every year and drop billions of their hard-earned bucks on the gaming tables and in the slot machines. The Strip has started to gain back some of its hip and cool allure. Celebrities are flocking there again, and gangsters from Russia and Japan are making the casinos their personal playgrounds. The Rat

Pack may be gone, but their cultural impact on Vegas will not be forgotten. Although the mob was taken out at the knees by the skimming cases, where there's money, the Mafia always finds a way to sneak back in.

Fat Herbie

Herbert "Fat Herbie" Blitzstein was one of the last remaining Spilotro soldiers in Sin City. After his bosses ended up in a cornfield under a couple thousand pounds of dirt, Blitzstein decided to lay low and rake in the cash. He ran a lucrative loansharking and insurance fraud operation out of his automotive repair business. At sixty-three years old he figured he could live out the rest of his years making a few bucks and living the life of a Vegas retiree. But low-level clowns from the Los Angeles and Buffalo crime families had different ideas. They wanted to muscle in on Herbie's measly rackets.

Herbie's End

Over a series of meetings recorded by the FBI, the gangsters plotted to rob Herbie and push him out of his business. The feds knew because they had a snitch, a con named John Branco, in on the action. Probably thinking that the bumbling gangsters wouldn't actually go through with the hit, they failed to let Herbie know of the plot against him. But they underestimated the drive of the wise guys. For a few thousand dollars, the mobsters hired two hit men to rub out Fat Herbie. They hid in his house and shot him dead as he was relaxing in an easy chair.

The Last Stand

Not long after Blitzstein's death the mob's carefully constructed house of cards in Vegas fell apart. When the feds swept in, they busted a dozen of the last remaining mobsters on the Strip. From the fallout of Herbie's murder and the parallel racketeering investigation, over a dozen mobsters, including Los Angeles underboss Carmen Milano, were convicted of a variety of crimes, many penny ante. The mob's heyday in Vegas came to an end.

CHAPTER 12

Did the Mafia Kill Kennedy?

November 22, 1963, is one of the pivotal dates in American history. It may also be one of the most controversial. Since President John F. Kennedy was killed that day in Dallas, there have been millions of theories as to who killed Kennedy. The official report is that a former Marine, and practicing Communist, Lee Harvey Oswald, was the lone gunmen, shooting the president as the presidential motorcade drove by the Texas School Book Depository. But from there, the facts get messy. One constant among the various theories is that the Mafia was involved. Whether acting alone, or with the help of anti-Castro Cubans or the CIA, the "Mafia-did-it" theory is one of the more popular conspiracies in the Kennedy assassination.

Papa Joe and Booze

The Kennedy dynasty was founded in part on the bootleg whiskey trade during Prohibition. The family patriarch, Joseph Kennedy, was a rumrunner during the Golden Age of the mob. He was an associate of none other than Frank Costello and Meyer Lansky. He was part owner of a racetrack and a heavy gambler. Even after Prohibition his mob ties continued. This came into play during his son's ascension to the White House and may also have played a role in the assassination.

FACT

Joseph Kennedy lived to bury three of his sons (Joseph Jr., John, and Robert), plus endure many other family tragedies, including a crippling stroke that left him paralyzed and speechless in his last years. This was after he promised the Mafia to reign in his son Bobby's crusade against organized crime. He was never able to fulfill that promise to the mob.

Like many men with mob ties, Joe Kennedy craved respectability. His fortune was made in the underworld of violence and criminality, and he pushed his sons to succeed in the legitimate world. In 1938 he was appointed ambassador to the Court of St. James (a fancy phrase for England) by President Franklin Delano Roosevelt. This was ironic because Kennedy came to America as a poor Irish immigrant, and the relations between the English and the Irish had been strained over the millennia. Kennedy had to resign after he advocated the policy of appeasement regarding Nazi Germany. This gave him the reputation as a Nazi sympathizer at a time when Roosevelt was inclined to enter the war as an ally to Great Britain against Hitler. The Kennedy name became tarnished, but better days were on the horizon.

Sins of the Father

Joseph Kennedy's firstborn son, his namesake and the first one on whom he had transferred his dreams, died during World War II. The burden then fell on his second son, John F. Kennedy. A hero in that same war, he was elected to the House of Representatives and then later the Senate. As a senator, he announced his intentions to seek the presidency in the election of 1960.

His opponent was Richard Nixon, who had served as vice president for eight years under the popular Republican president Dwight Eisenhower. In addition to his formidable wealth and good looks, Kennedy had an arsenal in the liberal glitterati of Hollywood. And foremost among the constellation of stars was Frank Sinatra and his pals.

Rumble in West Virginia

John Kennedy had one significant obstacle in his quest for the White House—he was a Catholic. There was a strong anti-Catholic sentiment among some, particularly in the Bible Belt Protestant South. The ostensible fear was that JFK would be taking his orders from the pope in Vatican City.

John Kennedy's main opponent in the Democratic primaries was Minnesota Senator Hubert Humphrey. Beating Humphrey in Southern states was key, and the primary in West Virginia (a state that was 95 percent Protestant) was seen as a make-or-break vote for Kennedy. It would take a miracle for the New England Catholic to score a win in this unfriendly land. Divine or diabolical intervention was required.

One assassination conspiracy theory places the blame on right-wing oil men in Texas who were not fond of Kennedy's religion or politics. Some of these shadowy characters also pop up theories involving the Mafia, Lyndon Johnson, and anti-Castro Cuban groups.

The rumor is that Joe Kennedy persuaded Frank Sinatra to ask his "friends" to use their influence to help JFK win the primary. Sinatra approached his pal, Chicago mob boss Sam Giancana. Giancana exerted pressure on the rank and file of the Teamsters and other unions to vote for Kennedy. This may have made the difference. JFK won the primary, Humphrey bowed out of the race, and JFK was assured the nomination of the Democratic Party.

One Brief Shining Moment

Kennedy beat Nixon in what was the closest election in history until the 2000 Bush versus Gore contest. And he allegedly had help with it, too. Mobster Sam Giancana, Mayor Richard Daley, and other allegedly crooked politicians in the city of Chicago supposedly stuffed ballot boxes to ensure a Democratic victory. Similar deceit is said to have occurred in Texas. Even with their help, the difference was only about 100,000 votes. John Fitzgerald Kennedy became president.

FACT

John Kennedy's decision to make his brother Robert the attorney general of the United States was a very controversial move. Many Washington insiders despised the Kennedy family, and in their eyes this was just another example of the unrestrained arrogance of the patrician Kennedy clan.

Bobby Kennedy—Double Cross

When Bobby Kennedy was appointed attorney general by his brother, he went after the Mafia in a big way. His two main targets were New Orleans boss Carlos Marcello and Teamsters head Jimmy Hoffa. Bobby made it his mission to take on organized crime, unaware of the serious repercussions his actions may generate. Increasing the federal budget for Mafia busting, the Justice Department under Bobby Kennedy was gearing up for a major battle. In looking at the Mafia-did-it theory, the most popular motive is that the Mafia was not happy with the double cross its members felt they were getting from the Kennedys.

Marcello on the Plane

The first casualty of Bobby's war on the mob was Carlos Marcello. Marcello had never bothered to become an American citizen. As a result he was subject to deportation. To combat this, he had a bogus birth certificate created that said he was born in Guatemala. He did not want to be returned to Italy or to his actual birthplace, Tunisia, in North Africa. Bobby Kennedy took this opportunity to rid the country of one of its top wise guys. He deported the Cajun don to Guatemala. Marcello was humiliated. He had a terrible ordeal trying to get back into the United States, including being stranded in the Central American jungles by the local military and wandering lost in the rain forests for three days. He was not without influence, however, and eventually made it back to the United States. He sued Robert Kennedy for illegally deporting him. Mafia informants maintain that he spoke openly of killing not the pesky Robert but his brother President John Kennedy.

Hoffa

Robert Kennedy also angered Jimmy Hoffa. The Teamsters president had ties with mobsters from all over the country. He shared a lawyer, Frank Ragano, with Santo Trafficante Jr. In the early 1990s Ragano came out with an unbelievable story. He maintained that he delivered messages from Hoffa to Marcello and Trafficante, setting in motion the plot to kill President Kennedy. Hoffa was a hothead, but he would have had to go through Mafia channels to pull off an assassination this large.

The Havana Connection

Many of the conspiracy theories center on the island nation of Cuba. Located just ninety miles off the coast of Florida, Cuba was a paradise for gamblers and gangsters in the years prior to the Cuban Revolution in 1959. The Mafia was partners with the Batista government, a cruel dictatorship that was very friendly to United States business, both legitimate and illegitimate. Meyer Lansky was the hood who personally dealt with Batista in a mutually beneficial business arrangement. Santo Trafficante Jr. took over his father's interests in a number of casinos, including the lavish Sans Souci. The Mafia flourished under Batista's regime, but the peaceful existence was in jeopardy with the rise of Fidel Castro.

In 1959 Fidel Castro won a hard-fought revolution and ousted the Batista regime. While he was fighting the Batista government, Castro was also receiving guns and money from the mob. The gangster casino bosses reasoned that if they supported both sides in the conflict, whichever side won would be eager to do business with them. They made a huge mistake. A former major-league baseball player and one-time seeming friend of the United States, Castro became allied with the Soviet Union after his victory, and the island became a communist enclave, which caused alarm in the U.S. intelligence community. But Castro also kicked out the mobsters and jailed a few of them, including Santo Trafficante Jr.

The Mafia families involved in Cuba included Pittsburgh, Chicago, New York, Kansas City, St. Louis, Cleveland, and Tampa. The role of Tampa was cemented when Ignazio Antinori used his friendships and associations with Cuban politicos to set up a smuggling operation for narcotics as well as raw materials for illicit liquor production during Prohibition.

Bay of Pigs

Before Kennedy became president, there were plans to invade Cuba and oust Castro. It would not be an attack by American armed forces, however; instead the assault would come from exiled Cubans who had planned and trained in the United States with the help of the CIA and the Mafia, who helped staff the operation with Cuban gangsters. Kennedy did not veto the plan when he took office, but when it was launched, he refused, at the last minute, to aid the assault with air cover from the United States Air Force. It was a total disaster, and thousands of exiled Cubans were killed or captured. Those taken alive probably came to wish that they had died on the beach.

Kennedy made many enemies in many circles by his refusal to provide air support in the Bay of Pigs invasion. He earned the hatred of the Cubans who wanted their nation back, those in the CIA who felt betrayed and humiliated, American big business, which had enjoyed great profits in Cuba, and, of course, the Mafia, for whom Cuba was once a cash cow and pleasure palace. Many of the Cubans who felt betrayed by the Kennedy administration drifted into covert operations run by the CIA out of Miami.

FACT

After he was released from Cuban prison, Santo Trafficante Jr. settled in Miami, where he led a crew of Cuban gangsters who left Cuba in 1959. This group conducted gambling operations, drug trafficking, loansharking, and anti-Castro activities.

Jack Ruby

Mere hours after JFK's murder, lone oddball Lee Harvey Oswald was picked up for the murder. With forty years of hindsight, many people feel it was all too convenient, a neat and tidy solution to the murder. Making things especially tidy was Oswald's murder in the Dallas Police headquarters by a local strip club owner and small-time hoodlum, Jack Ruby.

Ruby burst out of the crowd and shot Oswald, thus ending the possibility of a trial in which potentially explosive information might have come to light. Ruby claimed his reason was the desire to spare first widow Jackie Kennedy the pain and suffering of a protracted trial, where she would have to relive the horrific event over and over. There appears to have been more to the story, however.

Chicago Youth

During his youth, Ruby was a runner for the Chicago Outfit. He sold horseracing sheets and was involved in bookmaking. There are some rumors that Ruby actually worked for Al Capone. While he was making the rounds on the street he became friendly with David Yaras and Lenny Patrick, two hoods that became high-level operatives in the Outfit. Ruby also became involved in the Teamsters Union, where he was suspected in the murder of a union rep.

Jack Ruby

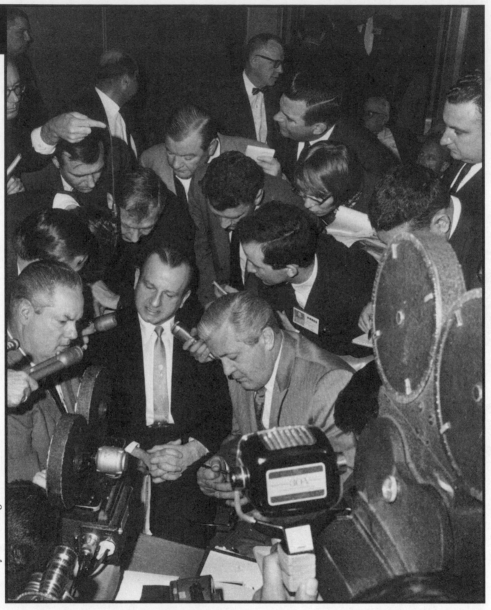

Courtesy of AP Images

▲ Jack Ruby, charged with the slaying of Lee Harvey Oswald, the accused assassin of John F. Kennedy, is surrounded by photographers and reporters before the start of his change of venue hearing in Dallas, Texas, Feb. 10, 1964. Seated with Ruby are two of his attorneys, Joe Tonahill, left, of Jasper, Texas, and Melvin Belli, right, of San Francisco.

More than Just a Nightclub Owner

Ruby moved to Dallas in the 1940s and became a well-liked nightclub owner. His burlesque shows were well attended by gangsters and cops alike. He kept up with his contacts in the mob, as well as with Dallas gangsters. There are some who say that Ruby had no connections to organized crime. This is unlikely.

Ruby—the Nexus

There are a lot of interesting coincidences that tie Jack Ruby to organized crime figures. Chief among them was Santo Trafficante Jr. In 1959, Santo was the guest of Fidel Castro in one of the Cuban dictator's swank jails. According to an eyewitness, Trafficante was visited there by an American gangster, Jack Ruby. As improbable as that may sound, Ruby admitted that he was in Cuba around the same time. The idea that Jack Ruby may have allegedly visited Trafficante in a Cuban prison surprises many because there doesn't seem to be any outward connection between a Dallas nightclub owner and a Florida mob boss.

Ruby's connections to Trafficante start with his companion on that 1959 Cuba trip, Lewis McWillie. Also a Chicago native, McWillie worked in the Deauville casino for Trafficante and a few others owned by the Florida mob boss's associates. McWillie was close with two other Trafficante cronies, Russell D. Matthews and Norman Rothman. In addition to involvement in gambling, all the men, including Ruby, were involved with smuggling weapons to Castro prior to his victory in the civil unrest.

Ruby, McWillie, and Matthews were also in the sphere of influence of Joe Civello, the mob boss of Dallas. Civello's name crops up in numerous conspiracy theories, as do McWillie, Matthews, and of course, Jack Ruby.

Lee Harvey Oswald

Lee Harvey Oswald was no doubt a strange loner. At age seventeen he enlisted in the Marines, worked in top-secret facilities, learned the Russian language, and ultimately renounced his American citizenship and defected to the Soviet Union. The circumstances of his defection and his return are curious and full of fodder for conspiracy theorists.

Lee Harvey Oswald's uncle, a man named Dutz Murret, was a bookie for the New Orleans Mafia. Oswald's mother was linked to several soldiers in the mob. The man who killed Oswald, Jack Ruby, had ties to the Dallas crime family, which was more or less a subsidiary of the Marcello organization. Is it possible that the Mafia used this outcast and oddball Oswald for their hit and then had him whacked to avoid discovery? Future generations will know when the classified files are revealed. Carlos Marcello was conveniently in a New Orleans courtroom being found not guilty of his false birth certificate charges on the afternoon of President Kennedy's murder.

Some Suspects

According to the most popular Mafia-did-it theory, the gangsters Santo Trafficante Jr. and Carlos Marcello were responsible for Kennedy's assasination. Other mob names that turn up include Johnny Roselli, Charles Nicoletti, and Sam Giancana. There are dozens of other suspects with ties to the intelligence community, anti-Castro Cubans, right-wing politicians, left-wing Castro supporters, the KGB, and Lyndon Johnson, but this book will concentrate on the gangsters.

QUESTIONS

Who were some other mobsters that people say were killed because of the Kennedy assassination?
Although the life of a mobster is rife with pitfalls, including the very real possibility of getting whacked over a business deal, the murders of Trafficante associate Eladio del Valle, Chicago boss Sam Giancana, and Johnny Roselli may have been linked to the Kennedy assassination.

Santo
Trafficante

Courtesy of AP Images

▲ Mafia Boss Santo Trafficante, of Tampa, Fla., waves before a grand jury appearing, Sept. 30, 1966, Queens, New York. He was one of thirteen reputed Mafia leaders arrested in a Queens restaurant September 22 and held as material witnesses on bail totaling $1.3 million.

Charles Nicoletti

Charles "Chuckie" Nicoletti was a hit man for Sam Giancana. A coveted player in Giancana's stable, Chuckie was reportedly hired by anti-Castro Cuban and CIA figures to be part of the conspiracy to murder Kennedy. Giancana and Johnny Roselli are also part of this particular theory. The main evidence against Nicoletti comes from the confessions of James Files, his one-time driver. Files stated that he and Nicoletti were two of the gunmen that shot Kennedy that

November day in Dallas. Chuckie himself was shot in the back of the head just days before he was scheduled to appear before the House Select Committee investigating the JFK assassination. His was just one of dozens of suspicious assassination-related deaths that occurred during the Committee's hearings.

Bill Bonanno's Story

Salvatore "Bill" Bonanno was the son of legendary crime boss Joseph Bonanno. In 1999 Bill came out with a book about his life in the Mafia. It contained a far-fetched story of who killed Kennedy. Bill maintained that Johnny Roselli was one of the shooters and that he shot at the president from a sewer hole in front of the motorcade. Bonanno also said that French/Corsican mobsters were involved in the hit. Bill offers little evidence to back up the claims.

Means, Motives, and Opportunity

If the Mafia was sufficiently angry with the Kennedys for their crusade against organized crime, the logical move would be to kill Robert Kennedy. But Carlos Marcello remarked that the best way to kill the dog was to cut off the head. In fact, after his brother's death, Robert Kennedy thought the mob may have had a hand in it. The Justice Department scaled back their assault against organized crime, though only temporarily. But if the mob wanted to kill the president, how would they have done it?

Bosses like Santo Trafficante Jr. had ties to the intelligence community. The Dallas Mafia was tight with the local police force. Carlos Marcello had a lot of political pull. So the matter of a coverup could be accomplished. Also, Trafficante and Roselli's connections to the anti-Castro Cuban operations gave them access to top-shelf hit men. It would be easy to send them to a mob-friendly town like Dallas.

And what better way to cover their tracks than to set up a patsy whose uncle worked for the Marcellos in New Orleans. This patsy would then be killed by a Chicago mob associate with ties to the local police, giving him access to the parking garage where Oswald was killed. We may never know the truth, but the circumstantial evidence is scintillating.

CHAPTER 13

Family Ties

The Mafia in America was always much more than just the figures in Chicago and New York; yet in most people's minds these two cities were synonymous with organized crime. At one time, dozens of crime families controlled America from coast to coast, as well as outposts in smaller cities and open territories like Miami. The Mafia in a real sense controlled American crime, though most of the families numbered less than 100 made soldiers. This chapter looks at some of the lesser-known, but no less infamous, Mafia families across the country.

East Coast Mafia Families

Gangsters were a dime a dozen on the East Coast in the Mafia's heyday. The region from New England through New Jersey and out to Pennsylvania was home to thousands of made guys, associates, bookies, loan sharks, dope peddlers, grifters, and hit men. The immigrant neighborhoods, readily corruptible electorate, and the economic activity of the area—dominated in the early part of the twentieth century by manufacturing, unions, and the docks—gave the wise guys just what they needed to expand their rackets.

Buffalo, New York

The Buffalo, New York, mob was founded by Stefano Magaddino. He was a member of the Commission from its inception and one of the elder statesmen of the Mafia. Buffalo's location near the Canadian border made it ideal for the bootleg business. The Buffalo mob was integral in the pipeline of transporting whiskey from Canada into the United States. Magaddino also had another business that catered to those who ran afoul of him—a mob-run funeral home. The Buffalo mob extended its influence west into Ohio and up into Canada.

Buffalo Mafioso Stefano Magaddino was the older cousin of New York City gangster Joseph Bonanno. They were not cousins on the best of terms however. The Buffalo resident was intensely jealous of his more successful younger cousin, and neither would have been displeased to see the other whacked.

When old man Magaddino died of natural causes at the ripe old age of eighty-two, his succession was thrown into upheaval as various gangsters made a grab for power. By the 1980s the Buffalo family was in control of Joseph Todaro Sr., who spent most of his time in Florida. The remnants of the Buffalo family are still involved in gambling, loansharking, and construction unions.

New England

The New England family had an identity crisis. The power base shifted back and forth between Boston, Massachusetts, and Providence, Rhode Island, depending on who was in charge. The first dons, Gaspare Messina and Phil Buccola, sipped espressos in Boston's North End. Buccola's successor, Raymond L.S. Patriarca Sr., moved the headquarters of the family to Providence, where he had his vending company—one of many mob bosses who worked in the vending-machine industry. Patriarca remained the don until he died in 1985. His son, Raymond Patriarca Jr., took over, causing turmoil in the family. He was replaced by Francis "Frank Cadillac" Salemme. The Salemme reign was marked by a war between the established Mafiosi and a younger group of renegades. After a series of murders and successful prosecutions, the New England Mafia was damaged. The crime family still lives on, with the power center shifting back once again to Providence.

Northeast Pennsylvania

This Mafia family operates out of the old coal mining cities of Scranton, Wilkes-Barre, and Pittston, Pennsylvania, extending its reach north into New York State and westward to Erie. This area attracted a large number of Italian immigrants to its coal mines and industrial operations in the beginning of the twentieth century. The local Mafia was founded by Santo Volpe, who was succeeded by John Sciandra as head of the family. Joseph Barbara had Sciandra whacked in 1940 and was the don until 1959. Russell Bufalino took over the crime family in 1959 and became the namesake of the group until his death in 1994. The current boss of the nearly dormant family is William D'Elia, who maintains close contacts with the mob in Philly.

Newark, New Jersey

When most people think of the New Jersey Mafia, *The Sopranos* comes to mind. There was a New Jersey crime family long before Tony Soprano and his cronies hit the small screen. The first don was Stefano

"Steve" Badami. He was succeeded by "Big Phil" Amari, who reigned for over twenty years. He was replaced by Nicholas "Nick" Delmore. Simone Rizzo DeCavalcante, known as "Sam the Plumber," took over after that, and the crime family became known by his name.

FACT

The New Jersey crime family is believed to be the basis for the hit HBO series *The Sopranos*. During the investigation that led to the 1999 indictment of the DeCavalcantes, agents listened into mobsters comparing characters on the show to real mobsters they knew.

Considered a "farm" team by the larger crime families, the DeCavalcantes stayed under the radar for decades. They were involved in the ever-popular union infiltration as well as those old mob standbys of gambling and loansharking before the conviction of boss Giovanni "John the Eagle" Riggi in the early '90s. Following his conviction the remaining hierarchy was swept up in a massive indictment in 1999. They are still active, though their numbers are diminished. The current boss is said to run his operations from the Peterstown section of Elizabeth, the last vestige of a thriving ethnic neighborhood.

The Rust Belt Mafia

The decaying steel towns and old industrial centers of the Great Lakes region were the perfect settings for Mafia families. Though at one time the gangsters were attracted to the area due to its thriving union-based economy, as the jobs left, the mob simply took advantage of the situation. The Mafia families in these cities may have been small potatoes, but they brought in big money.

Rochester, New York

Rochester, a small city in upstate New York, was under the thumb of the Buffalo crime family for over forty years. It broke away in the 1960s courtesy of the ambitious Valenti brothers, Frank and Stanley. As in all Mafia break-ups, the parting of ways was not an amicable one. Through the 1970s and early 1980s a war for control of the family led to a series of murders, indictments, and the complete implosion of the crime family. Though there have been a few members released from prison in recent years, the family is no longer functioning.

Pittsburgh, Pennsylvania

Stefano Monastero was the first Mafia boss of Pittsburgh. He was whacked, as was his successor, Giuseppe Siragusa. The longest running boss of the family was John Sebastian LaRocca. LaRocca didn't have the deep political connections that other mob bosses enjoyed. But his family controlled gambling, narcotics, loansharking, and extortion. The Pittsburgh family was even involved in the pre-Castro Cuban casinos. Like many Mafia families in smaller American cities, the once powerful family has contracted to a much smaller organization. While they still run some rackets, their ranks are dwindling. The last official boss, Michael Genovese, died on October 31, 2006, at the age of eighty-seven.

Detroit, Michigan

The Motor City is home to a small but tightly knit Mafia family that's still thriving. Gaspare Milazzo established the Detroit family in 1921. He was retired in a shower of bullets in a hostile takeover by a rival named Gaetano Gianolla in 1930. Gianolla remained in charge until 1944. Joe Vitale took over and had a twenty-year run as boss. He was followed by Joseph Zerilli and later by Jack Tocco. Tocco often picketed city hall with the audacious charge that the persecution of the Mafia was based on anti-Italian prejudice. The hierarchy of the Detroit Mafia was ravaged by a series of indictments and convictions in the late 1990s. Despite the efforts of law enforcement, the family remains active, with Jack Tocco still reigning.

Jack Tocco

Courtesy of AP Images/Richard Sheinwald

▲ Mafia boss Jack Tocco, seventy-two, of Grosse Pointe Park, MI, enters his automobile after he was found guilty on two racketeering counts and one extortion count. He was found innocent of ten related extortion charges in U.S. District Court in Detroit April 29, 1998.

Cleveland, Ohio

The Cleveland Mafia was originally led by Joseph "Big Joe" Lonardo. His adversaries were the Porellos. While waiting for the Porellos to arrive at a summit to smooth over their differences, Lonardo was killed. The Porellos were succeeded by Frank Milano. Milano fled Cleveland in the 1940s and was replaced by John Scalish. During Scalish's thirty-year run as boss, he failed to make many new members, and the family's numbers began to dwindle. And a car bombing war with Irish mobster Danny Greene brought a lot of law enforcement heat on the small family. After a series of setbacks and bosses, John "Peanuts" Tronolone, owner of a travel agency, took over the Cleveland mob, but he opted to lead the remnants of the family from sunny Florida. The last recognized boss of a much-diminished Cleveland mob was Joseph "Joe Loose" Iacobacci, though it is not known if he is still in charge.

FACT

The Detroit crime family's specialty was labor racketeering, since Motor City was a big union town. Its most infamous son, Jimmy Hoffa, was president of the Teamsters Union and had known mob connections. Detroit Mafiosi reportedly arranged for Hoffa's permanent disappearance.

Midwest Families

The families across the Great Plains were as varied as they come. St. Louis was a city rocked by a bombing war between mob factions, while Springfield's boss rarely raised his voice. The mile-high gangsters in Denver were local celebrities, while Madison's mob boss was virtually unknown. Unlike the good-natured Midwest temperament and folksy ways, the Mafia out West was just as dangerous as back East.

Kansas City, Missouri

Kansas City was a town that was raucous in its own right before the Mafia arrived. Scarface DiGiovanni arrived from Sicily in 1912. Like many Sicilian gangsters he left the old country with a price on his head. DiGiovanni and his gang made a bundle of money and terrorized the town during Prohibition. They preyed on their own, as was often the case. It was the law-abiding Italians and Sicilians who suffered before the gangs grew powerful enough to menace the general population. Anthony "Fat Tony" Gizzo was a major early Mafia power in the city. After his death and the death of his predecessor Charles Binaggio, the Kansas City mob fell under the control of Nick Civella. Nick brought the family immense power and wealth, and law enforcement scrutiny. He was indicted for skimming casinos. Nick died before he went to trial. His brother Tony Ripes reportedly took over the reigns and, though he has since died, the small crime family is still active.

Most of the Midwest Mafia families were under the thumb of the Chicago Outfit. The Outfit represented their interests at Commission meetings and often partnered with the smaller families in criminal operations.

Springfield, Illinois

The city of Springfield, capital of Illinois and one-time residence of Abraham Lincoln, never registered a big blip on the national crime scene. But the cozy town of 100,000 had its own homegrown Mafia family under the leadership of Frank Zito, who ran the family for decades before his death by natural causes in 1974. Zito was active in jukeboxes and vending machines, and he operated a number of bars. He was referred to by a newspaper reporter as one of the most dangerous mobsters in the state of Illinois. But his neighbors, of course, described him as a quiet man who kept to himself.

Madison, Wisconsin

This may seem an improbable locale for a Mafia family, but the FBI says one existed there, and its don was a man named Carlo Caputo. Caputo and the alleged Mafia family are like Bigfoot sightings. People swore it was out there, but it was not an "in your face" family like the boys in New York and Chicago.

The shadowy Caputo is alleged to have had ties to the Chicago and Milwaukee mobs, but less is known about him than his more famous associates. Caputo came to Madison in 1940. He was successful in real estate and ran restaurants, bars, and liquor stores. Caputo did thirty days in prison for income tax evasion and continued to expand his seemingly above-board businesses. When an associate of Caputo's named Joseph Aiello died a natural death, the FBI probed into his affairs and determined that the men were a two-man operation, the smallest Mafia family in history. Caputo died in 1993 at the age of ninety and went to his grave denying the government's charges. When asked to comment on the don's death, however, a local businessman said, "This is one man I don't want to discuss."

Milwaukee, Wisconsin

The Milwaukee Mafia family began as a subsidiary of the Chicago organization. The first don was Vito Guardalabene. Guardalabene was followed by his son Peter. When the Commission was formed, they determined that Milwaukee would remain an extension of Chicago. Frank Balistrieri took over the family and led it until his death in 1993. The Milwaukee and Kansas City mobs, with the help of the corrupt Teamsters Union, got in on the Las Vegas casino boom in the 1970s. Unbeknownst to the hard-working rank and file of the Teamsters, their pension fund funded the Stardust Hotel and other casinos. And the mob made plenty of money "skimming" off the top in the casino counting rooms before it was reported to the IRS. After Balistrieri's death, his sons reportedly took over, but the family has faded from the underworld scene.

St. Louis, Missouri

The St. Louis crime family thrived during Prohibition and had more than its share of gang violence. Vito Giannola was the first St. Louis don. The most famous was Anthony Giordano. The St. Louis mob appears to have had an independent streak. Its leadership did not attend the Apalachin conference that ended in disaster. Giordano was a skilled leader, and as a result he projected an image of power and influence that the family did not really have. It was a second-tier family. This was evident after Giordano's death—the family went into its death throes after the don's demise. His succeeding boss, Matthew Trupiano, was busted for running a high-stakes poker game, a far cry from the millions the family once made skimming from the casinos in Vegas. Trupiano died of a heart attack in October 1997, but some say the small family has hobbled along.

FACT

The gangsters of St. Louis had colorful names for their families in the days of Prohibition. The most powerful organizations called themselves the Green Ones, the Pillow Gang, the Egan's Rats, the Hogan Gang, and the Cuckoos. Eventually one familiar name, the Mafia, reigned supreme.

Denver/Pueblo, Colorado

This underworld outfit began in the 1880s and was more like a Western movie than a gangster melodrama. The first boss was a French-Canadian named Lou Blonger. He ran saloons that also featured prostitution as an attraction. This was common in the Old West. Blonger's career lasted from the wild and woolly 1880s until the 1920s, when he was finally imprisoned.

To counter the mob violence, the citizenry turned to an equally unsavory organization, the Ku Klux Klan, to restore order. The mayor, chief of police, and many cops were Klansmen. The KKK did not vanquish vice in Denver; they controlled and profited from it. The American Legion took on the Klan and won, eliminating the KKK's influence in the police force.

The Italians finally arrived in the 1930s in the persons of Pete and Sam Carlino. They brought their brand of bootlegging into the Wild West. The Mafia was split into two groups, both trying to stake their claim as the rightful racket kingpins of Colorado. The Smaldone brothers, with such fearsome nicknames as "Chauncey," "Checkers," and "Flip-Flop," ruled their factions out of Denver, while Jim Coletti ran Pueblo. Without new recruits the local mob family dwindled. The Smaldones were reduced to a crime family of three. Checkers died in 1996, Flip-Flop died in 1998, and Chauncey died in 2006. The Denver/Pueblo family is no more.

The West Coast Families

California was not quite the immigrant bastions that states back East were. Consequently the Mafia presence in cities like Los Angeles and San Jose were comprised mainly of transplants from New York and Chicago. But while the mobsters that made up the bulk of these small-time gangs were from some of the biggest crime families in the country, their exploits out West were decidedly minor league.

Los Angeles, California

The mob in Los Angeles never got much respect, even though they oversaw gambling, loansharking, and pornography. Founded by Joseph Ardizzone, the most influential Los Angeles Mafioso was Jack Dragna. He oversaw a small family of mostly East Coast transplants, nicknamed the "Mickey Mouse Mafia" by the Los Angeles Police Department. Dragna was involved with Hollywood unions and bookmaking. Dragna died in 1956 and was replaced by Frank DiSimone, followed by Nick Licata and then Dominic Brooklier. After Brooklier died, the family fell under the control of Peter Milano. The continually down on its luck family was plagued by informers, constant law enforcement surveillance, and a complete lack of respect on the streets. Though they should have faded away long ago, Milano still leads the now long-in-the-jaw Mickey Mouse Mafia.

San Francisco, California

Concentrated in the heavily Italian North Beach neighborhood, the Bay Area crime family remained a small, local criminal organization, never achieving much power outside their territory. The first don was named Frank Lanza, and he was the boss during Prohibition. Two other dons followed before Lanza's son James took over in the 1960s. He was not a grandiose hood who loved the limelight. The family received some notoriety after Jimmy Frattiano became a government witness, but faded into obscurity after Lanza's death.

QUESTIONS

Did a mobster ever sue the press for libel?
Joseph Cerrito of San Jose, California, sued *Life* magazine when the periodical identified him as the head of the San Jose crime family. The case was eventually dismissed.

San Jose, California

Onofrio Sciortino was the lyrically named founder of this low-key California family. He was replaced by Joseph Cerrito, a Sicilian native who operated a successful auto dealership in Los Gatos. Cerrito died in 1978 of a heart attack and the San Jose Mafia family died with him.

The Gulf Coast Connection

The humid Deep South was not only home to one of the earliest mob families in the country but boasted two of the most powerful mob bosses in the history of crime. Between the crews in Tampa, New Orleans, and the small outpost of Dallas, the Mafia controlled illegal gambling, narcotics trafficking, and even moonshine production. These crime groups were small, but their influence in world affairs was enormous, including the alleged involvement of all three families in the assassination of President John F. Kennedy.

Tampa, Florida

Though Miami and South Florida has been host to mobsters from around the country, Florida has a homegrown Mafia family, based in Tampa. The Tampa family made its initial fortune in gambling, specifically *bolita* (Spanish for "little ball"), a numbers game popular in the ethnic enclave of Ybor City. The Tampa family also had no compunction about getting into the narcotics business. They were one of the first families to aggressively get into the game. The Tampa mob also had connections in Cuba. The island nation was a paradise and a playground for the mob and wealthy Americans who went there to gamble and indulge in other vices. This all changed when Castro seized power in 1959.

FACT

Florida actually had another homegrown "Mafia" family, the Cracker Mob. This group of rural mobsters controlled gambling, drugs, prostitution, and moonshining throughout rural Florida and was closely tied in with the Tampa crime family.

Some of the earlier mob powers in Tampa were Ignazio Antinori, Ignazio Italiano, Salvatore Italiano, Alphonso Diecidue, and Santo Trafficante Sr. The most famous Tampa Mafioso was Santo Trafficante Jr., who succeeded his father as boss of the family after Sr.'s death in 1954. Trafficante Jr. became one of the most respected Mafia leaders in the country, forging alliances with mobsters from the United States, Canada, Italy, Spain, and Southeast Asia. Trafficante died in 1987 and was allegedly succeeded by Vincent LoScalzo.

New Orleans, Louisiana

In the twentieth century, the name of Carlos Marcello was synonymous with the New Orleans Mafia. Born in Tunisia, Carlos Marcello was a five-foot-four-inches tall, stockily built powerhouse. With a thick Cajun accent, Marcello did not fit the mold of the stereotypical American gangster.

The New Orleans mob was always very independent. It went its own way and did not answer to the Commission up North, which regulated just about every other Mafia family large and small. Just as the American South is regarded as laid back, with people and events that move along at a leisurely pace, so too the New Orleans Mafia's structure was a looser confederation of individuals and groups of criminals.

The Mafia in New Orleans operated bars and restaurants in the famous French Quarter, site of the yearly Mardi Gras celebration. It was a popular surveillance assignment for the local FBI!

Carlos Marcello continued to thrive and feign influence and prestige in the New Orleans rackets. He had his sticky fingers in drugs, gambling, and also in less harmful enterprises that the Mafia has always had an interest in—pinball machines, jukeboxes, and vending machines.

What is the longest reign of a Mafia don?
Stefano Magaddino ruled the Buffalo crime family for fifty years until his death in 1974. No other don approaches this tenure. They were ousted by either natural or unnatural causes long before they could celebrate this milestone anniversary.

Carlos Marcello became the don of the New Orleans crime family in 1947. A conference was held, and he was appointed by the other members of the New Orleans crime family. It created bad blood but no bloodshed. It was an unusual example of Mafia power transference. Most involved someone getting whacked.

Marcello shared the philosophy of most of his fellow gangsters. In a sense they were akin to the political Libertarian Party, which endorses the legalization of drugs and prostitution. Marcello believed he was giving the

Carlos
Marcello

Courtesy of AP Images

▲ New Orleans underworld figure Carlos Marcello, left, leaves federal court with Shreveport, La., attorney Michel Maroun, where Marcello's trial on charges of assaulting an FBI agent went to the jury, in Laredo, Texas, May 28, 1968.

people what they wanted. He wasn't concerned with whether or not people's lives were destroyed by drug abuse or alcohol addiction—that was the individual's responsibility.

His sphere of influences included most of the southern and western states, including California, plus pre-Castro Cuba, the Caribbean, and Mexico. His illegal income funded numerous and diverse legitimate businesses.

Carlos Marcello and the New Orleans mob continued to prosper and avoid the long arm of the law for many years. But nothing lasts forever, and eventually the FBI caught up with him. In 1981, after decades of seeming invulnerable, the don of the New Orleans Mafia was found guilty of violating the RICO law. He bounced around several federal prisons in the six years he was incarcerated, most of them minimum-security "country club" institutions. He developed Alzheimer's disease in prison and was released. The mighty little man who ruled a massive criminal empire degenerated into dementia and infantilism and died in 1993. The family leadership was picked up by his brother Joseph, who continued his ties with the Tampa and New York Mafia families. After Joe, Anthony Carolla took over, until the feds busted him for involvement in a gaming scam.

Carlos Marcello spoke with such a thick Cajun accent, other mobsters complained about having a hard time understanding him. And though small in stature, Carlos Marcello was a feared man. He had an ominous credo posted on the wall in his Metaire headquarters: "Three can keep a secret if two are dead."

Dallas, Texas

The Dallas mob is most famous for one of its low-level members, Jack Ruby, who gunned down Lee Harvey Oswald after he was arrested and charged with the assassination of President John Kennedy. Ruby was an intimate of the local don, Joe Civello, a native of Baton Rouge. Civello ascended to power after the reigns of Carlos and Joseph Piranio. The Dallas family was under the thumb of the larger New Orleans Mafia, as was a small off-shoot mob group in Galveston led by the Maceos. After Civello died in 1972, the FBI considered the family inactive, but Joe Campisi oversaw some operations for the New Orleans family until his death in 1990.

"Open" Cities and Outposts

Mobsters need vacation time too. For this reason the sunny paradise of Miami (as well as the gaming destination of Las Vegas) was considered an "open city," meaning any Mafia family could operate there without having to get permission. Things got so bad with mobsters from around the world descending on the South Florida city that Miami was declared "the international headquarters of organized crime."

Then there were the outpost cities. Comprised of small mob crews from larger families, they were sent out to set up operation in cities without a sizeable mob presence. This enabled bosses to expand their empire with little bloodshed.

Miami, Florida

Since the 1920s Miami has been the playground of vacationing mobsters. Gangsters from the frigid north took a train or plane to the luxurious hotels and sandy white beaches of the quasi-tropical paradise. Many of the major mob figures like Meyer Lanksy, Al Capone, and John Gotti spent time and ran operations in the southern port city. The close contact between the mobsters gave rise to a lot of interfamily schemes. Gambling, stock fraud, stolen property rings, and narcotics were the big moneymakers. By the 1990s authorities estimated that over 600 members and associates of all the crime families in America were either living full or part time in South Florida. Cuban, Colombian, Haitian, Russian, and Israeli gangsters joined them. In recent years Mafia activity has moved north from Miami to Ft. Lauderdale and Boca Raton.

Des Moines, Iowa

Iowa would be the absolute last place anyone would think of having a Mafia family, but a small offshoot of the Chicago mob operated there. Louis Fratto was the longtime mob "boss" of Des Moines. A capo in the Chicago Outfit, Fratto ran labor racketeering and gambling with a small crew. He was a close associate of San Giancana and Tony Accardo. He died in 1967 while under indictment for interstate fraud. His son Johnny is a minor celebrity and a frequent guest on the Howard Stern radio show.

San Diego, California

There was an active Mafia presence in San Diego, though it was never an official family. Los Angeles capo, and FBI informant, Frank Bompensiero operated lucrative rackets there before he ran afoul of the LA leadership and was murdered in 1977. Chicago sent down Chris Petti to oversee their interests in Indian gaming. Petti died in 2006. The final group was the Matranga family. The Sicilian-born mobsters operated restaurants and were suspected of being major international drug traffickers in the 1950s.

Youngstown, Ohio

Youngtown was not an open city in the traditional sense. Rather, it was split between the Cleveland and Pittsburgh families. For years the two families worked side by side running gambling, loansharking, stolen property rings, and narcotics in town. But as the city's fortunes declined as the steel industry collapsed, the mobs started warring with each other for control. Lenny Strollo, a Pittsburgh mobster, became the de facto "boss" of the Mahoning Valley. Following the murders of gangsters Joey Naples and Ernie Biondillo in the 1990s, federal authorities moved in with sweeping indictments of mobsters and politicians. Strollo decided to cooperate and became a government witness, eventually providing information against representative James Traficant.

CHAPTER 14

Just Say No

For years the Mafia had a love/hate relationship with the world of illegal drugs. The Mafia protested much about its involvement with drugs, but to some extent they always were, and finally the allure of the big money became too great. Narcotics has become a massive moneymaking entity, dwarfing the gross domestic product of most countries. And from the beginning the Mafia was right there in the thick of it. This chapter will look at the Mafia's involvement in the drug trade.

14

Drug Abuse in America

Contrary to what many people believe, drug use in America did not begin with the hippies in the 1960s. Drugs have been popular since humans first discovered the natural kick in certain chemicals in plants and then learned to refine and fine-tune them for greater potency.

In the late nineteenth century, "opium dens" were easy to find. Patrons could go into these dimly lit and seedy establishments—usually run by Chinese immigrants—smoke opium, and be provided a cot to recline on to enjoy their drug-induced reverie. When opium was outlawed, addicts turned to a legal substitute—heroin. Yes, heroin was legal in the United States. In 1898 the Bayer pharmaceutical company touted heroin as a non-addictive substitute for the highly addictive painkiller morphine. Astoundingly, even Coca-Cola was laced with cocaine for a time in the nineteenth century. Drugs have always been around, and there has always been a subculture of addicts.

Many drugs that are now illegal were once readily available and enthusiastically consumed by the general public. Vin Mariani was a popular drink in the nineteenth century. Made of cocaine-laced wine, it was served in saloons and bistros in Europe and America.

Some people were aware of the gravity of the drug problem. Sir Arthur Conan Doyle, author of the Sherlock Holmes stories, was also a medical doctor like his fictional character Dr. Watson. Doyle's fictional mouthpiece regularly warns Sherlock Holmes about the dangers associated with Holmes's cocaine use. Dr. Doyle, through the voice of Dr. Watson, was in the minority in his belief about the insidious nature of cocaine, but he and other medical men were ahead of their time in their belief that it was much more than a harmless recreational drug.

The Narcotics Cops

The first attempt by the government to control the use of narcotics by Americans was the Harrison Narcotics Act of 1914. It did not do much good. It required businesses that dealt in opium and cocaine products to register with the federal government and, of course, taxed them a penny per ounce on items they shipped through the United States Postal Service. Doctors were allowed to dispense heroin, opium, and morphine to patients for medicinal purposes. This resulted in the first versions of "rehab centers." Like the methadone clinics of later decades, these facilities tried to break people's morphine addiction by giving them heroin. Morphine addiction became a serious problem for many American soldiers during World War I. In 1923 the Supreme Court decided to make it illegal for doctors to prescribe heroin and morphine for any reason. Did government interference end the scourge of drug addiction in America? Of course not. All it did was make the trafficking of drugs go underground. And there was an organization in place ready, willing, and able to take up the slack and make billions over the remainder of the twentieth century. Enter the Mafia.

The Mafia and Drugs

There is evidence that some Mafia dons were unwilling to let their soldiers dabble in narcotics. Paul Castellano barred the Gambinos from dealing, though that did not stop John Gotti and his crew from trafficking in heroin. Buffalo don Stefano Magaddino wanted to give his soldiers a bigger cut of the profit to steer clear of drugs. But the allure of easy, and big, money was too much to avoid.

The Chinese Connection

Prior to the Mafia's entrance into the drug business, most of the heroin consumed by America's addicts came from China. A smaller supply came from the Middle East and the Corsican gangs in Marseilles, who would ultimately team up with the Mafia. During World War II this whole network was nearly broken by the fortunes of war. The fighting on land and sea in and around Europe and North Africa and Japan's invasion of China effectively dismantled the source of the heroin's manufacture and the trade routes over which the drug was shipped. Since the supply was not there, the demand diminished in the United States. Then the United States intelligence community made it possible for the Mafia to become extremely wealthy drug kingpins and flood the land with the addictive poison.

Just as the Sicilian Mafia had problems when the fascist government of Mussolini came to power, so too did Chinese organized crime fail after the Chinese communist revolution of 1949. The peasant class suffered either way, whether it was from the menace of the criminals or the cruelty of the totalitarian regime.

Just Say Yes

Even before the Supreme Court decision made these drugs illegal, the Mafia had dabbled in drugs. Mafiosi acted as though it was beneath them, but they greedily salivated at the money to be made. The New Orleans Mafia was dealing drugs, including marijuana, in the nineteenth century. Marijuana was popular in the local African-American community in turn-of-the-century New Orleans. The Mafia talked a lot about keeping it away from children and from Italian and Sicilian neighborhoods. There was always racism within the Mafia in addition to its deep insularity, so it did not much care what drugs did to destroy other ethnic groups.

Business Opportunity

The Mafia crime families in the North were slower to jump on the narcotics bandwagon. The old guard from the Old World wanted nothing to do with it. There was plenty of money to be made in the bootlegging, gambling, and prostitution rackets. These were regarded as "harmless" vices by many people, even law enforcement officials, who often turned a blind eye when these activities were going on right under their noses.

Drug trafficking was another matter altogether. When the Young Turks wiped out the old guard in the Castellammarese War, the new leaders of the Mafia reconsidered staying out of the drug trade. They had a peripheral role in the business anyway. Their Jewish pals such as Meyer Lansky, Dutch Schultz, and Legs Diamond were already involved in the heroin business in the 1920s. The new Boss of Bosses, Lucky Luciano, decided that the Italians should get a piece of the action.

The vagrancy charges against Meyer Lansky, fifty-five-year-old gambler and who is reputed to have large gambling interests in Cuba, were dismissed, February 26, 1958, after a short trial before magistrate Reuben Levy in New York City's Manhattan Arrest Court. When Lansky arrived from Cuba on February 11, he was followed by a detective to midtown Manhattan where he was taken into custody and charged with vagrancy. ▶

Meyer
Lansky

Courtesy of AP Images

The Bureau

When Prohibition was repealed in 1933 after the election of Franklin Delano Roosevelt, the Mafia turned its sights on the heroin racket. The decision made good business sense. Though there were fewer drug addicts than drinkers in the country, the profit margin would be much higher, and drugs would be easier to smuggle. Packets of powder do not noisily clink-clank in crates when being unloaded off ships in the dead of night.

ALERT!

As the Mafia's power and influence has dwindled, other forces have moved in to take up the slack. The Mexican cartels are supplanting the Colombians as suppliers of cocaine. Outlaw motorcycle gangs are manufacturing methamphetamine. Israeli mobsters control the ecstasy trade. Italian-based crime groups control both cocaine and heroin in Europe.

Part of Luciano's plan was to turn the approximately 1,200 prostitutes (who earned him $10 million a year) under his control into heroin addicts. They would not create problems, and they could be easily manipulated that way. The prostitutes would work to support their habit and buy the product from the Mafia. They would be immediately returning the pittance they earned back into the pockets of their Mafia masters. During his exile in Italy, Lucky Luciano masterminded the modern heroin trade.

Cops in the Know

The first federal law enforcement agency to realize that the Mafia were the new bad boys on the block was not the FBI, but rather the Federal Bureau of Narcotics (FBN), the precursor to the Drug Enforcement Agency (DEA). The FBN compiled extensive lists of major drug dealers and financiers across the country. In addition, rather than hiring all Ivy League WASPs, the BNR hired agents of Italian, Middle Eastern, and Asian descent to effectively infiltrate the drug underworld. By the 1960s the FBN had a far more extensive database of mobsters than any other law enforcement agency.

The Italian Connection

The United States government thought they were getting rid of a rotten apple when they deported Lucky Luciano back to Italy. What they really did was send him off to the old homestead so he could organize a very efficient and effective drug trafficking empire. They kicked him out, and he sent back tons of heroin that filled the Mafia's coffers. Luciano immediately renewed old acquaintances in the Sicilian Mafia when he returned to the Mediterranean region.

Middle East Mayhem

It was a labyrinthine trail that took the heroin from its source to its destination as nickel bags in American cities and towns. And Lucky Luciano oversaw the whole sordid affair until his death in 1962. It is estimated that the number of heroin addicts in the United States increased from 20,000 to 150,000 in the twenty years after World War II.

The trek began in the Middle East, where it was in its morphine base form. Luciano's main source for the morphine base was a shady character in Beirut, Lebanon. Sami El-Khoury secured the raw opium from Turkey, oversaw its transformation into morphine base in Lebanon, and sent it along to the laboratories in Sicily and Marseilles, France, for its final metamorphosis into heroin. It seems that just about everyone in Lebanon was on the take. Members of the police force and airport and customs officials were generously bribed, which enabled the trafficking to run smoothly with no interference from pesky law enforcement officials.

On to Sicily

In Sicily, Lucky Luciano had several secret laboratories where morphine was processed into heroin. Luciano had minimal interference from the law from 1949 to 1954 until some investigative journalists ran some pictures and a story in a Rome newspaper. One lab was shut down, but the impact to the business as a whole was negligible. Luciano's ties with other major mob drug figures, like Santo Sorge and Santo Trafficante Jr., helped him maintain control.

Luciano was not the only Mafioso who was deported after World War II. More than a hundred big and little fish were kicked out of the United States, but their penchant for larceny did not diminish. Nor did they all return to Italy when deported. Luciano had his men placed in big cities throughout Europe. Therefore he had many agents and operations in places across the European continent. If one tentacle of his hydra-like empire was cut off, it would not have jeopardized the enterprise as a whole.

FACT

The Mafia's involvement with drugs and the increasing number of snitches is directly connected. Since drug trafficking carried very serious jail time and law enforcement officials were less likely to look the other way, low-level hoods were more likely to cut deals.

Back in the USA

Meanwhile, Luciano had stayed in close contact with his old pals back in America. Meyer Lansky was controlling Luciano's interests in America, and Lansky organized the American end of the drug empire. Lansky worked with the Trafficante crime family of Florida to oversee drug smuggling from the Caribbean and Cuba. Smugglers also delivered through Canada, and some audaciously unloaded their product right off the shores of New York City, much as they had done in the bootlegging days. The Cotroni family was the major player in the Great White North.

Luciano was not allowed back into the United States, but nothing prevented him from visiting Cuba, a mere ninety miles off the coast of Florida. Cuba was a haven for the Mafia until 1959. Luciano went to Cuba in 1947 for a meeting with the American crime bosses to discuss their plans. The famous Havana conference had representatives from almost every mob family in the country. The Mafia bribed the entire corrupt government of Cuba and secured their services in making Cuba the last stop before drug distribution in the United States. The United States government was well aware of Luciano's presence in Cuba, and it put pressure on the Cuban government to revoke Luciano's visa and force him to return to Italy. He did return there, but not before he had accomplished his goals. The distribution network in America was established.

The French Connection

Vast poppy fields stretched for miles in areas like Turkey and Afghanistan. When the poppy bloomed, the head was cut off and the juice was cultivated. The raw materials were then transported over land or by boat to either the tiny island of Corsica or the port city of Marseilles. There the French Connection took over. The French Connection was not just the name of a famous action movie, it was an operation overseen by Coriscan crime lords, French intelligence, the Mafia, and various middlemen.

Pure Product, Pure Profit

In the mid-1950s a kilogram of pure heroin was smuggled into Marseilles at a cost of $500. It was then sold to a middleman for $1,500 in Marseilles. The heroin was then cut at least twice with milk powder or sugar. By the time the final product reached the street the value of a kilo came to over $20,000. That kind of money brought attention from the underworld, as well as from law enforcement. The Corsican mob was bringing in over 5,000 pounds of heroin into the United States.

Corsican mobsters have been implicated in the assassination of President John F. Kennedy. Jailhouse confessions from a Corsican gangster fingered Lucien Sarti as one of the gunmen. The theory has been dismissed, but the involvement of Corsican mobsters is an intriguing possibility.

The Corsican mob lacked the elaborate organization of the rest of the Mafia. It was comprised of close-knit and insular clans who worked together for the greater evil. They have always had a track record of working for the highest bidder and have occasionally been employed by the Americans. It is generally accepted that the CIA paid the Corsican mob to break the striking communist labor unions. The Corsican mob's association with the CIA made them an extremely powerful crime family and in effect made Marseilles the largest heroin producer in the Western world.

ALERT!

> The Mafia's involvement in the drug trade has diminished, but other groups are picking up the slack. Some of them are funneling drug money into terrorist networks. These new transnational Mafias pose a serious threat to national security.

Popeye

The movie *The French Connection* followed New York City cop Eddie "Popeye" Doyle and his partner Sonny Grasso as they attempted to unravel the French mob's heroin racket. The case began when they noticed a Bonanno family member tossing money all over the place at a bar. The tenacious detectives set out a stakeout at the mobster's place of business and soon uncovered a heroin ring. Though nowhere near as exciting as the famous car chase through Brooklyn featured in the movie, the case was a test for the detectives as they matched wits against the Mafia and French traffickers. In the end the mobsters lost, though the disruption of the Connection was temporary at best.

Loss of Control

By the late 1970s the FBI, DEA, and various local and state law enforcement agencies had made some serious inroads into the Mafia's drug network. Another development was the rise in popularity of cocaine, a drug that was provided to countless partiers by the Colombian and Cuban crime groups. The Mafia was slow to get onboard with the cocaine trade, instead clinging on to heroin. As the law was pressuring the Mafia from one side, other crime groups were coming in from the other. Even homegrown Mafia groups from the inner city were starting to stand up to the Mafia.

Passage to Bangkok

The inner cities of America had always been under the grasp of the Mafia. They preyed on the inhabitants, often black. But starting in the 1960s, up and coming black crime groups started standing up to the Mafia and moving drugs on their own without having to buy them for inflated prices from their mobbed-up suppliers. Gang boss Frank Lucas took things one step further—he went to the source.

Frank Lucas was the subject of the 2007 movie *American Gangster*. In the movie Denzel Washington played the flamboyant drug kingpin. Though some law enforcement officers complained their roles in the demise of Lucas's reign were trivialized, Lucas helped with the movie to try to keep it somewhat accurate.

The Golden Triangle was an area of Southeast Asia that became the new source for much of the heroin that had previously gone through the French Connection. Lucas set up his own distribution network to bypass the mob and bring the profit to his gang. Others emulated his model for a short time, until the heroin trade was taken over by Chinese organized crime groups.

The Purple Gang was the name of a famous bootlegging syndicate. It was also the name of a group of Mafia drug dealers that operated out of East Harlem in the 1970s. Also known as the Pleasant Avenue Connection, they represented a cross-section of the New York five families as well as sellers from various other crime organizations.

Dumbed-Down Dons

Back on the United States home front, the Mafia adapted to the times, and the drug trade became more and more a part of Mafia business and more and more in the open. The Mafia's pretense of civility and its vaunted code of honor gave way to the inherent greed of its members. The Mafia went from avoiding involvement in narcotics to involvement with reservations to outright and enthusiastic drug trafficking. As the old dons died and the Young Turks took over, they were less concerned about the nasty nature of the drug trade and more interested in the profits they made.

The Mafia went from wholesalers and controllers of routes to low-level street salesman, peddling bags of coke and joints in their own neighborhoods. This embarrassing downgrading of their power in the drug world led to numerous busts from both the cops and feds, not to mention an exponential increase in the number of wise guys ready to testify against their former cohorts in crime.

CHAPTER 15

The Gotti Mystique

The last of the flashy and flamboyant Mafia dons was John Gotti. In 1985, he became the boss of the Gambino crime family. He was the first hoodlum since Al Capone to become a media darling. Like Capone, he contributed undeserved positive publicity and bogus charm to a nasty and brutish lifestyle. Although his reign lasted only seven years, he was on the cover of *Time*, a favorite target of the New York City media, and a celebrity in his own right. This notoriety ultimately led to his downfall, and the fall of a number of his capos.

15

Coming Up in the World

The glory days of the Mafia were long gone by the 1980s. The FBI was using wiretaps, turncoats, and the latest technology to battle organized crime. Unlike the Hoover years, the FBI considered the Mafia to be one of their top priorities. While most of the new dons were content to lay low and out of the limelight, Gotti thrust himself in front of a camera whenever he got the chance.

John Joseph Gotti Jr. was born in the Bronx in 1940. He came from a poor family. His family moved to Brooklyn, and the angry young kid found himself in the land of the wise guys. They became his heroes. Like Al Capone a few decades earlier, he began his life in crime running errands for the local mobsters.

He became the member of a criminal street gang. Gotti was no "Fonzie," however. The gang was involved in car theft, robbery, and other criminal activity. He was arrested five times while still a teenager but avoided any jail time, a bit of luck that would follow him through most of his career. His luck did run out eventually.

It is not always easy when you are "married to the mob." The Gotti marriage was a tumultuous one. The hundreds of hours of FBI wiretaps reveal John Gotti complaining, "That woman is driving me crazy," referring to his wife.

Married to the Mob

John Gotti married Victoria DiGiorgio in 1962. His marriage was volatile, full of separations both by mutual consent and imposed by trips "up the river." After a brief flirtation with the legitimate world he quickly returned to a life of crime. The couple had five children. One would die tragically young, and another, Victoria, became a successful author, fundraiser for charities, reality TV show star, and tabloid fodder. His namesake, John Gotti Jr., ascended to the boss of the family briefly in the 1990s, but the FBI were hot on his tail. After serving a sentence for racketeering he beat three other indictments. He was arrested yet again and indicted in Tampa, Florida, in 2008 for overseeing a crew into robbery, drug dealing, and murder.

The Ozone Layer

Gotti hooked up with the Gambino crime family when he joined a group of low-level hoods that reported to Aniello Dellacroce, who hung out at the Bergin Hunt and Fish Club, a storefront in Ozone Park, Queens. Gotti's beat was nearby John F. Kennedy International Airport. The pack of thieves hijacked stuff that landed at the airport and had yet to make it to its final destination. Gotti and his crew would steal anything; one of their favorite things to steal was women's designer clothing. In 1968 Gotti was nabbed in the back of one of his heist trucks by the FBI and went to jail for three years.

ALERT!

Got any John Gotti memorabilia? It might be worth more than you think. A person who attended Gotti's wake and grabbed a memorial card from the funeral home sold it on eBay for over $300. A newspaper from the day he died, the *Time* magazine with his picture on the cover, and various items he supposedly owned have all been sold for good money online.

Gambino underboss Dellacroce took a liking to Gotti and promoted him to capo. When Dellacroce went to prison, Gotti's star rose even further. His leadership enamored him to his crew, and they became as close-knit as a mob crew can get, with little of the petty bickering that plague the Mafia at every level.

Irish Need Not Apply

Kidnapping was a common means of intimidation among Mafia families in the 1970s. Members of one family would snatch someone from a rival family and demand ransom in the form of loot or other conditions. Often the kidnapped hood was released intact; on other occasions he was sent home on an installment plan, one piece at a time. Carlo Gambino's nephew was kidnapped and killed, and the old don wanted to put an end to the practice.

An Irish gangster with the pugnacious sounding name of Jimmy McBratney was believed to be the killer. Gotti curried favor with his boss Gambino by sending the errant Irishman to meet his maker. It turned out that McBratney was less of a brat than that. He was not the killer. Gotti got the wrong guy and did two more years in the slammer, but he got in good with his boss. That is an example of upward mobility, Mafia-style.

Clawing Up Through the Ranks

Carlo Gambino died of a heart attack in October of 1976, while watching the New York Yankees in the World Series. He had named Paul Castellano to succeed him. Castellano was adept at managing the family's white-collar crimes, which Gambino realized were the wave of the future. Aniello Dellacroce's feelings were hurt. And when a sensitive mobster's feathers are ruffled, the fur usually flies.

Boss in Training

Gotti had been consolidating his power base and rising within the ranks. The McBratney murder had granted him the exalted position of "made" man. The heists crew that operated out of the Bergin Hunt and Fish Club were his guys now, loyal to the up-and-coming capo. The boss, Paul Castellano, did not have as high an opinion of Gotti. That in itself thwarted Gotti's ambitions. Gotti in turn did not like or respect Castellano.

FACT

A week before John Gotti's death, his brother, Peter, acting head of the Gambino crime family, and several others were indicted on sixty-eight counts of racketeering, including another brother and a nephew, both named Richard. It was yet another blow to the Gotti era of the Gambino crime family.

Much of Gotti's success occurred because he violated an old Mafia rule: no involvement in drugs. Castellano eschewed the drug scene and ordered his men to stop. But there was a lot of money to be made in the drug trade.

Paul Castellano, known as "Big Paul," sixty-nine, arrives at federal court in Manhattan for his arraignment on Feb. 28, 1985. Castellano is the reputed head of the Gambino crime family and described by law enforcement officials as the most powerful man in organized crime. ▶

Paul
Castellano

Courtesy of AP Images/Mario Suriani

Other criminal organizations were deeply involved in drug trafficking, and the Mafia was notorious for wanting a cut of someone else's profits.

The rules were bending in that it eventually came down from Castellano that anyone caught dealing in drugs would be killed, emphasis on the "if they were caught" loophole. Eventually the old dons turned a blind eye to drug dealing when they saw the vast wealth that filled the family coffers.

Shooting at Sparks

Paul Castellano was in hot water. In the early 1980s the government was aggressively going after the heads of the five New York families, including Genovese boss Fat Tony Salerno, Lucchese boss Tony "Ducks" Corallo, Colombo boss Carmine "the Snake" Persico, and Bonanno boss Phil Rastelli. They were being prosecuted under RICO charges.

Family Troubles

Castellano was also losing respect in his own family. His insistence on white-collar crimes was not going over well with the blue-collar crews, who were aligning behind Gotti. The street tough seized upon the old don's vulnerability and began planning his demise.

It was December 1985, and Christmas shoppers crowded the busy city sidewalks, dressed in holiday style. Paul Castellano and his driver Thomas Bilotti pulled up in front of Sparks Steak House in midtown Manhattan. The venerated restaurant was a favorite dining place of Castellano's. No sooner did he exit his car then he was ambushed by assassins-in-waiting. Four gunmen administered six bullets to Castellano's head. John Gotti cruised by in a passing car and surveyed the carnage. Another Mafia transfer of power had been successfully staged. Gotti was the Big Boy now.

The New York media covered John Gotti's death and funeral for days, focusing on everything from the dapper suit he donned in death to man-and-woman-on-the-street interviews where naive New Yorkers came to praise the murderer, not to bury him. The extensive news coverage drew some criticism, but it sold papers.

Castellano had not been respected as a don, and Mafia experts believe that the fact that he did not see this hit coming and take precautions was an indication of his lack of competence.

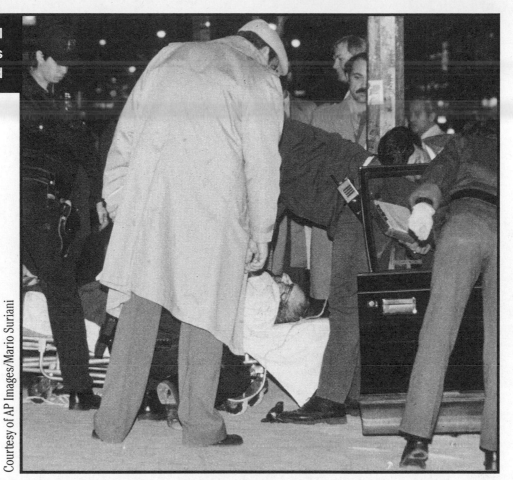

Paul
Castellano is
assassinated

Courtesy of AP Images/Mario Suriani

▲ The body of mafia crime boss Paul Castellano lies on a stretcher outside the Sparks Steak House in New York after he and his bodyguards were gunned down, Dec. 16, 1985. At the mob's peak, when dozens of top-echelon mobsters from around the country assembled in 1957 for the infamous Apalachin meeting, more than two dozen families operated nationwide. Disputes were settled by the Commission, a sort of gangland Supreme Court. Corporate change came in a spray of gunfire. Mob executions are a blast from the past; the last boss executed was Castellano.

Little Boy Lost

The tragic story of the death of Gotti's son, Frank, epitomizes Mafia justice. John Gotti's twelve-year-old son, Frank, was puttering around their Howard Beach, Queens, neighborhood when he was struck and killed by a car. The driver, John Favara, was a neighbor of the Gottis. Favara's son and little Frank Gotti were friends. They even had overnights in each other's homes. Favara had been blinded by the setting sun and had not seen Frank pull in front of his car.

Shortly thereafter, Favara began receiving death threats. The local police suggested that he move. He did not take these threats seriously at first. After all, it had been an accident.

FACT

John Gotti was a rebel and a hero to many a misguided citizen. He thumbed his nose at the New York City ban on fireworks with a lavish pyrotechnic display every Fourth of July. He was greeted on the street like a movie star, kissing women and babies on their cheeks and shaking the hands of star-struck gawkers.

The word *Murderer* was spray-painted on Favara's car, and one of his friends, the son of an old mobster, urged him "to take a powder," slang for hastily leaving the scene. After Gotti's wife, Victoria, attacked Favara with a baseball bat, he changed his mind. He put his house up for sale and decided to get out of town.

He did not get very far. He simply disappeared one morning, never to be heard from again. Veteran crime reporter Jerry Capeci pieced the story together years after the fact. Witnesses saw Favara get clubbed and thrown into a van. The witnesses were intimidated and remained silent. It is believed that his body was dumped in a barrel that was filled with cement and ended up at the bottom of the Atlantic. The offending automobile was turned into scrap metal.

In January 2009 another wrinkle was added to the saga when an informant related that he was told by Favara's killer that Favara's body was put in an oil drum that was filled with acid, dissolving it.

Mr. and Mrs. Gotti were in Florida when these events transpired. They were questioned upon their return, but as usual, there was no evidence to link them to Favara's disappearance.

The Favara murder truly shows the depravity to which gangsters could sink. It wasn't all honor and criminal ethics. They do what they please, usually in the shadows, and to get on their bad side, intentionally or inadvertently, is invariably bad news.

Celebrity Gangster

Gotti was a Mafia superstar in the 1980s, always elegantly dressed and not the least bit camera-shy. Throngs of admirers lined up in front of the Ravenite Social Club just to get a glimpse. Andy Warhol painted Gotti's picture for the cover of *Time* magazine. No murderous thug since Al Capone enjoyed the adulation of a perverse press and public. The government continued to go after Gotti, with no success, further cementing his dashing Robin Hood image.

From Teflon to Velcro

Gotti was a target from the moment he assumed control of the Gambino crime family in 1985. Even before that, he had been caught on FBI wiretaps over the years discussing all sorts of things, from criminal activities to complaining about his wife. Big Brother was monitoring Gotti.

Gotti beat his first rap as don in 1987. The government thought it had an airtight case and was stunned by the verdict. Gotti was acquitted again on another RICO charge. As is often the case with bureaucracies, in organized crime and the legitimate world, there were rivalries and infighting among the prosecution attorneys and the FBI agents who brought them the evidence. Gotti was acquitted again, and as a result he earned another nickname, the "Teflon Don." No matter what the feds threw at him, nothing stuck.

Gotti was also acquitted on an assault charge in 1990. He had been accused of hiring a gang of "Westies" to shoot carpentry union boss John O'Connor. It was alleged that O'Connor demolished the restaurant of a man who had dared employ nonunion workers. The restaurant happened to belong to a soldier in the Gambino family. The Westies are an

John Gotti

Courtesy of AP Images/Richard Drew

▲ Reputed mob boss John Gotti sits in New York Supreme Court in Manhattan, N.Y. on Jan. 20, 1990. Gotti listened to the opening arguments of his trial. He and a co-defendant were accused of ordering the shooting of a union official.

organization of Irish gangsters who operate out of a neighborhood once known as "Hell's Kitchen" on Manhattan's West Side. The Irish hoods shot O'Connor. If they were aiming for his head, they truly were the gang that couldn't shoot straight—he was shot in the butt. O'Connor told police that he had no idea who would want to take a shot at him. He knew that next time the marksman might take better aim if he squealed on Gotti.

One of Gotti's trusted capos was Carmine Lombardozzi, known as the King of Wall Street. Carmine attended Apalachin as a representative of the Gambinos. By the time Gotti took over the top, Carmine was in the September of his years but still was respected.

Witnesses always tend to lose their memories when questioned about their relationship with John Gotti. The *New York Post*, always good for a clever headline, once ran "I *Forgotti*" on their front page about one such witness, a trucker who Gotti assaulted over a parking spot.

John Gotti's son John, known as Junior Gotti, made a mistake following in the family business. He lacked both the acumen and the dubious charm of his father. He eventually plead guilty to, among other things, lying on a mortgage application.

Fourth Time's a Charm

The next time around the prosecutors were more successful. In fact, they were luckier than they could ever have imagined. They found the biggest "rat" ever to scurry into their midst, with enough information to turn the "Teflon Don" into the "Velcro Don," as Gotti later came to be called when his world began to fall apart.

Sammy "the Bull" Gravano was John Gotti's underboss in the Gambino crime family. He confessed to murdering nineteen people over a twenty-year period, an average of about one whack per year.

When Gotti got wind of another indictment, probably charging him with the murder of Paul Castellano, he ordered Gravano to go into hiding. Gotti knew Gravano would be subpoenaed to testify. Sammy the Bull stayed in various resort areas: the Poconos, Florida, and Atlantic City. When he retuned to New York City, Gotti demanded he meet him at the same social club that everyone on both sides knew was wired better than a home entertainment center. They were not there fifteen minutes before the feds raided the joint.

QUESTIONS

What do John Gotti and Grandpa Munster have in common?
Believe it or not, John Gotti's defense team trotted out celebrities as character witnesses to tell the press what a great guy he was. Among them was the ancient Al Lewis, most famous for playing Grandpa on the beloved television classic *The Munsters*. Other celebrities who attended his trail were actors Mickey Rourke and John Amos.

The two men and others were arrested and denied bail. At a hearing, excerpts from the hours and hours of tapes were played. Gravano learned what Gotti had been saying about him when he was not around. He was putting the blame for the Castellano hit on Gravano's shoulders. Locked up together for months before their trial, the two men developed an even deeper dislike for one another. Gravano saw the writing on the wall and decided to cut his losses. He became one of the most important mob informants in history.

The feds knew Gravano would be an invaluable asset in nailing the Teflon Don, so despite his many crimes he was granted immunity. His testimony not only brought down several members of the Gambino family, but also members of the Colombo and Genovese crime families. The Bull entered the Witness Protection Program, getting five years for all his murders.

Many mobsters believed that, while the Bull's testimony was certainly damning, the Dapper Don's rampaging ego was in large part to blame. Most mobsters prefer the shadows, and those who strutted and swaggered in the limelight invariably had their comeuppance. Membership in the Gambino family dropped considerably. Many modest low-level capos and underlings were ordered to meet with Gotti at his social club, despite the fact that everyone knew that it was under constant FBI surveillance. Camera-shy hoods were obliged to have their picture taken lest they earn the wrath of Don John. It was common knowledge that the FBI was watching and listening to everything that was said in the club, but Gotti would make his minions line up and pay homage. He would also speak with self-destructive candor. The Bull and the others were alarmed and angered by the Dapper Don's egotism and big mouth. He had begun, as many celebrities do, to believe his own publicity and consider himself as "untouchable" as Eliot Ness.

John Gotti became a pop culture icon. Starting with his portrait by Andy Warhol on the cover of *Time*, Gotti became a cottage industry, spawning books, T-shirts, songs, and name-dropping across the media spectrum. His daughter Victoria became a successful novelist and star of a reality show.

Circus, Circus!

The final John Gotti trial was, to no one's surprise, a media circus. Sammy the Bull was now Sammy the Rat in the local papers. Gotti's people initiated a smear campaign, calling him everything from a homosexual to a compulsive womanizer. The defense team did not have as much ammunition as they did in previous cases, and the sequestered jury was impossible to influence.

When Gravano, who had been sequestered at a Marine Corps base in Virginia, took the stand, that was, as they say, all she wrote. He placed Gotti at the scene of the Paul Castellano murder and fingered him as the man who orchestrated the hit.

In 1992, Gotti was convicted and given a life sentence without the possibility of parole. At his sentencing an angry mob loudly protested the verdict, but to no avail. Gotti was sent to a maximum-security prison. For many years it is believed he ran things from behind bars. But eventually health problems took over. He was diagnosed with cancer and lingered gravely ill for many years in a prison infirmary.

John Gotti's funeral procession

Courtesy of AP Images/Robert Spencer

▲ Cars with floral arrangements lead the funeral procession of reputed mob boss John Gotti as it winds its way through the Queens borough of New York, Saturday, June 15, 2002. Gotti died in prison of cancer. He was sixty-one.

Death of a Don

John Gotti succumbed to cancer on June 10, 2002, at the age of sixty-one. The Associated Press eulogized him as follows: "John Gotti, who swaggered, schemed, and murdered his way to the pinnacle of organized crime in America only to be toppled by secret FBI tapes and a turncoat mobster's testimony, died at a prison hospital Monday while serving a life sentence."

FACT

Sammy the Bull has made it back into the news in recent years. Living in Arizona as "Jimmy Moran," he became involved in trafficking the popular drug known as ecstasy. He was arrested along with his wife, son, daughter, and son-in-law. A real family affair.

John Gotti delivered his own obituary right before he was sent to jail. It is naturally more colorful and more hubris-laden than the press reports that covered his death. The Dapper Don was nothing if not full of himself. "I'll always be one of kind. You'll never see another guy like me if you live to be 5,000." And as his hearse wound its way through Queens, thousands of people were there to witness his last drive through town.

CHAPTER 16

The Rats

Despite the code of Omerta, the vow of silence every "made" Mafioso makes, there have been many "rats" in the mob's violent history. Turning on fellow gangsters has become commonplace, though there have always been snitches and informers who used the police to take out enemies and competitors. If found out, the informers were marked for death. But on the flipside, the turncoats gave the public a firsthand account of what life was like in the underworld. This chapter introduces you to some of the more famous, or infamous, Mafia informants.

The Valachi Papers

Joseph Valachi was the first informant to get national attention. Press from around the country covered his testimony. The events that transpired to land Valachi on the witness stand were of soap opera caliber and could rival anything a writer could dream up.

Joe Valachi became a member of Salvatore Maranzano's organized crime family in the 1920s. He was officially "made" in 1930. After Maranzano's murder, Valachi was moved into a crew led by Vito Genovese.

Valachi was a gangsters' gangster. He was a numbers runner, leg breaker, ruthless murderer, and in later years a drug trafficker before he was finally locked up. He was in prison on a fifteen- to twenty-year sentence for a drug charge when he decided to re-evaluate the oath he took when he was made.

FACT

Attorney General Robert F. Kennedy's war on organized crime turned up the heat and made turncoats of many Mafiosi. He called the Mafia "the enemy within," a hostile force within our borders out to undermine the American way.

Two's Company

Joe Valachi was in a federal prison in Atlanta, sharing a cell with his former skipper, Vito Genovese. Vito was now the boss of the former Luciano family. He enjoyed the trappings of success, including a home in Atlantic Highlands, overlooking Raritan Bay in New Jersey. But Genovese's forays into drug trafficking netted him a prison sentence.

While in prison with Valachi, Genovese began to suspect that his loyal soldier was a traitor. Vito suspected Valachi was giving information to the authorities in exchange for a lighter sentence. He got the word out that Joe had to go.

Kiss Me, Guido

Vito Genovese publicly gave Joe Valachi the "kiss of death," meaning that he was now a marked man. His days were numbered. There were three attempts on his life while behind bars. Even in prison, the Mafia could conduct business and have men killed. Valachi knew he would soon be whacked.

He got wind of who the hit man was, a fellow mobster also serving time. However, Joe mistakenly killed the wrong man after he thought he was being ambushed. The stone-cold killer who had seen so much violence in his life perhaps felt his first pangs of conscience when he learned that the man he clubbed to death with an iron pipe was not the man he thought he was. His sentence was amended from fifteen to twenty years to life imprisonment. It was then that Valachi fulfilled Vito Genovese's prophecy and become an informant.

There is much braggadocio and one-upmanship among low-level Mafiosi. It is therefore necessary to take much of Joe Valachi's testimony with the proverbial grain of salt. A man in his position would not be told much about his superior's plans, and his fellow soldiers tended to lie about their exploits to feed their egos and enhance their reputations.

Sing, Sing a Song

Valachi was placed under witness protection and guarded by 200 United States marshals. They were not going to let the Mafia get their hands on their prize songbird. The mob offered a $100,000 reward for Valachi's head on a platter. Valachi appeared before the McClellan Committee in 1963. He fingered 317 organized crime members and brought the name *La Cosa Nostra* into the vernacular. The testimony was enlightening but produced no quantifiable results. Not one Mafioso was jailed based solely on Valachi's testimony, but the one lasting vestige was that the five New York families were given the names of the bosses who were leading them at the time: Bonanno, Colombo, Gambino, Genovese, and Lucchese.

Valachi had no real view into the inner workings of the Commission, but his vast experiences gave the McClellan Commission and the general public an idea of how pervasive the Mafia's influence was, as well as a look at some of the stranger customs of the gangsters, including the lack of work on

Mother's Day. There was probably much braggadocio in his testimony, and plenty of unreliable hearsay. Nevertheless, his pronouncements painted the picture of a brutal, nasty, and ruthless world: speaking of honor and codes while double-crossing and backstabbing, going to church on Sunday and

Joseph Valachi's Senate hearing

Courtesy of AP Images

▲ New York City gangster Joseph M. Valachi sits at the witness table, right, facing members of the Senate Investigation subcommittee as he reveals more of the inner workings of a major crime syndicate in Washington, DC, on Oct. 8, 1963. In the background are four charts of crime families with names and pictures of mobsters indentified by Valachi. From left are Giuseppe Magliocco family, top; Joseph Bonanno family, bottom; Carlo Gambino family; Gaetano Lucchese family; and the Vito Genovese family.

beating a man to death on Monday, sexually distancing themselves from their wives when they became the mothers of their children while keeping girlfriends on the side.

Spin City

The Mafia orchestrated something akin to a publicity campaign against Valachi's testimony. Not everyone on the side of the law bought a lot of Valachi's claims either.

There have been some notable informants since the Mafia's inception. Camorra gangsters Raffaelle Daniello and Tony Notaro testified against their bosses in 1918. Gangsters from New York, Chicago, and New Orleans provided information to police long before the FBI became interested in the Mafia.

Vito Genovese was not considered the Boss of Bosses by most in the know. Even in far-off Italy, Lucky Luciano remained the boss until his death in 1962. And Luciano's mouthpiece in America was his old friend Meyer Lansky. Valachi, not the brightest bulb in the underworld, and more than a little xenophobic, did not give Lansky his due simply because he was Jewish.

Other Mafia informants claimed Valachi talked out of both sides of his mouth long before he turned rat. And claims surfaced that he might have been an informant long before he officially went to the feds.

Another attack on his character was in his Mafia nickname. He had been called Joe Cargo as a young man but over time other Mafiosi began calling him "Joe Cago." According to mob sources, they were not simply mispronouncing his moniker. It was a sign of how they felt about him. *Cago* is an Italian word for "feces."

Joe Valachi tried to commit suicide in 1966 but failed. In 1971, in a Texas prison, Valachi died after an acute gall bladder attack (or heart attack, depending on the source). He was sixty-six years old. Before his death, Valachi cooperated with bestselling author Peter Maas on the book *The Valachi Papers*. It was later made into a movie starring Charles Bronson. At least

Valachi exacted revenge on his old boss. Vito Genovese lost much of his power as a result of Valachi's testimony, and he died in 1969.

Always a Gangster

Another infamous rat in the history of Mafia informants is Henry Hill. Henry Hill was played by Ray Liotta in one of the best and most realistic gangster movies, Martin Scorsese's *Goodfellas*. And in a very appropriate twist for these very twisted times, he is the first Mafia informant to have his very own website. Hill also appears regularly on the Howard Stern radio show and has become a restaurant owner after overcoming drug and alcohol problems.

A Brooklyn Tale

When Hill was a small boy on the mean streets of East New York, Brooklyn, he was enthralled with the local wise guys. Like many a wannabe mobster before him, including Big Al Capone, he got his start running errands for the neighborhood gangsters, much to the chagrin of his parents.

A Mafioso must be fully Italian in order to become a made man. Jimmy "the Gent" Burke and Henry Hill could never be made men because they were not full-blooded Italian. Burke was given the affectionate and honorary title of "the Irish Guinea." In later years, some mobsters, like John Gotti Jr., were made despite being only half Italian.

Henry became entrenched in the seductive criminal underworld. One of his best friends was Jimmy "the Gent" Burke, a Queens-based mobster well known as a hijacker. Hill and Burke were half Irish, and because of that, no matter how many people they killed, they would never be admitted into the inner sanctum of the Mafia. For the record, Hill says he never killed anyone, though he was present at a few murders.

Hill was an associate of the Lucchese Mafia family. His biggest score was as part of the famous Lufthansa heist, at Kennedy Airport. But by the 1970s, his life was also spiraling out of control. Drug and alcohol addiction, plus the increasing stress of living in the dangerous underworld, were bringing him to the breaking point. He started dealing drugs and became a target for local narcotics detectives. In 1980 he was arrested for drugs and decided to become a turncoat for the feds. He knew he was on the outs with Burke and Paul Vario, his other mentor in the Mafia.

Witness for the Prosecution

In the wake of the Lufthansa heist, many of those involved in the robbery were snuffed out. Dozens more were murdered as they squabbled over the distribution of the Lufthansa airport heist money. Faced with his world coming in all around him, Hill went into the Witness Protection Program and was given a new identity. He remained in the program for seven years.

After the ill-fated Lufthansa heist, many of the robbers involved in the operation were murdered by Burke, who sought to keep the money for himself. Of those murdered, four bodies were never found, one corpse was frozen solid, one decomposed body was found in Ohio, and another dismembered body was found floating off New Jersey.

Under his new identity, Henry Hill continued to engage in criminal activity and even did sixty days in jail. He was arrested for drug dealing, assault, burglary, driving while intoxicated, and parole violation. The protection program, run by the United States Department of Justice, kicked him out, so he turned to the FBI, which has helped him remain in hiding since then.

Cyberfella

Henry Hill calls himself a "cyberfella" these days. He is also the author of a cookbook called *Cookin' on the Run*. Although his life will always be in danger, it would seem that his ego has compelled him to make potentially hazardous forays into the light. He has a website called *www.goodfellahenry .com*. He also owns a restaurant in Connecticut.

Those who log on can buy copies of Mafia-related books and chuckle over his version of David Letterman's Top Ten List. Hill's parody is a list of Mafia slang expressions for murder. You can take an interactive tour of his old neighborhood and the mob hangout called Robert's Lounge. You can even buy an autographed poster of the movie *Goodfellas* that he suggests you purchase before he gets whacked. Send him an e-mail and he might even answer.

The Sicilian Turncoat

Although turning informant is a dangerous decision for an American Mafioso, it can be dangerous for their entire family in Italy. But while the violence of the Italy-based groups kept their defectors to a minimum in the

Henry Hill

Courtesy of AP Images/Mike Derer

▲ Former mobster Henry Hill smiles during an interview at the Essex County Jail in Newark, N.J., Friday, May 9, 1997. Hill, fifty-three, whose autobiography inspired the movie *Goodfellas*, was arrested in a Newark hotel room with his girlfriend on parole violations in California.

early years of the Mafia, as time went on more and more mobsters decided to make the move to assist the police. One of the most significant was Tommaso Buscetta. His testimonies at trials in the 1980s resulted in the conviction of dozens of American and Sicilian gangsters.

The Sicilian Mafia was known for its violent vendettas. Throughout the twentieth century hundreds of mobsters and family members were killed due to personal conflicts, in addition to the many more who were taken out for business reasons. Police officers and judges were also vulnerable to attack.

A Gangster's Gangster

As one of seventeen children, Buscetta had to work hard to help out his family. He was born into poverty. But by the time he was a teenager he was running errands for local Mafia bosses. By the mid-1940s he was a full-fledged member of the Porta Nuova family, smuggling cigarettes and working in the narcotics trade.

The Pizza Connection case stemmed from an investigation into heroin smuggling activities. Authorities learned that a group of Sicilian mobsters had established an extensive network of heroin traffickers in pizzerias throughout the United States. The network was headquartered out of a Queens, New York, pizza parlor. In total, over twenty Mafiosi were convicted.

Fleeing an escalating Mafia war, Buscetta came to New York, where he worked for the Gambino crime family before moving to Brazil. In South America, he was picked up on an old murder warrant from Sicily. Deported back to Italy, Tommaso was sent away for life.

Turning Against the Sicilians

Prison is not easy for anyone, so they say, but Buscetta was having a difficult time. To make matters worse his two sons were murdered as part of yet another Mafia war that was turning the streets of Palermo red with the blood of gangsters and family members. Buscetta decided it was time to make his move. But rather than further the violence, he met with an anti-Mafia judge. Buscetta let loose the deep, dark secrets of the Mafia, as well as alliances with the American mob. He testified in the infamous Pizza Connection trial in New York as well as the Maxi-Trial in Italy, which led to the convictions of over 300 gangland figures.

Philly Breaks Down

There was little brotherly love for Philadelphia mobster Ralph Natale. He was the first Mafia boss to turn rat while still on the job. Not that a rat in the family was unusual for Philly, though usually the rats were small-time operators. This violation of Omerta was just the latest blow to the faltering Philadelphia family, a group that endured mob wars, RICO cases, and the turning of some of their top capos.

The Old-School Don

Prior to Natale turning traitor, the big boss of Philadelphia was the old-school Angelo Bruno. He was nicknamed "the Docile Don," because he was more loath to use violence than any of his predecessors or contemporaries. Under his leadership the Philly family maintained an even keel, making millions from gambling, loansharking, narcotics, unions, and other rackets. But Bruno's ambivalence toward Atlantic City angered some of the New York families, while his underlings wanted a bigger slice of the pie. The low-level punks in the Philadelphia family were either jumping ship or getting a piece of the lucrative drug trade. Bruno was losing power and influence, and the boys in New York finally ordered his assassination. He was murdered in 1980.

Power Grab

The resulting fallout from Bruno's assassination set a series of events in motion that rocked the underworld for the next twenty years. Underlings scrambled to be the top banana in the days after the Docile Don's demise. Over thirty New Jersey and Philadelphia mobsters were murdered in the bloody battles, including one of Bruno's killers, Antonio "Tony Bananas" Caponigro, and the man who replaced Bruno, Phil "Chicken Man" Testa. By the time Nicky Scarfo and his successor, John Stanfa, were put behind bars, the Philly family was under the thumb of Ralph Natale.

Two of the victims in the endless Philly mob war of the early 1980s were members of a loosely affiliated Hellenic crime group, referred to as "the Greek Mob." Led by Steve Bouras, the Greek Mob was engaged in many of the same rackets as the Philly family. There were also Greek crime figures in New York City, Chicago, Philly, and Tampa.

From Cop to Capo

The Natale-Merlino reign was a shaky one. One of the thorns in their side was a hoodlum named Ron Previte, who had been, interestingly enough, a Philadelphia police officer for ten years. He was the capo of a New Jersey crew.

Previte was unhappy with the leadership of Natale and Merlino, and their dynasty was built on sand. Previte turned back from the Dark Side to the Force. In this case, the Force was the FBI. He "wore a wire," meaning a recording device on his person. Hours of damning evidence was handed over to the feds. Natale and Merlino were indicted on drug charges.

Boss Rat

Feeling the heat, Ralph Natale became a federal informant and witness for the government. His former partner in crime, Merlino, and ten others were indicted, and the charges were expanded to include attempted murder and murder in the first degree. Merlino and most of his men were sent to prison, and Natale was shipped off to an undisclosed location. After Natale left, Joe Ligambi allegedly took control of the family. But if past history is any indicator, Ligambi's reign will be a short one.

The Bosses Start to Sing

In the early years of the rat phenomenon, many of those who chose to work with the government were low-level associates with the occasional soldier. But as time went on the turncoats came from higher and higher ranks. By the mid-1990s, former bosses and underbosses were jumping ship. But when Ralph Natale turned, all bets were off. From then on the top guys in the family were as apt to turn and the mob would never be the same.

Gaspipe

Anthony "Gaspipe" Casso was the underboss of the Lucchese family. He led an ostentatious life, wearing top-dollar suits, living in a mansion in Brooklyn, and going out to the top restaurants in Manhattan. When the boss of the family, Vic Amuso, went to prison in 1991, Casso became the acting boss. But he was hiding out from charges against him. When the police found him hiding in a shower in a mob safe house, his reign was over. Casso decided to take the easy way out and become a cooperating witness. The feds had high hopes. Casso disappointed. He became unreliable as a witness and was kicked out of the Witness Protection Program.

Big Joe

In the late 1990s the Bonanno crime family, which just a decade before had been kicked out of the Commission and was facing extinction, was back as one of the top Mafia families in the country. A big part of that reason was the leadership of Joe Massino. Joe took over in 1993 and brought the family back to underworld prominence. Wary of electronic surveillance, Joe took trips overseas with his brother-in-law and underboss, Salvatore Vitale. But the feds caught up with Big Joe in January of 2003. When he came to trial the following year, there was a stable of rats ready to pounce on the big cheese, including his own brother-in-law. Massino saw the writing on the wall and helped the feds nab his successor, Vinny Gorgeous. Massino is serving life in prison, but his testimony and cooperation with authorities saved him from the death penalty.

Joseph "Big Joey" Massino, the head of the Bonanno crime family for fourteen years, is seen in this undated file photo released by the U.S. Attorney's Office. Massino, sixty-one, has become the first family boss ever to turn cooperating witness. ▶

Joseph
Massino

Courtesy of AP Images/US Attorneys Office

The King of the Rats

James "Whitey" Bulger ran South Boston for the Winter Hill Gang. Rising through the ranks of the predominantly Irish mob group, Bulger became one of the most feared crime figures in Beantown. But every time the state police started to get close to capturing the gangster, he seemed to get wise to their operations. Whether it was a found bug or a snitch who disappeared, Bulger seemed one step ahead of the law. But things were coming to a head.

QUESTIONS

Who is Whitey Bulger's brother?
Whitey's brother is Billy Bulger, a controversial, yet popular, Boston politician. Billy was the president of the University of Massachusetts, the president of the Massachusetts State Senate, and president of the Boston Public Library. He is also on the board of various museums, hospitals, and banks.

In 1995, a joint task force comprised of Massachusetts State Police, the Boston Police Department, and the DEA closed ranks around Bulger's organization. They arrested the top leaders of the local mafia and the Winter Hill Gang, but Bulger was nowhere to be found. As it turned out, Bulger had been an informer for the FBI for over twenty years. In exchange for information he gave the FBI about the Mafia, they allowed him to continue running his criminal operations. In fact, Bulger developed such a close relationship with his field agent that he was tipped off about the impending DEA task force indictment.

Bulger fled on January 5, 1995, and disappeared with his longtime mistress. He met with his underlings a few times in Boston and Chicago. He lived for a while in Louisiana and Florida. He has also been seen in Ireland and England, and there was a false sighting of him in Italy, which made international news. As of January 2009, Bulger was still on the run. He is number two on the FBI's Ten Most Wanted, right behind Osama Bin Laden.

CHAPTER 17

Making Money

The single goal of the Mafia is to make money. That is the driving force behind many of their decisions. "It's not personal, it's just business" is a mantra that pop culture tells us is the principle by which mobsters live. But as with the distorted notion of honor, sometimes it is personal—usually if it involves the stealing of money from another mobster! The Mafia makes it money in a number of ways. This chapter looks at some of the more common schemes, scams, and rackets.

Policy, Numbers, Lottery, Bolita

Many nights, across the country, state governments run their lotteries. A collection of balls, numbered 1 to 100, are put into an air machine that mixes them up and spits out three balls, or six balls, or a number of other combinations. Millions of Americans bet money on what the combination of the balls will be. From this, the government takes in tens of millions of dollars to fund education and other programs, though no one really ever seems to figure out exactly where all the money goes. But the lottery was used by the mob for decades before states made it legal. Known as policy, numbers, or *bolita*, it was one of the mob's most profitable rackets.

Bolita

Bolita ("little ball" in Spanish) came to America via Tampa. It was brought there by Manuel Suarez. By the 1920s the game was flourishing. It was similar to the lottery. Balls numbered 1 to 100 were tossed around in a sack and the winning number was chosen. It wasn't long before gangsters started fixing the games, making it easier for certain numbers to be drawn. After that, the operators started taking their numbers from the Havana lottery or the stock market.

QUESTIONS

Where was the best place to make bolita bets?
Everywhere! During bolita's heyday in Tampa you could make bets at the local grocery store, the butcher, in the street, at work, and in any number of bars, cafés, and restaurants. Bolita was so widespread that you could even give bets to the ice cream man while your kid was buying a frozen treat!

Policy and Numbers

The numbers racket was a popular game in the poor sections of many cities. Black gambling kingpins amassed fortunes running these games. People would make bets, then the operators would get the winning number from the stock market, or the winning numbers at the dog track. This random selection made it more difficult to fix the numbers. But that didn't matter. With so many people making small bets, the profits were enormous. Even if a number hit and a bunch of people won, the organization would have enough money to cover it.

Wanna Bet?

Sports gambling is a multibillion-dollar a year business. Despite ever-increasing avenues for legal betting, the Mafia and its network of bookies still see more action that they can handle. In 2007 New Jersey authorities busted a mob-backed gambling ring that they estimate took in more than $1 billion. That's a lot of point spreads and over/unders. But be careful if you bet with a bookie. Low-level bookies, even Mafia-affiliated ones, have been known to welsh on winning bets. And it's not like you can go to the police and complain!

The Mafia has long been associated with funny business at horse tracks. The races have been known as places where big-time gamblers place loads of bets on a contest that can easily be fixed. But even with the seedy underbelly past, the races are still popular. Back in the day, mobsters like Meyer Lansky owned not only horses but had money invested in the tracks themselves. Saratoga Springs, Hallandale, and Aqueduct were some of the racetracks owned at least partially by the Mafia. The gangsters fixed races, beat up jockeys who didn't go along with their plans, and made sure that the horses they wanted to win came in first. In short, it was just as crooked as any other Mafia racket.

Paying the Sharks

When you are a compulsive gambler, it's not easy to go to the bank for a loan. If you are a business owner with no history of credit and you need a quick influx of cash, who do you call? In both cases your local neighborhood loan shark is more than willing to help out. For a higher-than-usual interest rate, they'll lend you money without any question. Watch out if you are late paying it back.

The Vig

The "vig" or "vigorish" is the interest or amount paid to get a loan. The vig can range from a few hundred to hundreds of thousands. By keeping money on the street at all times, the loan shark is maximizing his profit base. "Points" above the vig are usually increments of interest due each week. Since the interest compounds rather quickly, it doesn't take too long for the initial loan amount to balloon way out of proportion. This is when a little talking to or a leg breaking might be needed to keep the loan recipient in line and make sure he'll pay.

FACT

Bars are very popular businesses for mobsters to own. In addition to serving as a ready-made hangout, most of the bar's business is done in cash, making it an attractive business to launder money through. Also the bar clientele often buy ancillary products like drugs and prostitutes.

Your New Partner

If a debtor can't pay back the loan to the loan shark, this is one way in which the Mafia butts into legitimate businesses. Instead of taking payment of the loan, the Mafia takes a piece of the debtor's business. More often than not the Mafia would bleed the business dry, laundering money through it or using it as a de facto headquarters. Many a criminal act was planned in a "busted out" business.

Shakedown

In the Mafia's infancy, the modus operandi was to shake down local merchants for "protection." This code word simply meant that if the shopkeeper refused to pay the mobster, the mobster would have the shop trashed . . . or worse. The early Mustache Pete's preyed solely on their own fellow immigrants, rarely venturing outside the area to shakedown other groups. But as their influence expanded the extortion racket was brought to other neighborhoods.

The Mafia makes a lot of its money from imposing a "street tax" on independent criminals operating in its territory. Drug dealers have long been a favorite target. Why deal the drugs yourself when you can simply shakedown a dealer? It's less work and less risk. The street tax is usually applied to bookmakers, pimps, con men, and thieves, but can also include other criminals, as well as up and coming mob associates.

The term that the Mafia used to get money from local neighborhood merchants was "a little to wet my beak." That was enough to let the shopkeepers know that if they didn't kick up some of their hard-earned money, then retribution would be harsh.

Moving in Respectable Circles

In order to keep the flow of illegal money away from the prying eyes of the law, many mobsters own businesses to wash their cash through. While some own bars and lounges, others own restaurants and coin laundries—all cash businesses. But an increasing number of underworld figures are getting into legitimate businesses, blurring the lines between their illicit take and their business acumen. In fact, some alleged mobsters are far more successful in their legitimate endeavors than their street rackets. Car dealerships, manufacturing plants, car title loan companies, and construction companies are just a few of the myriad legitimate businesses currently owned by reputed Mafiosi.

High-Tech Rackets

While the Mafia still relies on the tried and true bookmaking and loansharking rackets, they have been able to capitalize on other ventures, some even high-tech. Not too shabby for a street-level tough with barely a high school education! In recent years the Mafia has been involved in sophisticated stock scams, money laundering operations, prepaid cell phone distribution, computer crimes, and insurance scams.

FACT

The Mafia's pump and dump scams on Wall Street were big moneymakers, but the mob also ran sophisticated stock scams out of Boca Raton, Florida. The community became so notorious for its stock rackets that it became a target for organized crime groups from around the world.

In June of 2000, the Justice Department announced the indictment of 120 people, many tied to the five families of New York. It was one of the largest busts of its kind, and it showed that some members of the Mafia were equally at home on Wall Street as they were in Brooklyn. Throughout the 1990s, gangsters were setting up fake brokerage houses and marketing worthless stocks to unwitting investors. The wise guys bribed brokers, threatened security personnel, and stole millions. It was money for the taking. And even though the busts brought their operations to a screeching halt, the gangsters only went away for a couple years.

CHAPTER 18

Fuhgeddaboudit!

The Mafia has its own unique "slanguage." Some words might be easy to catch on to, like using "whack" to mean killing someone. There's a whole host of terms that the mobsters use to talk about their illegal activities that won't appear in any dictionary. In many cases, however, these words and phrases have become part of the vernacular, especially in parts of the country where gangsters are or have been prevalent. And there is, of course, the influence of pop culture and its image of the all-American mobster, an image that some real gangsters have adopted for themselves!

What Are Youse Lookin At?

Why would a close-knit and insular organization also develop a language all its own, full of unique and colorful turns of phrase to describe brutal and barbaric actions? There are several reasons. Since what they do for a living is almost always illegal, the Mafia began to employ code words to describe many of their activities. This was designed to fool law enforcement officers that may be listening either within earshot or using sophisticated listening devices.

Warm and Fuzzy Hoodlums?

Perhaps members of the Mafia sometimes feel guilt or pangs of conscience about their unsavory lifestyle. They are known to be the masters of rationalizations and have the ability to put "spins" on their doings and dealings that rival any elected official. Maybe the clever language can psychologically blunt the harsh reality of their misdeeds.

The Italian and Italian-American Mafia are not the only organized crime outfits that have a vernacular all their own. Ethnic gangs from the Chinese triads to the Russian Mafia have words, phrases, and code names to keep outsiders from knowing too much.

The Neighborhood

Another source of the unique mob slang is rooted in the accents of places where the mobsters came from. New York City, being the main epicenter of Mafia activity for so long, has contributed the most, starting with the stereotypical New York Italian accent. "Youse" instead of "you" or "you all," "dem" instead of "them," or "tree" instead of "three" are just a few examples of how accents have become so associated with the mobster mystique.

Mobsters also have a broad sense of humor. They are the ones committing the crimes and inflicting the pain. They are the ones breaking the bones, corrupting the souls, and putting the bodies in "cement shoes." But many are also natural-born storytellers, embellishing their mishaps, conquests, and everyday struggles to make a buck. For every stoic mobster there is an equally flamboyant over-the-top character, like Bonanno capo Jerry Chili, regularly cited for his jokes, exaggerated mannerisms, and ruthless leadership.

The ironic part of the Mafia developing its own language is that many of the rank-and-file gangsters, especially in the early years of the mob, were barely literate. Even now, it's generally not the students at the top of the class who decide to turn to a life of crime as a viable career choice. To be sure, there are exceptions, but most mobsters have a hard enough time speaking English let alone in code.

How Can I Kill Thee . . .

There are many ways to kill a person in the Mafia handbook, and even more ways to describe it. Nowadays, with the numerous Mafia movies and the television hit *The Sopranos*, the secret is out. The general populace and the FBI wiretappers are not fooled by these once-cryptic code words and phrases.

The main phrase, one that has become an everyday part of the American vernacular, is "whacked." It's not clear where this term originated, but it has become the premier mobspeak term for the general populace. The popularity of the term is related to its prevalence on movies and television shows.

But a victim can also be hit, iced, clipped, offed, burned, rubbed out, or popped. The hit man can break an egg or give his quarry a serious headache. They could be fitted with cement shoes, a cement jacket, or put in a cement coffin. This type of murder is specifically for burials at sea, when the body, sometimes alive and sometimes not, is weighted for deposit in the deep blue, where the incriminating evidence will never be found. Such a victim is said to be sleeping with the fishes.

Putting Out the Word

A contract is put out on the target of a hit. The boss says to "take care of the situation," or "make him disappear." Johnny Rivera, a Tampa Mafioso, once complained that public killings were bringing too much heat on the mob. They started to "make people disappear" and covered them with lye to make sure the body decomposed quickly. A more intimate way to order a hit is to publicly give the person the kiss of death. This means that his days are numbered. That person is now a goner.

ALERT!

If a Russian Mafioso goes into a politician's office and offers him silver or lead, the bureaucrat is likely to opt for the silver. This is a slang expression that offers the man the choice of a bribe or a bullet in the head.

The hit man may have already been told to get a place ready, meaning to find a good location to dispose of the body. That means he is going, as in "going, going, gone." The victim will then be taken for a ride. Or perhaps go out for an airing.

Maybe he will get five times thirty-eight, which is five bullets in the head with a .38-caliber revolver, or maybe be on the receiving end of a Little Joe if he failed to pay a gambling debt. A Little Joe is four shots in the head in two rows of two bullet holes. Neatness counts. He could also receive the Italian rope trick. That is strangulation. Or maybe a Sicilian necktie, which means being garroted with piano wire. On very rare occasions, the person may be given a pass, meaning his life has been spared.

A Couple More

An ice pick kill means what it sounds like—an ice pick though the ear and into the brain. One thing you never want to hear a Mafioso say is the word *buckwheats*. He is not referring to the beloved tyke from the *Little Rascals* and *Our Gang* comedies. It is a slang expression for an especially grisly murder wherein the victim is mutilated and tortured for an extended period of time before being put out of his misery.

Native Tongue

One of the common ways that an ethnic group keeps outsiders from hearing its secret plans is to speak in its native language. Most of the new immigrants to America in the late nineteenth and early twentieth centuries spoke a language other than English. Most learned English with a desire to assimilate, but the native language was still spoken at home. The children of the immigrants were often bilingual, but their native tongues often faded from use in favor of the English language.

The native language was often spoken as a code to prevent others from understanding what they were saying. The Mafia employed this course of action, and many of the Italian expressions continued to be used by subsequent generations. There is something more musical about a "romance language" (Italian, French, and Spanish) than the "Anglo-Saxon" English language.

Mafiocracy is a slang word to describe the current state of affairs in Russia. When communism collapsed, the criminal element filled the void before true democracy could get a foothold.

In some areas mobsters were fluent in more than one language. In the Cuban-Spanish-Italian area of Tampa known as Ybor City, the local mobsters were often fluent in English, Spanish, and Italian, sometimes even mixing the three together to make a unique Tampa "slanguage."

Smack Talk

Gangster like to talk tough, and they like to "break balls," meaning they like to throw around insults, many times in jest. If you do not like the looks of someone, you can say *Che bruta*, which means "How ugly you are." A similar slur is *Facia bruta*, which can literally mean "an ugly face" or simply be used as a generic insult. However, it would be unwise to say this to anyone in the Mafia. If someone is a motor mouth they could be called a *chiacchierone*, or "chatterbox." *Gira diment* means "going crazy," and *pazzo* or *oobatz* (*u'pazzu*) means that you believe the person you are addressing is already crazy.

A *mortadella*, besides being a type of Italian bologna, is a loser. So is a *cafone*, also spelled and pronounced *gavone*. *Va fa napole* literally means "go to Naples" but in mobspeak means "go to hell."

Speak Like a Gangster . . . Guaranteed!

Most Mafiosi have a mistress on the side, even though they consider themselves to be fine husbands and fathers. A girlfriend is called a *comare* or *goomare*, while a male buddy is called a *compare* or *goombah*. Italian phrases that are used to denote "the Mafia" include *La Cosa Nostra*, which is translated as "our thing" or "this thing of ours," and *fratellanza*, which means "brotherhood."

Capo di tutti Capi is much more lyrical than "Boss of Bosses," but they mean the same thing. An *amico* is a friend of the family who is not a member of the crime family, and an *amico nostro* is a way to introduce a stranger who is also a member of a Mafia family.

Omerta is the Mafia's vow of silence. Once a mobster is "made," meaning he is inducted into a family, he takes this vow. Violating Omerta is a death sentence, or at least it once was.

FACT

The Russian Mafia calls a front company that launders money and serves as a front for illegal activities "a panama." This is probably derived from the common practice of using offshore, often Latin American, front companies by both legitimate and illegitimate organizations.

Pleasantries

On a lighter note, other expressions used by the Mafia do not imply malice or menace. *Piacere* is a greeting that means it is a pleasure to meet you. *Che peccato* is an expression of sympathy meaning "what a pity," and *buon'anima* is a condolence and meditation on mortality that translates as "rest his soul." And the Mediterranean mouthful *Col tempo la foglia di gelso diventa seta* is an old Italian proverb that is rendered in English as "Time and patience change the mulberry leaf to satin," meaning that patience pays off in the long run with great rewards.

Business Language

The Mafia does business in a similar fashion to any multinational corporation, murder and mayhem notwithstanding. It has executive officers, middle-management types, and drone-like workers. It also has a singular slang for its practices.

The mob is inherently capitalist, although its structure is a little different. Money is made from the bottom up. A soldier makes a score, or a successful criminal endeavor. He brings in a load of cash. Since he's a big earner, the Mafia's equivalent of Salesman of the Year, he's looked at favorably by his capo. The soldier gives the capo a taste, giving the capo a percentage of the take. In turn, the capo pays up to the boss. Associates, like bookies and loan sharks, who are not made into the mob may have to pay tribute, or pay a fee to ply their trade in a particular mob family's territory.

In an example of linguistic détente, the Russian Mafia slang expression for a hired killer is the same as one of the many used by the American Mafia. When they need someone whacked, they call a hit man a torpedo.

Drugs and Alcohol

Of course, much of the Mafia's business in its earlier days involved bootleg whiskey. In later years the Mafia dealt in drug trafficking. *Alkali* was a word for alcohol. *Alky racket* was slang for Prohibition, and an *alky cooker* was what they called a still, a device used for distilling alcohol. The *B-and-A racket* stood for beer and alcohol, another expression for Prohibition. When

Prohibition became law, all distilleries and breweries became illegal, but gangsters as well as the thirsty private citizens decided that the party was not going to end because of some lawmakers in Washington, DC.

Bootlegging seems innocent in comparison to the drug trade. *Babania* is a word for the drug traffic, especially heroin. It was forbidden for many years, but eventually the old dons looked the other way because of the big profits made in the narcotics business.

The Bangkok Connection refers to the drugs that wind their way from Southeast Asia to American shores for distribution at great profit by the Mafia.

Gambling

The Mafia also made a lot of money in the world of illegal gambling. Action covers the illegal gambling business. A bookmaker or bookie is the guy who takes illegal bets on horseracing and other sporting events. The numbers racket was the illegal precursor to state lotteries. A number was chosen at random and itinerant gamblers tried to divine the result. You had to be in it to win it. The gangster in charge is called a numbers operator. His assistant who takes the bets for the citizenry is called a numbers runner. And below the numbers runner is a low-level hood called a drop man. The percentage that the numbers operator and other Mafiosi have to pay to their bosses is called giveup or tribute.

Money Talk

The Mafia also has a unique language to describe money. A nickel is $500. Logically it follows that a dime is $1,000. Sometimes a dollar is also $1,000. So is the word *large*, as in "five large" being $5,000.

Frankenslang

A subset of mobspeak is "Frankenslang." This is the phraseology developed by Frank Sinatra's "Rat Pack," a group of entertainers who were not Mafiosi per se, but who certainly moved on the fringes of that world. Any performer who worked in Las Vegas, especially in the '60s and '70s, had to rub elbows with the mob. It was inevitable. The Mafia owned the place. The Rat Pack worked for the Mafia and were friends with many Mafiosi. They attended the same parties and shared the same girlfriends. There was plenty of cross-over between Mafia lingo and the hipster patois of the Rat Pack. While not politically correct, there is a charm in the Rat Pack's idiom. In the 1950s and early 1960s the Rat Pack patter was the epitome of cool.

FACT

Unlike the American Mafia, each yakuza clan of the Japanese Mafia has its own unique slang. A capo in the Bonanno family can understand a member of the Gambino crime family, but in Japan the clans often have a deeply secret slang that no one else can comprehend.

Here's to the Ladies

The Rat Pack made many slang expressions for members of the opposite sex. They are interesting as curiosities from a bygone era, but male readers of this book should proceed with caution before referring to their significant other by any of these antiquated terms of endearment.

Some of the complimentary terms for a woman that a Rat Pack hipster would like to get to know better are barn burner, meaning a very attractive woman. A petite woman was called a mouse, and a beetle referred to a well-dressed woman. Broad and chick were not insults but expressions of affection. So was gasser. Dame was not affectionate; in Rat Pack slang dame was not a compliment. A woman who liked to dance was called a twist or a twirl, and a girl who appeared to be ready and willing for a little hey-hey (romance) was called a tomato, in that she was ripe for the picking.

Likes and Dislikes

The Rat Pack was an opinionated clan. They considered themselves big leaguers and did not suffer clydes gladly. They were not good on names, so they would be likely to call you Charlie or Sam. They might greet you with "How's your bird?" This was an inquiry into the health and well-being of your pelvic region. They had no time for creeps, crumbs, bums, bunters, finks, punks, or Harveys. If they said, "Let's lose Charlie," it meant that they found your company not particularly stimulating. Similarly, if Frank told Dean that they were in Dullsville, Ohio, it meant that he was bored and wanted to Scramsville. Also if Sammy told Peter Lawford that it was raining and it was not, that was another code for wanting to split the scene. "Cash me out" also meant a desire to leave that particular clam bake. And if another of them blurted out "Hello!" to no one in particular, it meant he had just noticed an attractive woman.

Much of the yakuza's elaborate slanguage contains naughty words and scatological phrases that are not fit to print here. And just as the yakuza adopted a dress code straight out of Hollywood gangster movies, they borrowed some English words in a linguistic hybrid called "Japlish."

Food

Food is an important part of the Mafioso's life. Every meeting had food; every family event had food. Italian food is the mainstay of American cuisine, and the gangsters love it too, whether from their neighborhood eatery, the back of a bar, or from their mother's kitchen. And while most mobsters were very masculine and would never stoop to doing "women's work," when it came to cooking they were right there stirring the sauce.

It's All Kosher

Growing up in multiethnic neighborhoods, some mobsters took a fancy to the delicacies of other cultures. In *The Godfather* there is a scene where the family is eating Chinese food. Asian cuisine was popular with mobsters who grew up in Little Italy, which was located right next to Chinatown.

Mobsters in New York were also fond of Jewish food, hearing scams and levying decision over hot pastrami sandwiches and matzo ball soup. In

Tampa, mobsters sipped Cuban coffee and ate yellow rice and black beans, while in New Orleans po' boys and crawfish were Cajun-inspired mobsters faves.

Events

A football wedding is a wedding reception where the food is not a fancy catered affair, but rather plates of cold cuts with sub rolls, called footballs. It was one of the most popular ways to celebrate weddings in the more blue-collar, working-class neighborhoods where most of the gangsters grew up. Caviar wouldn't fly at a neighborhood wedding!

Prison stays were also situations where food was important. As depicted in the movie *Goodfellas*, mobsters sometimes had cells that were different from the accomodations for the general population, and they could get Italian delicacies brought in. Even in tougher conditions, mobsters often bribed guards to bring in salamis and cheese.

CHAPTER 19

The Mafia on Television

The two most famous mob shows on television are ABC's *The Untouchables* and HBO's *The Sopranos*. Both shows were and are controversial and also ratings blockbusters. They have been accused of defaming the reputation of Italian Americans, yet are enormously popular with Americans of all ethnicities. But much the way that the mobster has been a staple of the movies, gangsters have been bad guys in television for as long as the little box has been beaming signals into households across the country.

A 1950s Hit

Eliot Ness was a stalwart young federal agent when he was assigned to the Chicago office and began his campaign against Al Capone. He and his elite corps were called "untouchable" because they couldn't be bribed. This set them apart from many of their brother officers at the federal level and on the Chicago police force.

. Ness got Capone on tax evasion charges, despite his many more malevolent transgressions. J. Edgar Hoover was intensely jealous of Ness's successes and did his best to thwart his upward mobility. Ness wrote his memoirs in the 1950s and died shortly thereafter, bitter and in obscurity. He did not live to see his autobiography become the source material for one of the most successful television shows in the new medium's history.

The First TV Gangland Hit

Robert Stack played Eliot Ness in *The Untouchables* TV series, which first aired in October 1959. The show ran until September 1963. After the 1987 movie was a big hit, Stack starred in the TV movie *The Return of Eliot Ness*. This was a purely fictional rendition, and Stack was a little long in the tooth to play Ness, who died in his middle fifties.

Staccato Delivery

The machine guns were not the only things with a rat-a-tat-tat delivery on *The Untouchables*. The show was narrated by the notorious newspaper and radio personality Walter Winchell, no stranger to covering real-life gangsters. Winchell's delivery was as rapid-fire as the Tommy guns in the garage on St. Valentine's Day. A slower yet nevertheless measured staccato was intoned by TV's Eliot Ness, Robert Stack. Stack later used his trademark delivery on *Unsolved Mysteries*.

The two-part pilot revolved around Ness's pursuit of Al Capone. The earlier episodes were done in documentary style, and the gangsters Ness battled were based on real people, hence the controversy and the lawsuits. When real-life crime figures were exhausted, Ness took on fictionalized hoods and some real hoods that the real Ness never encountered, such as the malevolent matriarch Ma Barker. Though the real Untouchables were long gone by World War II, the fictional Ness was still operating in Chicago in the 1940s and matching wits with Nazi saboteurs. *The Untouchables* ran for four seasons and has been in reruns ever since. It even inspired a movie version in 1987 (see Chapter 20).

There was also a 1993 television version of *The Untouchables* that emulated the look and feel of the 1987 movie. Elliot Ness was played by Tom Amandes, who later went on to star on the show *Everwood*. Al Capone was played by character actor William Forsythe. While Capone's bribes and bullets could not touch Ness and company, bad ratings could. The show lasted only two seasons.

Critical Responses

The Untouchables was a violent program, a Tommy gun shoot-'em-up on the mean streets of 1930s Chicago. By today's standards it is rather tame, but it shocked many viewers in its initial network run. CBS received many protests from parents who were concerned about the impact the show would have on their children. The violence was a forerunner of what later TV shows would become. In that sense, *The Untouchables* might be considered one of the more influential shows in television history.

Ethnic Backlash

Most of the protests about the show came from Italian-American groups. The old Cagney and Bogart films rarely used Italian surnames for their characters, but *The Untouchables* made no secret of the ethnicity of its villains. Capone and his cronies were mentioned by name, and many felt this was an ethnic slur. In fact, the producers were sued by, among other people, Al Capone's widow!

Far-Reaching Implications

Desilu Productions, a company run by two classic TV icons, Lucille Ball and Desi Arnaz, produced *The Untouchables*. At one point Desi received death threats and was obliged to travel with bodyguards. The ever-volatile Francis Albert Sinatra even accosted Arnaz in a Hollywood restaurant and chided him for his involvement in such a scandalous show.

Eventually, some compromises were made. Once the series had exhausted the many historical figures in the Chicago mob, they decided to give the fictional villains non-Italian-sounding surnames. And the actor who played "Nick Rossi," one of Ness's team, got more lines as a result. This was to highlight an Italian-American good guy on the show.

FACT

Robert Stack, now so associated with the role of Eliot Ness, was actually a last-minute replacement for actor Van Johnson, who bowed out at the eleventh hour. Stack went on to make television history, imbuing Ness with a stoic manner and clipped speech patterns that were affectionately parodied by everyone from Leslie Nielsen to Dan Aykroyd.

Money Talks

The mob was not pleased with their depiction in *The Untouchables*. One of the sponsors of the show was L&M cigarettes, back in the days when tobacco advertising was allowed on TV. Rumor has it that the mob threatened to use their clout with the mobster "Tough Tony" Anastasia threatened to use his clout with the Longshoremen's unions to see that millions of cartons of L&M cigarettes would sit on the loading docks, unpacked by the longshoremen and undelivered by the truckers. L&M dropped its sponsorship of the show in short order, costing the network and all those concerned a lot of money.

Crime Story

Oftentimes a television show fails to find its audience but gets a huge amount of critical praise. One such show was a gangland drama from the mid-1980s,

Crime Story. The series was produced by Michael Mann, who later went on to fame as a movie director. It follows the story of the head of a special Chicago police unit dedicated to fighting the mob. But unlike *The Untouchables*, this period piece was set in the early 1960s, reflecting the Chicago mob at the height of its power.

The main character was an Italian-American flatfoot, Lieutenant Mike Torello, with a penchant for straight talk. Torello was played by Dennis Farina, a former Chicago cop and no stranger to mob roles. He played the mob boss in the comedy *Midnight Run*, a mobster in the female gangland movie *Bella Mafia*, a low-level wise guy in *Get Shorty*, and another mobster in *Men of Honor.*

Wiseguy

The 1980s brought one of the more interesting shows about organized crime, the critically acclaimed *Wiseguy.* The show starred Ken Wahl as Vinnie Terranova, an undercover FBI agent who investigates some of the biggest crime groups in the country. The show was darker than most prime-time shows back then. But unfortunately the show was plagued by low ratings and battles between Wahl and the producers. Wahl left before season four, and the show fell apart.

Ray Sharkey brought a hard-edged yet flamboyant persona to mobster Sonny Steelgrave. He was the boss of the Atlantic City Mafia and responsible for the murder of Terranova's mentor at the FBI. Sharkey's manically comic performance was one of the highlights of the show. Unfortunately Sharkey's hard partying lifestyle offscreen took its toll. He died of AIDS in 1993.

This Week's Villain . . . the Mobster

Gangsters served as the weekly foil for an intrepid detective or a nemesis for the police. In many of the PI shows that were popular on television in the 1970s, mobsters began making an appearance as a staple villain for most of the shows. As the genre reinvented itself, gangsters were there, changing from old-time bosses to slick, young players, but their purpose remained the same.

Big Actors, Bad Guys

Many big-name entertainers have jumped at the chance to play small-screen mobsters. Before his turn as mob capo Rusty on *The Sopranos*, singer Frankie Valli played a mobster on the ultimate '80s cool TV show, *Miami Vice*. Harry Guardino played a mob boss on the '70s PI series *Vegas*, a natural setting for stories involving racketeers.

QUESTIONS

Have their ever been any shows with female gangsters?
Actually, yes. There was a Neapolitan mob boss in *The Sopranos*. Vanessa Redgrave led a women-run Mafia group in *Bella Mafia*. And in a Lifetime movie (hardly the place you'd expect to see a gangster flick), Alyssa Milano was a mob gal who took over her boyfriend's rackets in the TV movie *Wisegal*.

Cartoon Gangsters

One of the most recognizable mob bosses on television is the suave and brooding Fat Tony, the mob boss of Springfield, home of *The Simpsons*. From his post as head of the Legitimate Businessman's Social Club, Tony and his thugs have tried to muscle in on Marge's pretzel business (resulting in an all-out battle with the yakuza), recruit Bart for a spot in the mob family, and bribe the borderline incompetent Chief Wiggam. Fat Tony was the real nickname of Anthony Salerno, the late boss of the Genovese crime family.

The Sopranos: *Cultural Phenomenon*

Coming onto prime time on a cable channel and under the radar, *The Sopranos* became not only a cultural phenomenon but easily one of the best shows on television, both from a writing and acting perspective. It took the mob mythos into the modern era and added new riffs and spins to old themes. But more than any portrayal of the Mafia before, it delved into the inner workings of the mob family, domestic life, and a mob boss who was becoming unhinged.

Sopranos actors Tony Sirico and James Gandolfini

Courtesy of AP Images/Mike Derer

▲ Actors Tony Sirico, left, who plays Paulie Walnuts and James Gandolfini, right, who plays Tony Soprano, shoot a scene from the mafia drama, *The Sopranos*, outside the fictional Satriale's pork store in Kearny, N.J., in this Wednesday, March 21, 2007 file photo.

Jersey

The Sopranos chronicles the life of Tony Soprano, a Mafia don beset by modern problems that Al Capone and Lucky Luciano did not have to deal with. The story provides a sly counterpoint between the ordinary and the violent. Soprano, who lives in the dangerous underworld, goes home to the pedestrian problems that beset any American family. He has marital problems. He has strained relationships with his kids. And he sees a psychiatrist. Yet when he goes to the office, his daily workload most often involves criminal conduct and occasionally murder. This is what separates him from the other family men living in suburban New Jersey.

The Jersey setting gives the story an authenticity often lacking in other mob projects. From the grimy industrial backdrop of the Newark skyline to the McMansion-filled suburbs, it shows how far the Mafia has come, and how they are now more of a suburban phenomenon than an urban one.

Actors in *The Sopranos* have run afoul of the law. Michael Squicciarini, who played an enforcer in a couple episodes, was charged with a gangland hit before his death from natural causes. Robert Iler, who played AJ Soprano, got into a couple minor squabbles with the law. Lilo Brancato, who played Matt Bevalaqua, was sentenced to 10 years in prison for robbery in January 2009.

Mafia for the New Millennium

The Sopranos is a new Mafia image. The old Warner Brothers gangster movies presented hoodlums that suited the allegedly simpler times. Perhaps the times were not so simple in real life, but the movies portrayed them as such, and a conversation with your grandparents is likely to have them waxing nostalgic about the "good old days."

The show was filmed on location throughout New Jersey, but the interior scenes were filmed at a sound stage in Queens, New York, located at Silvercup Studios. Some cities refused to allow the show to be filmed there, but others, like Kearny, Caldwell, and Lodi, embraced the notoriety and gave the show the authenticity it needed.

The Untouchables television show continued that classic tradition with archetypal good guys and bad guys. Often there was more complexity given to the gangsters, but basically things were black and white with the occasional shades of gray.

In *The Sopranos* you do not see bigger than life. You see a representation of a Mafia in decline that mirrors the culture as a whole on the decline. Tony Soprano laments the loss of the "good old days" of the Mafia. He presides over a Mafia family whose glory days are long gone and are never going to return. But at the same time it shows a vibrant, rich tapestry of ethnicity, family, and success—from Lorraine Bracco's psychiatrist to the Italian FBI agents pursuing Tony.

There is much culture shock comedy as old mobsters have difficulty adapting to the changing world. One aging Mafioso laments that the mob did not get in on the Starbucks bandwagon, because that is where the real money is these days. Tony Soprano reads self-help books to deal with his many problems. You see a Mafioso picking up tips, tools, and techniques from current trends like pop psychology and applying them to the often grisly business of the Mafia.

ALERT!

The Sopranos generated much ancillary merchandise, including the books *The Psychology of the Sopranos* and *The Sopranos Family Cookbook*. There are Sopranos bus tours through New Jersey and a multitude of pop culture references in other TV shows, magazine articles, songs, and movies. It's safe to say that the show has become as much a part of the culture as *The Godfather*.

Hero Worship

The Sopranos constantly referred to the Mafia epic of all time, *The Godfather*. In a humorous recurring theme, all the members of the Soprano crime family grew up on the *Godfather* movies and regularly quote them. The fictional Corleones are the gods and goddesses on Mount Olympus for these less epic, less empathetic, and less inspired hoodlums.

One area where the Sopranos differ from the Corleones is in the desire for legitimacy. While the Corleones suffered great angst over their lifestyle and career choices, and always claimed that they sought to emerge from the shadows and into the light of respectability, Tony Soprano expresses no such beliefs. He likes his job, and probably would not mind seeing his son go into the "family business." Don Corleone wept when he learned that his son Michael killed two men and thus entered the Mafia life. Tony Soprano did not sweat such things.

Just as *The Untouchables* made many people angry, *The Sopranos* was no stranger to controversy. Italian-American groups have complained that it presented negative stereotypes. One New Jersey congressman wanted to pass legislation to have it banned. There was concern that it would create controversy when it first aired on Italian television, but it was a ratings hit in the birthplace of the Mafia.

But the most controversy was reserved for the shows' final episode. Fans were bitterly divided over the shows' quick cut to black. Some felt that show copped out at the end, while other thought it was brilliant, encompassing everything unpredictable about the show.

CHAPTER 20

The Mafia in the Movies

Gangsters have been boffo box office in the movies since the Golden Age of Hollywood. From *Public Enemy* and *Little Caesar* to *The Godfather* films and beyond, the criminal element has been portrayed as misunderstood Robin Hoods, tragedians of Shakespearean scope, lovable goombahs, and as nasty and ruthless killers that continue to fascinate us.

The Early Mob Movie Stars

From the 1930s and 1940s, Warner Brothers produced classic gangster movies starring the likes of James Cagney, Humphrey Bogart, and Edward G. Robinson. These films and their antiheroes differ dramatically from the more realistic cinematic portrayals of gangsters in later years. Rarely were the mobsters overtly identified as being of Italian ancestry. James Cagney had the map of Ireland on his pugnacious puss. Robinson was the product of the Yiddish theater. Bogart was English and Dutch.

Robin in the 'Hood

James Cagney usually played a basically good guy who grew up on the mean streets and inadvertently stumbled into a life of crime. These films were made during the Great Depression and thus it was often the lack of opportunity for the immigrant underclass to break out of their station that led the prototypical Cagney hero to a life of crime.

The gangster was not a total victim, however. Most movies had a character, usually the hero's friend or brother, who chose the straight and narrow and did not fall into a life of crime. In *Public Enemy*, it is Cagney's brother who remains crime-free. In *Angels with Dirty Faces*, it's Cagney's boyhood friend who becomes a Catholic priest while Cagney's character becomes a hoodlum.

FACT

Despite the repetition by impressionists for decades, James Cagney never actually said "You dirty rat" in a movie. But he did scream "Top of the world ma!" in the movie *White Heat*.

The Cagney persona was guilty of romanticizing the urban outlaw, making him into a kind of metropolitan Robin Hood. In *White Heat*, Cagney broke his own mold with a powerful and unsympathetic performance as Cody Jarrett, a psychotic killer with an Oedipus complex. Cold-blooded yet perversely pathetic, he is a murderous mama's boy who blows himself sky-high rather than be taken alive.

Play It Again, Bogie

The other legendary screen gangster of the Golden Age was Humphrey Bogart. He started out playing secondary villains but eventually became an A-list star and often played the good guy, particularly later in his distinguished career.

Bogart achieved stardom with the part of the vicious gangster in *The Petrified Forest*. It has the now-familiar theme of a group of gangsters holding a collection of characters from "central casting" hostage. Almost twenty years later, Bogart played a suspiciously similar role in the movie *Desperate Hours*. In between he played a variety of good and bad guys. His most famous gangster roles were opposite Cagney in *The Roaring Twenties, Angels with Dirty Faces*, and his very moving portrait of an aging and tired gangster on the run in *High Sierra*. He went against the Mafia in the underrated 1951 gangster pic *The Enforcer*.

George Raft, probably best known for his role as Spats Colombo in *Some like It Hot*, was a big star of the day and of Italian ancestry. He was also a good friend of Bugsy Siegel and Santo Trafficante Jr. Siegel visited Raft on movie sets, and Raft even helped arrange a screen test for the handsome gangster. Trafficante used Raft as a greeter in the Havana casinos in pre-Castro Cuba.

End of an Era

Bogart teamed with another famous gangster icon, Edward G. Robinson, in John Huston's classic *Key Largo*. Robinson plays the leader of a group of gangsters who hide out and harass the locals in the Florida Keys as a hurricane looms offshore. Bogart is the hero and shoots it out with Robinson's evil and froglike hood, Rocco. But by that time, the straight-ahead gangster pics were being overtaken by a darker, more stylish genre.

Gangland Noir

The term *film noir* refers to a particular style of movie featuring spectacular cinematography, dark angular shadows, heroes of questionable morals, femme fatales, private eyes, shifting alliances, and the underworld. The unique thing about noir is that some of the best were low-budget, under-the-radar movies. These movies, filmed mainly in the 1940s and 1950s, feature some of the best portrayals of gangsters ever captured onscreen. And lots of dames.

Private investigators are the staple character in film noir. Often times they are investigating mobsters or trying to rescue femme fatales. They are shot, stabbed, double-crossed, and left for dead. But the PI in the film noir is a staple movie character.

One of the classic film noirs is *Out of the Past*, starring Robert Mitchum as a former private eye who is living as a gas station attendant in a small town. When a gambling boss (Kirk Douglas) sends one of his goons to ask Mitchum to meet with him, the story goes into flashback—a common film noir device. At the end, back in real time, Mitchum finds that the life of a film noir private eye has only one ending, and it's not a happy one. With his hat and dangling cigarette, Mitchum's PI became an iconic image forever associated with noir.

FACT

One of film noir's most prolific actors was Sterling Hayden. He appeared in such crime classics as *The Asphalt Jungle, The Killing*, and *Naked Alibi*. But he may be best known to fans of Mafia movies for his performance as Capt. McCluskey in *The Godfather*. His memorable death scene is one of the movie's more gruesome moments.

The one role that transcended the film noir genre and one of the most memorable onscreen gangsters was Tommy Udo. Portrayed by Richard Widmark, Udo is a maniacal, sadistic killer who rampages through *Kiss of Death*, tracking Victor Mature, a gangland snitch who sent Tommy to the clink. Along the way Udo pushes a wheelchair-bound woman, the mother of the snitch, down the stairs, laughing the whole time. For audiences in 1947, it must have been shocking.

Widmark starred in a few more noir gangland thrillers. In *The Street with No Name*, Widmark is an undercover FBI agent who infiltrates a mob crew with a penchant for robbery and murder. In *Night and the City*, Widmark plays a low-level con man who lurks among the gangsters of London's underworld. Looking to break into the wrestling game with a new discovery, a hulking wrestler named Gergorius, Widmark is the poster child for noir losers, a man with big ideas who gets caught up in double-dealings and his own failings as both a businessman and a criminal.

The Godfather Trilogy

In the 1960s, Mario Puzo's novel *The Godfather*, one of the most talked about bestsellers of the time, introduced millions of voracious readers to the world of La Cosa Nostra. The film version was inevitable, but no one was prepared for just how successful it would be. *The Godfather I* and *II* became American classics, transcending the screen and becoming not only an essential part of pop culture but part of the American vernacular as well. How many times has someone made you "an offer you can't refuse"?

Dramatis Personae

The Godfather may have been an entirely different experience if other actors considered for the roles had been cast. Imagine Frank Sinatra as Don Corleone. Often linked to the mob and the basis for the Johnny Fontaine character, Sinatra physically attacked novelist Puzo in a restaurant after the novel was published. Apparently he got over it, because a few years later he expressed interest in playing the titular don. Laurence Olivier and George C. Scott were also considered. Of course, the coveted role went to Marlon Brando, who mumbled his way to an Academy Award he refused to accept.

The Godfather also made a relatively unknown Italian from New York, Al Pacino, a star. He went on the play numerous other gangster roles, including non-Italian hoodlums in *Scarface* and *Carlito's Way*. But can you imagine

Robert Redford or Ryan O'Neal as Michael Corleone? Strange indeed, but they were the producer's choices. Fortunately, director Francis Ford Coppola insisted on Pacino, and the rest, as they say, is Hollywood history.

The Godfather films tell the story of the Corleones, an immigrant family that achieves the American Dream through crime. But the movie is much more than just a simple crime drama. It touches on issues of sin, redemption, revenge, forgiveness, and the twisted machinations of a mob boss looking to stay one step ahead of his enemies.

Many mob buffs argue over exactly who the titular character was modeled after. Some speculate that Carlo Gambino was the model for Don Corleone, while others point to Sam Decavalcante, Vito Genovese, or Joe Bonanno.

The main character through the three-film epic is Michael Corleone. The audience first meets him as a returning war hero who loves his family but has no interest in the family business. Life does not always unfold as per our plans, and by the last scene of the last movie, Michael Corleone has lived and died a very different life than he planned.

Part One

In *The Godfather*, we first meet the Corleones. The movie is as much about an American family as it is a gangster movie. It eloquently chronicles the dark side of the immigrant experience and the American Dream. The old don is a powerful crime lord who made his fortune in the criminal underworld yet craves respectability, if not for himself then certainly for his children. The fates have other plans for him. Though he dies rather benignly of a heart attack in his garden, one son dies in a hail of gunfire, and the other becomes the new Don Corleone. He could have been Senator Corleone or Governor Corleone, but there wasn't enough time.

Several famous scenes in *The Godfather* are inspired by real incidents in mob lore, including the shooting of Don Corleone at a fruit stand, based on the real-life shooting of Gambino boss Frank Scalise in 1957. True, too, is the message sent to notify the Corleones of Brasi's murder—a fish wrapped in newspaper. "Luca Brasi sleeps with the fishes" has entered the pop culture vernacular.

Michael Corleone's fate is sealed when he assassinates the men who attempted to kill his father (resulting in the famous line "Leave the gun, take the cannoli"). From then on he is corrupted, and his destiny is an inexorable juggernaut deeper and deeper into the underworld of the Mafia and a Hades-like underworld of his own tortured soul. Even though he does evil things, such as orchestrating the murder of the heads of the five families and his own brother-in-law, he is an oddly sympathetic character. However, his behavior only gets worse in the second movie.

Part Two

The Godfather: Part II tells the parallel stories of the young Don Corleone, played by Robert De Niro, and Michael Corleone at the height of his power. The story follows the orphaned Vito Corleone's arrival in America at the turn of the twentieth century and his immersion into a life of crime. It counterpoints Michael Corleone's gradual descent into material and spiritual corruption.

FACT

The town of Corleone, Sicily, was too developed by the time the first *Godfather* movie was filmed, so instead filmmakers shot the Sicilian scenes in the countryside town of Savoca.

Real events also inspired elements of the script. The mob's involvement in Cuba before Castro took over is a major element of the plot, as is the mob's involvement in Las Vegas. Corruption of senators and politicians is of course one of the hallmarks of the mob's dominance in the underworld. Another event that was captured was the congressional hearings in which Frank Pentagelli recants his previous testimony against Michael Coreleone. The colorful Jewish gangster Hyman Roth is based on the less colorful but chillingly competent real hoodlum Meyer Lansky.

Michael, who was somewhat sympathetic in the first film, becomes colder and more ruthless, finally ordering the execution of his own brother, the simple and harmless Fredo. Rival gangsters used Fredo as a dupe and Michael finds it hard to forgive, as he tells his brother, "Fredo, you broke my heart." This is a sin of a biblical scale and Michael seems beyond redemption.

Part Three

Fredo's death weighs heavily on Michael in *Part III*. It is a compelling final installment in the saga of a man who took the wrong path and spent the rest of his life trying (and failing) to get back on track. The old and ill Michael Corleone is still trying to go legit, but just when he thinks he's out, they pull him back in. And just as the sins of Don Vito Corleone were visited on his offspring, Michael Corleone watches his sweet and innocent daughter murdered in front of his eyes.

ALERT!

There had been talk of a fourth *Godfather* film, but it looks like it isn't going to happen. Just as *The Godfather: Part II* told the parallel stories of the young Don Corleone and son Michael, the fourth film would have counterpointed the lives of the young Sonny Corleone (played by Leonardo DiCaprio) and his illegitimate son Vincent.

The plot is somewhat convoluted but parallels the Vatican banking scandal of the late 1970s and the activities of Sicilian and American Mafiosi. The final scene, a series of assassinations occurring during an opera, was similar to the assassinations that were carried out during the baptism scene in the first movie. *The Godfather: Part III* brings closure to a family saga that tapped into the collective unconscious and captured the imagination of filmgoers.

The Scorsese Legacy

One of the most successful Mafia movie directors is Martin Scorsese. A modern artist, Scorsese took his New York Italian background and transformed not only the Mafia movie but the film world in general. His movies are street-level visceral and gritty. Scorsese also knew how to pick talent. Martin Scorsese and Robert De Niro are one of the great actor-director teams in the history of film, rivaling John Ford and John Wayne, and Akira Kurosawa and Toshiro Mifune. Their collaborations include *New York, New York, Taxi Driver, Cape Fear, The King of Comedy*, and *Raging Bull*. And, of course, the mob classics *Mean Streets, Goodfellas*, and *Casino*.

FACT

Marin Scorsese's first movie, *Mean Streets*, was partly based on his years growing up in Manhattan's Little Italy. But by the time it came to shoot the movie, Scorsese had to film in Brooklyn to get a real Italian neighborhood feel, as Little Italy had become a tourist destination more than a real ethnic neighborhood.

Goodfellas

Goodfellas is based on the book *Wiseguy: Life in a Mafia Family* by crime reporter Nicholas Pileggi. It is the story of Henry Hill, an ex–wise guy turned "rat" who entered the Witness Protection Program to save his skin. The story chronicles the unsavory activities of the Lucchese crime family from the 1950s through the early 1980s, though the names have been changed to protect the innocent and the guilty.

Here one can see the Mafia in all its sleazy splendor. You meet a cast of low-life hoods and dangerous psychos who populate the landscape of New York City and its suburbs. You see how absolute power corrupts absolutely. *Goodfellas*, more than any mob film before it, shows that day-to-day drudgery and internal petty squabbling of the real street-level hoods who make up a majority of a Mafia family.

You also get a glimpse of how the mob members treat their women. The men all have girlfriends on the side while their wives turn a blind eye. It is a given that a Mafioso has a mistress. She is the one he squires about town and lavishes with gifts while the wife stays home with the kids and becomes no longer an object of desire but rather a maternal figure.

The most outrageous character in the movie is Tommy D., a deranged, psychotic cowboy played by Joe Pesci. He is disarmingly affable at one moment and he viciously kicks a man to death the next. He is exchanging quips with a gopher (played by a pre-*Sopranos* Michael Imperioli), but when the kid doesn't get him his drink quickly enough, he shoots him. He is too much of a loose cannon even for his handlers, and he is eventually killed by some made guys as vengeance for killing another made guy without permission (and without being a made guy himself). This character is based on a real person, Tommy DeSimone. Joe Pesci won a Best Supporting Actor Oscar for the role. Unlike his over-the-top character, after receiving the award Pesci demurely said, "This is an honor and a privilege. Thank you."

The most famous scene in *Goodfellas* may be the walk into the Copa through the kitchen. The stedicam follows Henry and his soon-to-be-wife Karen from the streets of Manhattan through the kitchen of the hottest nightclub in town. This widely praised shot is coupled with another stedicam scene, this one introducing all of the mobsters around Henry Hill, as he enters the Bamboo Lounge.

Casino

Another great Martin Scorsese, Robert De Niro, Joe Pesci collaboration is *Casino*. It is the story of Las Vegas in the waning days of the Mafia's control of Sin City. De Niro plays a Jewish gambler who runs a casino for the mob, and Pesci plays another of his patented frenetic psychos who meets an even more grisly fate than he did in *Goodfellas*. The characters were based on real-life Las Vegas gangland figures Frank "Lefty" Rosenthal and Anthony "the Ant" Spilotro.

This movie details the Mafia's practice of "skimming." The audience sees how money is taken off the top before being reported as income and how much of it is sent back to the bosses back East. You see the ruthless way that card cheats are dealt with. As in medieval times, the hand that cheats is crushed in punishment. You see an embittered Mafioso assigned to kitchen duty spit in the soup of a customer he does not like. The Corleones, one suspects, would never do such a thing. They are nothing more than sleazy and despicable punks in Scorsese's films.

Irish Gangland

In 2007, Martin Scorsese finally won what he has deserved for decades, a Best Picture Oscar. He won it for *The Departed*, a remake of a Hong Kong flick, set in the Irish-dominated Boston underworld. The movie has an all-star cast: Jack Nicholson, Matt Damon, Leonardo DiCaprio, Alec Bladwin, Mark Wahlberg, and Martin Sheen. Nicholson plays Frank Costello, an Irish mob boss modeled after noted fugitive and former Winter Hill Gang boss Whitey Bulger.

One other Irish gangster picture of note, though not made by Scorcese, is the 1990 film *State of Grace*. Based on the Westies, a violent Irish mob in New York City's Hell's Kitchen neighborhood, *Grace* teams Ed Harris as an Irish mob boss and Scan Penn as a former neighborhood tough who becomes a cop and works undercover to infiltrate the gang.

The mob bosses in *Casino's* courthouse scenes are never named; nor is it made clear what cities they represent. In real life, the bosses who were indicted for skimming the casinos in Vegas included: Nick Civella, boss of Kansas City; Joe Aiuppa and Jackie Cerone, boss and underboss of the Chicago Outfit; and Frank Balistrieri, boss of Milwaukee.

International Gangster Flicks

While Hollywood may have given the world the works of Coppola and Scorcese, there have been many memorable gangster films from across the globe, in particular England. The Mafia's homeland Italy contributed movies about their homegrown criminals. Asian cinema has taken gangsters and combined them with explosive action to create memorable movies about the triads and yakuza.

Brit Flicks

One of the best gangster movies ever, and certainly the best portrayal of a gangster on the edge, was the movie *The Long Good Friday*. Bob Hoskins plays Harold Shand, a London crime boss who wants to partner with an American Mafioso in some real estate deals. Harold wants to go straight but in one day his world falls apart as murders and bombs rock his world. He thinks it's a rival but it turns out to be the IRA, who one of Harold's underlings crossed. The final scene, with Hoskins not uttering a single word, is simply amazing.

In the movie *Get Carter*, versatile actor Michael Caine virtually invented the British gangland movie persona with his visceral portrayal of a gangster looking into his brother's murder. Unfortunately Sylvester Stallone did a remake and failed to capture any of the screen magic of the original. Caine went on to star as a crime boss in another classic British gangster pic, 1986's *Mona Lisa*, also starring Bob Hoskins.

A modern Brit gangster classic is *Sexy Beast*. Ben Kingsley plays a feared London hit man who is called in to recruit a retired mobster, played by Ray Winstone, to do a bank job. Crime boss Teddy Bass (the always impressive Ian McShane) is the mastermind behind the heist. But while most gangster movies focus on the business of crime, *Beast* focuses on the personalities. Kingsley is out of control as he psychologically tortures Winstone at his Spanish estate, badgering him and his wife incessantly until Winstone snaps.

Asian Crime Cinema

Hong Kong is the headquarters of the Asian film industry. And because the territory is inundated with triads, the Chinese Mafia, they have often been a popular subject of movies. Director John Woo has made some modern-day classics, including *A Better Tomorrow* and *The Killer*. Known for his outlandish action sequences and otherworldy gun battles, Woo's movies were some of the first to break through to American audiences.

A recent Asian gangster movie was *Election* and its sequel *Triad Election*. The story has a *Godfather*-like tone to it, telling the story of a triad civil war and the ascension of a new boss. The two movies dig deep into the modern-day triad and how they succeed by corrupting law enforcement in Hong Kong and mainland China. Some of the scenes are particularly brutal, but the action is secondary to the intricate plot, weaving Machiavellian machinations with humor.

The Untouchables *on the Big Screen*

Brian De Palma's *The Untouchables* movie does not have much in common with the TV series of the same name, other than the setting and the antagonists. A young Kevin Costner plays a less assured Eliot Ness, tutored by Sean Connery in an Academy Award–winning performance as tough Irish cop Jimmy Malone. Perennial gangster movie star Robert De Niro gained a few pounds for a cameo performance as Al Capone.

FACT

Sean Connery won an Academy Award for his moving performance as Jimmy Malone, the Irish cop who serves as a mentor to Kevin Costner's Eliot Ness. The character was a purely fictitious addition to the story. Ness had many brave men on his team, but giving him an elder mentor was purely a dramatic device.

The Chicago Way

Award-winning playwright David Mamet's screenplay does not adhere to the historical facts any more than the television show did. Novice Treasury agent Ness arrives in Chicago, and his gung-ho naiveté is mocked by basically the whole Chicago police force and political machinery. He finds "the one good cop in a bad town" in the person of Connery, and together they assemble their version of the Untouchables.

Connery plays a more rough-hewn Obi-Wan Kenobi to Costner's Luke Skywalker as he tutors him in the ways of "the Force," Chicago style. He delivers the famous advice, "He pulls a knife; you pull a gun. They send one of yours to the hospital; you send one of theirs to the morgue. That's the Chicago way. And that's how you get Capone."

Three Strikes and You're Out

Perhaps the most famous scene in *The Untouchables* movie is the De Niro/Capone baseball bat scene. Capone lectures his tuxedo-clad associates about the importance of teamwork as they are enjoying a fine meal and cigars in an elegant setting. He circles the table comparing their business to a baseball team, before savagely bashing the skull of one of the henchmen who allowed a valuable stash of bootleg booze to be impounded by Ness and company. In real life, Capone is alleged to have personally murdered at least three men with a baseball bat.

CHAPTER 21

The Other Mafias

You don't have to be Italian to be in a Mafia. Although technically the term Mafia is of Italian origin, many ethnic groups have formed organized crime gangs over the centuries. And while the ethnicities are different, the modus operandi is the same: drugs, gambling, vice, extortion, fraud. But some of these crime groups have expanded into the world of arms trafficking, nuclear weapons trafficking, and terrorism. This chapter will look at some of the more noteworthy and notorious "other Mafias."

The Russian Mafia

The Russian mob has been around for a long time. But after the collapse of the former Soviet Union in 1991, the organized crime community in Russia came into its own. The underworld went above ground and thrived as it never did in the era of communism. There had been an American-Russian mob in Brooklyn since the 1970s, but in the early 1990s New York City saw an influx of fresh mobsters from Russia and some of the breakaway republics.

Like the crime families of the American Mafia, the Russian Mafia is not a monolith but rather a loose confederation of crime outfits. This makes them difficult to track and adept at moving from crime to crime. And though their presence in America is on the rise, their hold over Russia is staggering.

Nuclear Threat

Perhaps the most infamous activity the Russian gangsters are involved in is far removed from low-level scams and bookmaking. Since the Soviet Union fell, it has been a primary concern of both Russia and the United States to keep an eye on Russia's nuclear stockpile. There is a great fear that the Russian mob would not hesitate to get its hands on nuclear material and sell it on the thriving black market that emerged as the former communist countries were exposed to the world of capitalism.

This unthinkable horror is no longer the farfetched plot of a James Bond movie. Starting in the mid-1990s, intelligence agencies in Europe began receiving indications that Russian gangsters were actively looking to get their hands on nuclear material, including enriched uranium.

Yearning to Breathe Free

In the 1980s, when the Cold War between the United States and the Soviet Union was at its most frigid, it would appear that the sneaky Soviets played a nasty trick on America. Anti-Semitism was rampant in Russia, and as part of the many negotiations that went on during the Cold War, the communist government agreed to let many Russian-Jewish refugees leave the country. They also used it as an excuse to open their jails and rid themselves of their worst criminals by shipping them off to the United States under the guise of a liberal and compassionate policy.

Fidel Castro did the same thing with the Mariel boat people in 1980. Soviet Russia and communist Cuba simultaneously got rid of the lowlifes in their society and inflicted them upon the United States. Hundreds of thousands of criminals came to America to continue their criminal activities in the New World.

In January of 2008, Russian police commandos swarmed over a group of men leaving a supermarket in Moscow. They grabbed a sixty-one-year-old man, wearing jeans and a leather jacket. He was Semyon Mogilevich, the most notorious Russian Mafia boss around. Worth an estimated $100 million, he was wanted for multiple murders, drug running, and arms trafficking.

Pax Europa and America

The Russian mob has moved beyond its homeland to every corner of the globe. They are most active in Eastern Europe, where they merged with native ethnic gangs there, and in America, where they teamed up with the traditional Mafia as well as other criminal organizations to further their nefarious career. The shifting alliances and structure of the Russian mob has made it difficult for law enforcement to take out large numbers. But as intelligence grows, so does the ability of the cops to understand them and work to remove them from the crime world.

Brighton Beach Memoirs

Initially, the Russian Mafia operating in America preyed mostly on other Russian immigrants who had settled in the United States. Shakedowns and extortions were common crimes inflicted on the decent hardworking Russians. They also engaged in the usual crimes such as thievery and prostitution.

The Brighton Beach section of Brooklyn, New York, was a hotbed of activity for the Russian Mafia in the 1970s. It even formed an uneasy alliance with the Italian boys who had been in place for decades. The homegrown Mafia was not about to let these newcomers start muscling in on their territory. The Italians let the Russians operate, but at a price that must have stunned those raised in a communist regime. They had to pay a hefty "tribute" to the Italian Mafia for the privilege of operating in New York. La Cosa Nostra's aggressive capitalism was a rude awakening for the Russian Mafia.

FACT

The Russian Mafia is causing trouble in America, but its influence in the United States pales in comparison to the power it wields in Mother Russia. Dozens of political assassinations have been linked to the Russian mob, as well as assassinations of leading journalists, including the editor of the Russian edition of *Forbes* magazine.

Mafia Family, Russian Style

The Russian Mafia equivalent of the don is called the *pakhan*. This boss controls four operating "cells" through his second in command. This number two man is called the *brigadier*. Given that this crime family structure originated in Russia, where secret police once ruled with terror and fostered a paranoid environment, the pakhan employs spies to keep an eye on the brigadier. The cells are made up of the usual suspects—soldiers who deal in drugs, prostitution, extortion, bribery, and all manner of criminality. But the viscous nature off these groups makes it harder for authorities to track who's really on top.

The members of the individual cells do not know members of the other cells, though they all report to the pakhan. This is a crime family of the Eastern European variety. Just as the American Mafia mirrors the legitimate capitalist world, the Russian Mafia reflects the communist regime where it was spawned.

Vyacheslav Ivankov

Courtesy of AP Images/Monika Graff

▲ Vyacheslav Ivankov, center, allegedly a top boss of the Russian mob in Brooklyn, is flanked by FBI agents while being led in this file photo from the agency's New York headquarters on Thursday June 8, 1995. Ivankov, fifty-six at the time, was convicted Monday July 8, 1996, with three co-defendants of trying to extort $3.5 million from two owners of Summit International, an investment advisory firm for Russian emigres.

ALERT!

Nothing is sacred, not even the Olympics. Russian gangster Alimzhan Tokhtakhounov is accused of putting the fix on the 2002 Winter Olympics in Salt Lake City, compelling judges to vote for the Russian figure skating team in exchange for votes for the French ice dancing team.

California Schemin'

The Russian Mafia sent emissaries out to the West Coast and established a foothold in San Francisco and Los Angeles. There is a steady stream of Russian Mafiosi heading across country to the sun and fun of California. Authorities believe this is happening because the American Mafia is least powerful on the West Coast. The Russian Mafia has to pay a heavy "tax" to the American Mafia when doing business in its territories. California represents more freedom and higher profits for them, not to mention a large pool of immigrants from which to draw recruits and victims to extort.

FACT

The first major Russian gang leader to be arrested in America was Vyacheslav Ivankov. He arrived in Brighton Beach in 1992 and immediately built a gang of more than 100 soldiers. He started extorting local businessmen. That led to his arrest in 1995. He was extradited to Russia in 2004 for murder charges but was acquitted. He is now in Russia.

The South American Connection

Since the breakup of the French Connection in the early 1970s, South American drug cartels, particularly those from Colombia, took up the slack with drugs. But unlike the heroin-dominated drug scene of the Mafia, the cartels were into marijuana and a new drug that was taking the party scene by storm, cocaine. Buoyed by celebrities and Studio 54, the coke scene became the hottest new trend and helped the emergence of a new organized crime force.

The Colombian Drug Cartels

The DEA as well as dozens of local and state agencies had its hands full with the Colombian drug cartels, especially in the 1980s and 1990s. These crime families are responsible for most of the cocaine that finds it way into the United States. Another DEA agent, Michael T. Horn, testifying before the Senate Foreign Relations Committee, compared the American Mafia with these vicious new interlopers:

"In the twentieth century, 'traditional organized crime' in America rose to what was then considered unparalleled heights. These organizations were built around a hierarchy of leaders and members. This form of organized crime, although of immigrant background, was rooted on American soil. From our earliest exposure to traditional organized crime, a common thread has been and continues to be the violence with which these organizations are operated, expanded, and controlled."

Like the Russian Mafia, the Colombian drug lords became the bad guys of the moment in television shows and movies in the 1980s and early 1990s. Tom Clancy's intrepid hero Jack Ryan took them on in the novel *Clear and Present Danger*.

Ruthless People

The DEA agent quoted above minimizes the brutality of the Colombian drug cartels. Unlike the Mafia, who for the most part killed only their own, the drug cartels were notorious for slaughtering the entire families of their enemies in particularly nasty ways, including women and children. This would have horrified many of the older Mafia dons had they lived to see the horrors that the drug traffic wrought on the innocent.

Colombia produces coca, which is the plant from which cocaine is produced. The nation is geographically ideal for a brisk drug traffic industry. It is at the tip of the South American continent with hundreds of miles of coastline on both the Caribbean and the Pacific Ocean and a little over two hours as the plane flies from the United States.

The Colombian drug cartels also worked with Mexican drug smugglers to transport cocaine into America across the United States/Mexico border. There is rampant corruption in the Mexican government and military, and it is not uncommon for military armored vehicles to accompany drug smugglers across the border and even fire upon the American border patrol officers.

Cartel Organization

The DEA assessed the structure and effectiveness of the Colombian drug cartel operations within the United States in one of its reports to Congress:

Members of international groups headquartered in Colombia and Mexico today have at their disposal sophisticated technology—encrypted phones, faxes, and other communications equipment. Additionally, they have in their arsenal aircraft, radar-equipped aircraft, weapons, and an army of workers who oversee the drug business from its raw beginnings in South American jungles to the urban areas within the United States. All of this modern technology and these vast resources enable the leaders of international criminal groups to build organizations that reach into the heartland of America, while they themselves try to remain beyond the reach of American justice. The traffickers also have the financial resources necessary to corrupt enough law enforcement, military, and political officials to create a relatively safe haven for themselves in the countries in which they make their headquarters.

Colombian cocaine trafficking groups in the United States—consisting of midlevel traffickers answering to the bosses in Colombia—continue to be organized around "cells" that operate within a given geographic area. Some cells specialize in a particular facet of the drug trade, such as cocaine transport, storage, wholesale distribution, or money laundering. Each cell, which may be comprised of ten or more employees, operates with little or no knowledge about the membership in, or drug operations of, other cells.

The head of each cell reports to a regional director who is responsible for the overall management of several cells. The regional director, in turn, reports directly to one of the drug lords of a particular organization or their designee based in Colombia. A rigid top-down command-and-control structure is characteristic of these groups. Trusted lieutenants of the organization in the United States have discretion in the day-to-day operations, but ultimate authority rests with the leadership in Colombia.

The upper echelon and management levels of these cells are normally comprised of family members or long-time close associates who can be trusted by the Colombian drug lords—because their family members remain in Colombia as hostages to the cell members' good behavior—to handle their day-to-day drug operations in the United States. The trusted personal nature of these organizations makes it that much harder to penetrate the organizations with confidential sources. That difficulty with penetration makes intercepting criminal telephone calls all the more vital. They report back to Colombia via cell phone, fax, and other sophisticated communications methods. Colombian drug traffickers continually employ a variety of counter-surveillance techniques and tactics, such as fake drug transactions, using telephones they suspect are monitored, limited-time use of cloned cell phones (frequently a week or less), limited use of pagers (from two to four weeks), and use of calling cards. The top-level managers of these Colombian organizations increasingly use sophisticated communications and encryption technology, posing a severe challenge to law enforcement's ability to conduct effective investigations.

Medellin Cartel

The first of the major cartels was the Medellin cartel. This was perhaps the most famous cartel, due to its flamboyant and internationally recognized leader, Pablo Escobar. In the 1970s and early 1980s the Medellins, named for a city in Colombia where they originated, controlled the vast distribution network of drugs coming into North America, mainly through Florida. They had a fleet of American pilots who evaded radar and the peering eyes of law enforcement to bring kilos of coke into the United States.

The cartels also caused instability in their own country. They put bounties on the heads of police departments and infiltrated the government.

The Medellins were represented in Florida by a murderous psycho, who also happened to be a sweet-faced stocky Colombian matriarch named Griselda Blanco. She was so obsessed with crime, she even named one of her sons Michael Corleone! Her paranoia and murderous reign brought a lot of heat down on the organization. Before long the police, FBI, and DEA formed a task force to take the cartel down. Blanco and her underlings were taken out. Colombian police killed Pablo Escobar in 1993.

The Cali Cartel

The heads of the Medellin cartel were gradually murdered and arrested in the 1980s, and the drug outfit that achieved prominence in the lucrative cocaine trade was the Cali cartel. This organization had a little more finesse than its predecessor. Gone were the routine massacres and rampant violence. It was not eliminated entirely, but the Cali cartel was more adept at using legitimate businesses as fronts.

The Cali cartel has extensive operations in the United States. In upstate New York, the state police and the DEA raided a laboratory that had the equipment to produce more than $700 million worth of cocaine a year. And that was just one of their many facilities. It is estimated that the cartel made billions of dollars a year in a period from the late 1980s through the early 1990s.

Like the Medellin cartel, the Cali group had an elaborate network of cells in the United States. Each cell handled a particular aspect of the drug trade, from traffic to storage to bookkeeping. The Cali leadership insisted upon the names of family members of their employees. This was a form of blackmail. As stated earlier, the Colombians would murder entire families of their enemies and employees who fell out of favor either through incompetence or corruption.

Colombia does not have an extradition treaty with the United States. As a result it was illegal for the United States to bring Colombian drug lords to justice in the American justice system. Eventually, the combined efforts of the DEA and the Colombian National Police finally produced results after many years of failures. By 1996, the Cali cartel collapsed and its leaders were either in jail or dead. The Mexican problem continues, however.

When the Colombian drug cartels became known in America, much was written about their tendency to slaughter the whole families of their enemies, including women and children. This is something the American Mafia did not do. It is something that the Sicilian Mafia did. In the Old World, if they killed a man they also killed his sons lest they grow up and exact vengeance.

Mule Train

Heroin is also produced and shipped from Colombia. Poppies, the flower from which opium is produced, grows freely in Colombia and Peru. It goes from the poppy fields to laboratories to be converted into heroin. It is smuggled into the United States via many means, one of which is to use "mules." People who are called "mules" swallow condoms filled with heroin, fly into the United States, and pass through customs. One would not want to be around when the "mule" discharges the heroin for delivery to the local drug dealer.

The Yakuza

This Japanese crime organization, known in Japan as *boryokudan*, is one of the oldest crime organizations in the world. The name derives from a Japanese card game called Oicho-Kabu; the worst hand in the game is 8-9-3, "ya-ku-sa." The yakuza are regarded as losers in the austere and rigid Japanese culture. For losers, they have enjoyed great success in the underworld of crime. In addition to the homeland, the yakuza have spread across the world from Hawaii to Western Europe. The tattooed gangsters are among the most adept at exploiting new and profitable rackets.

FACT

From 1958 to 1963, membership in the yakuza grew an astonishing 150 percent, to more than 184,000 members. The average membership of a Mafia crime family during the Mafia's glory days was never more than a few hundred per family. The largest yakuza gang is the Yamaguchi-gumi, based out of Kobe.

The yakuza tradition maintains that they were once proud citizens of medieval times who defended their cities and towns against marauding bandits that were terrorizing the countryside. The tradition paints them as heroic Robin Hood types. This is not entirely accurate. The modern yakuza really originated in the seventeenth century, when professional gamblers and other miscreants joined forces.

When Japan began to interact and trade with Western culture, it began to experience its version of the Industrial Revolution. Like its American criminal counterpart, the yakuza began to worm its way into the docks. They also began the age-old practice of bribing politicians.

While Al Capone was in effect the mayor of Chicago, halfway around the world the yakuza were terrorizing Japan. Yakuza hit men assassinated numerous politicians who refused to play ball, including two prime ministers.

The Modern Yakuza

After World War II the American forces occupied Japan and established a military government led by General Douglas MacArthur. The lower classes of the defeated nation were living in poverty, and a black market developed for the necessities and amenities that people had come to expect. Just as people in America had to pay through the nose for a shot of booze during Prohibition, the Japanese had to pay inflated prices to the yakuza. The yakuza fared well under the American occupation. The American military disarmed the citizenry but weren't able to disarm the criminal underworld. As a result the yakuza ran roughshod over the law-abiding populace. While the Americans jailed some crime figures, one man was actually working with the intelligence community to combat Communism. His name was Yoshio Kodama and he is recognized as the liaison between the gangsters, spies, and politicians.

QUESTIONS

Who was the longest serving yakuza boss?
Kazuo Taoka was the boss of the Yamaguchi-gumi from 1946 until his death in 1981 from a heart attack. Following his demise, the streets of Kobe were filled with bodies as different factions fought for control.

As the American influence began to rise in postwar Japan, the yakuza became influenced by gangster movies and turned in their swords for guns and began to wear dark suits and sunglasses. The simple extortion rackets that were prevalent during the black market days gave way to a wide variety of moneymaking schemes from the usual—drugs and prostitution—to the unusual—corporate shakedowns.

Going Straight

Japan began to crack down on the yakuza in the early 1990s with surprising success. A series of laws were passed (and actually enforced) that diminished the yakuza's ability to conduct business. In addition there was a change in the public's attitude. Rather than viewed as benevolent neighborhood protectors, yakuza were being viewed as the criminals they were, bringing out more public scrutiny. Yakuza members began calling the authorities and inquiring about how they could get real jobs. Japanese companies even began to hire reformed yakuza in an effort to encourage more and more of them to go straight.

Like many other groups and individuals before it, the yakuza looks to the "decadent" West as a source of income and base of operations. But their operations here are not as widespread as other Asian criminals. The yakuza are feeling pressure from another Asian powerhouse of crime, the Chinese triads.

One of the major sources of money for the yakuza is the trafficking and distribution of ice, known in America as methamphetamine. The Japanese thugs who deal in this illicit narcotic have turned some section of Japanese cities into slums filled with addicts. The ice merchants have also spread their operations to other parts of Southeast Asia.

Triads

The triads are underground secret societies in Chinese culture that date back centuries. In the past, like the Mafia, they were quasi-patriotic organizations dedicated to helping out the less fortunate. As the years went on the groups morphed into organized crime syndicates. Headquartered mainly in Hong Kong, these gangs have become some of the most powerful crime organizations in the world, controlling heroin trafficking, illegal alien smuggling, high-tech fraud, production of counterfeit electronics, and a host of other crimes, including murder.

War in Macau

Macau is a former Portuguese colony in China that has become the Las Vegas of the Far East. Home to dozens of high-class casinos and resorts, Macau is trying to break from its past, a past that includes a vicious gangland war between rival triads. The main group was the 14K, still the largest triad gang in the world. The gangs were fighting over the usual—money, turf, and power. But the government had too much riding on Macau's reputation as a tourist mecca, handing out death sentences to some of the gangsters in the hopes of getting rid of triad influence.

The Triads in America

America has long been a magnet for Chinese immigration. Since the late 1800s Chinese have settled in major metropolitan areas around the country. Because they were often the victims of prejudice, the gangster set out to help each other. They formed mutual aid societies to provide business and financial support to newly arrived immigrants. These societies were named *tongs*, which literally means "hall." In these storefront social clubs, the Chinese gangsters established themselves. The tongs themselves were not criminal, but they attracted an element that used the tong's influence in the neighborhood to gain control of extortion, prostitution, and especially gambling, a particularly lucrative vice in the Asian ethnic communities.

Just like Apalachin brought the Mafia to the attention of mainstream America, it was the Golden Dragon massacre that brought Asian crime to the news. One early morning in September 1977 members of the Joe Boys street gang went into the restaurant with guns blazing, attempting to take out members of the rival Wah Ching gang. No gang members were shot, but five people, including two tourists, were.

By the late twentieth century, street gangs affiliated with tongs were operating in the Chinatowns of Boston, New York, and San Francisco. The street gangs were the low-level soldiers who strong-armed the local storekeepers, the ones who dealt the drugs on the street corners and the ones who did the dirty work for the higher-ups. The street guys were also the first that the triads started to recruit when they began arriving in greater numbers from Hong Kong and settling across the United States and Canada. While these gangs have stayed mainly in their respective communities, they are beginning to spread out, teaming with other Asian crime groups (Korean, Vietnamese, Cambodian) to commit ever-more sophisticated crime from credit card fraud to identity theft.

African Organized Crime

Africa is often in the news for the civil wars and humanitarian crises that plague many of the countries. Other countries, though, are in the news as hotbeds of organized crime activities. Some rackets are run by corrupt governments; others run in direct contrast to progressive governments. The criminal operations are as varied as the continent itself—from drug trafficking through the north to e-mail scams and diamond smuggling in the central and south. And it's not all homegrown. Russian, Israeli, and Chinese crime groups have gained a foothold in local crime.

E-mail Scams

Have you ever received an e-mail from an African prince promising millions of dollars for help in getting his money out of Africa? Of course, you may have been drawn in by the proposition that for only a few thousand of your dollars, to help grease the wheels, the prince would repay you ten times for your effort. After all, you are exactly the kind of person a prince would look for to help with complicated monetary transactions. Unfortunately many people fell for the ruse and put money in the pockets of African organized crime

The FBI estimates that Americans fall for Nigerian-based scams to the tune of $1 billion a year. In addition to the now-well-known e-mail scams, Nigerian crime groups engage in health care fraud, insurance scams, auto accident scams, and life insurance fraud. The FBI set up a task force specifically to look into these rackets, and not a moment too soon.

Many state and local police departments have begun outreach events to teach the public about how to identify potential scams, including those operated by African crime groups. But everyone has to be on alert, because there are as many scams as ever being tried out every day to unsuspecting marks, just ripe to have their money taken from them.

Traffick

Drug trafficking is not as widespread an issue historically in Africa, but those wily gangsters have turned Nigeria and South Africa into the two biggest entry points for drugs into the continent. Heroin is the drug of choice. Many of the gangsters also set up operations in Europe to pad their wallets even further. In addition to trafficking, the crime organizations have made deals with corrupt dictators, stolen money meant for humanitarian needs, and turned the major cities into war zones.

Mafia, Mafia Everywhere

After the fall of communism and the formation of the European Union, the continent has become a playground for dozens of organized crime groups. Many are transplants from other regions of the world, but a number are homegrown. From Irish drug lords to the Albanian mob, the European underworld scene has become a patchwork of overlapping territories, personal vendettas, and unparalleled cooperation between ethnic groups that have never been particularly friendly. And their infiltration of Europe has brought them untold riches from a continent ripe for the picking.

The Celtic Tiger

On June 26, 1996, Irish journalist Veronica Guerin was sitting in her car at an intersection when a gunman on a motorcycle pumped her car full of bullets. Guerin had been investigating the upsurge in Irish gangland activities, specifically the drug scene. Her focus was on John Gilligan, one of the most feared gangsters in Ireland. Once the protégé of the famed General, Martin Cahill, Gilligan rose out of the ashes of Cahill's death to be the number one man in the Dublin underworld.

But taking out Guerin was not the smartest move. The resulting uproar brought the police down on him full force. Though he was found not guilty of her murder, he was sentenced to twenty years in prison for drug trafficking.

The Albanians

Albanian organized crime gangs operated under the radar for years before they had the spotlight shined on them as a result of the war in Kosovo. There were reports that tied the smuggling of heroin through the Balkan region to the Kosovo Liberation Army (KLA), an American-backed freedom fighter group battling the Serbian army. It was reported that the Albanian mob families were funding the KLA. As the war heated up and Albanians began emigrating throughout Europe, many of the crime figures followed suit. Albanian crime groups set up shop in Belgium, Germany, Austria, and even Italy, where they partnered with the Camorra, 'ndrangheta, and Sicilian Mafia.

FACT

One of the world's major drug dealers, Israeli crime boss Ze'ev Rosenstein was extradited to the United States in 2006 to face charges of ecstasy trafficking. It was one of the first times that Israel extradited someone to face criminal charges in another country. Rosenstein pled guilty and was sentenced to twelve years in an Israeli prison, another interesting twist.

The Albanian mob was into the usual rackets—drugs, loansharking, infiltrating legitimate business, and various scams. But like the Russians, they sometimes took it a step further, delving into human smuggling and arms trafficking. Not the nicest bunch of guys around.

The influence of this crime group even extended to New York City, where an Albanian crew out-muscled the Lucchese Mafia family from its former stronghold in Astoria. Known as the Rudaj Corporation, the group operated out of a social club, echoing the popular image of the espresso-sipping mobster. There were even some Italian associates in the group. But the Rudaj boys had little time to enjoy the spotlight as the feds quickly moved in and arrested the crew.

The Italian Scene

The Sicilian Mafia has always been the archetypical organized crime group. They gave rise to the crime lords of America and have carved out a significant niche for themselves across Sicily, Europe, and the rest of the world. However, with the increasing focus from law enforcement, internal warfare, and scores of mobsters turning against their former brothers in arms, the Italian criminal landscape has made some room for the other mobs to expand their operations: the Calabrian 'ndrangheta, the Neapolitan Camorra, and the Pugliese Sacra Corona Unita.

Italian journalist Roberto Saviano's 2007 book *Gomorrah*, an exposé of the Neapolitan Camorra, so angered the region's crime bosses that they put out a contract on him. He has a constant police escort to protect him.

The influence of these other mob groups has eclipsed the Sicilian Mafia. In 2007, the streets of Naples were piled with trash, after the Camorra-dominated trash industry stopped picking up refuse to flex their muscle. Then in short order was a report that the 'ndrangheta controlled a vast amount of Europe and Australia's drug market, and in fact have become the most powerful Italian crime organization in the world. And the Corona Unita are little-known outside the "boot" of Italy, avoiding the police attention afforded the other groups.

The Hit List

Big Jim Colosimo—May 11, 1920

Colosimo was gunned down on orders from Johnny Torrio. This event set in motion the rise of Al Capone.

Dion O'Banion—November 10, 1924

The Chicago Irish crime boss was killed in his flower shop by Al Capone's gunmen as a result of an ongoing war over bootlegging profits. His funeral was the biggest in Chicago history.

Joseph and John Lonardo—October 13, 1927

Cleveland mob boss Joseph and his brother John were gunned down in a barbershop. Lonardo was succeeded by Joe Porello. Joe was taken down in 1930.

Arnold Rothstein—November 4, 1928

Legendary Jewish gambling boss Rothstein was stepping on some toes in New York. After allegedly welshing on a huge gambling loss, he was shot while leaving the Park Central Hotel in Manhattan and died two days later.

Sam Carlino—May 9, 1932

The Denver underworld was just starting to take shape when a vicious gangland war broke out. Bootlegging kingpin Sam Carlino was in his house with Jim Coletti, who later ascended to the throne of Pueblo boss. Both men were shot by unknown gunmen. Carlino was killed.

Vincent "Mad Dog" Coll—February 8, 1932

Notorious Irish hood Mad Dog Coll angered Lucky Luciano and everyone else in New York when he killed a child during a kidnapping attempt. After his acquittal on the murder charge, Coll was talking in a telephone booth when a car drove by and filled him with bullets.

John, Arthur, and James Volpe—July 29, 1932

The Volpe brothers were underworld figures in Pittsburgh. They were gunned down in a coffee shop on orders from John Bazzano, the family boss. Bazzano's body was found in a burlap sack on a Brooklyn street the following week.

Joe Roma—February 18, 1933

Joe Roma took over the rackets in Denver after the death of Sam Carlino. But his reign was short-lived. Less than two years after Carlino was ambushed in his own home, Roma was in his house, talking with some unidentified acquaintances. As they rose to leave, they took Joe out.

John "Big Nose" Avena—August 17, 1936

Big Nose became the leader of the Mafia in Philadelphia after Salvatore Sabella stepped down. A rival faction killed him in South Philadelphia.

Joe Tocco—May 2, 1938

Detroit gangland bigwig Joe Tocco took five pistol shots and twelve rounds from a shotgun to his back yet still held on for a couple days before passing away. His death brought about a consolidation of power in the local family.

Ignazio Antinori—October 22, 1940

When Tampa mob bigwig Ignazio Antinori went out for drink with a few friends, he became a victim of the first Tampa mob war, between the Mafia and the crime group led by Charlie Wall. He was shot through a window while drinking at a juke joint.

James Ragen—June 24, 1946

Ragen was the owner of the Continental Wire Service, providing services to dozens of gambling operations. He ran afoul of mob bosses and was gunned down in the middle of a Chicago street.

Charles Binaggio—April 6, 1950

Charles Binaggio was the boss of the Kansas City mafia. But on April 6, 1950, he was found with his bodyguard Charles Gargotta, dead in the Jackson County Democratic Headquarters. Both were shot at close range.

James "Head of the Elks" Lumia—June 5, 1950

Tampa mob power James Lumia was popped in broad daylight while talking to two employees of his oil company in Tampa. His death was part of an intrafamily war between the Red Italiano faction and the Trafficantes.

Phillip and Vincent Mangano—April 19, 1951

Vincent, the boss of the Mangano crime family (now known as the Gambinos), disappeared the same day as his brother Phillip was gunned down in Brooklyn. Albert Anastasia orchestrated the hit, taking the top spot.

Willie Moretti—October 4, 1951

Moretti was the underboss of the Genovese family and a family relation to Frank Costello. But his mind was going. He was heard babbling on and on about mob business as his mental health eroded (some said from syphilis). Three gunmen took him to lunch and finished him off.

Albert Anastasia—October 25, 1957

Albert Anastasia was also known as "the Mad Hatter" and "the Lord High Executioner." He met his demise in a barber chair at the Park Sheraton Hotel.

Gus Greenbaum—December 3, 1958

The manager of the Flamingo and Riviera in Vegas, Greenbaum was handpicked by Meyer Lansky to keep things running smoothly in Sin City. But his womanizing and heavy drinking took its toll. He relocated to Phoenix to stay out of trouble but the mob found him.

Anthony "Little Augie Pisano" Carfano—September 25, 1959

Augie was out on the town with Janice Drake, a former Miss America contestant. Carfano was a New York–based mobster, but he was instrumental in turning Miami into a gangster's paradise. But his usefulness was exhausted. He was gunned down in his car. Miss Drake did not survive the assault.

Bernie McLaughlin—October 1961

Bernie was the leader of a Charlestown, Massachusetts, Irish gang, direct competitors to the Winter Hill gang and the Boston Mafia. After an incident on Labor Day, a grudge quickly escalated into all-out war between the McLaughlins and the Winter Hill Gang. Bernie was shot and killed in the middle of a large crowd. No one saw anything.

Charles "Cadillac Charley" Cavallaro—November 23, 1962

Normally mobsters only kill their own kind or those who cross them in business. But this time, the eighty-second bombing in Youngstown, Ohio, resulted in the death of not only mob figure Cadillac Charley but his eleven-year-old son as well.

Frank Mari and Mike Adamo—September 18, 1969

Mari was a rising star in the Bonanno family and Adamo was his bodyguard. This was the last day either was seen.

James "Jimmy Doyle" Plumeri—September 17, 1971

Plumeri was a Lucchese mobster with ties to the garment industry. He was also part of anti-Castro operations in South Florida and may have been offshore in a boat during the Bay of Pigs invasion. That fact didn't impress the mobster who strangled Plumeri to death with his own tie.

Joe "Crazy Joe" Gallo—April 7, 1972

Gallo had returned from prison to reignite the Gallo war against the now-Colombo family. While eating seafood at the famous Umberto's Clam House in Little Italy, gunmen burst in the restaurant and cut him down. Gallo staggered out and died in the middle of the street.

Sam "Mad Dog" DeStefano—April 14, 1973

The Chicago Outfit's top hit man, Mad Dog DeStefano, was awaiting indictment with his crew for murder. His previous courthouse behavior worried the higher-ups in the Outfit. He was shotgunned to death in his garage.

Jimmy Hoffa—July 30, 1975

The legendary mystery of "where is Jimmy Hoffa buried" started this day. The most plausible explanation is that he was killed by members of the Detroit Mafia and chopped into pieces and/or crushed at a car wrecking plant. He is not, however, buried under Giants Stadium.

Jimmy "the Hammer" Massaro—November 23, 1975

"The Hammer" got himself caught up in an escalating war in the Rochester family. Following an intensive investigation, six men, including the boss of the family, were convicted of Massaro's murder. This event is chronicled in the hard-to-find cult mafia book, *The Hammer Conspiracies*.

Joe Barboza—February 12, 1976

Known as "the Animal," this Portuguese mobster testified against members of the New England Mafia, including boss Ray Patriarca. He was relocated to San Francisco, but the old boys back in Beantown found out where he was living. Barboza was paid a visit by Patriarca family member J.R. Russo. Only Russo left alive.

Frank Bompensiero—February 10, 1977

Frank angered the leadership of the Los Angeles family by criticizing their ineptitude. The head of the San Diego branch, the Bomp was killed while talking in a phone booth. It later came out that he was an FBI informant.

Charles "Chuckie" Nicoletti—March 29, 1977

Nicoletti was an alleged figure in the JFK assassination according to some sources. But he definitely was a Chicago Outfit hit man who was responsible for over twenty murders. Nicoletti made waves in the Chicago underworld; he was shot in the head and his car set on fire.

Danny Greene—October 6, 1977

Greene was an Irish gangland figure in Cleveland who was fighting with the local Mafia over control of rackets in town, following the death of Ohio boss John Scalish. The resulting war was characterized by car bombs, many of which failed. This time the bomb succeeded.

August Palmisano—June 30, 1978

Milwaukee boss Frank Balistrieri ran a tight ship. So when word came through the grapevine that there was an informer working with the police, Balistrieri put out the order. Taking a page from the Cleveland war, Palmisano was killed by a car bomb.

Carmine Galante—July 12, 1979

Bonanno crime family boss Carmine Galante was killed while eating at an Italian restaurant in Brooklyn. The now-famous murder scene photo shows Galante still clutching his cigar between his teeth.

Phil "Chicken Man" Testa—March 15, 1981

When Bruce Springsteen sung about the Chicken Man getting blown up, he was referring to the murder of Philly mob boss Phil Testa. After Angelo Bruno's murder the year before, the Philly family was thrown into upheaval. Following Chicken Man's demise, Nicodemo "Little Nicky" Scarfo took over.

Francis "Cadillac Frank" Salemme and William "Wild Guy" Grasso—June 16, 1989

This day was a pivotal one in the history of organized crime in New England. The body of mobster William Grasso was found along the banks of the Connecticut River with one bullet in his head. Later that day, Frank Salemme was ambushed at a pancake house, but he survived to become the boss of the New England family.

Henry "Hank the Bear" Smurra—November 23, 1991

Smurra was part of the Persico faction of the Colombo crime family. He was sitting in his car in front of a doughnut shop in Brooklyn when he was taken out by gunmen loyal to Victor Orena. It was the first casualty in the Colombo war; it resulted in twelve deaths.

Michael "Mickey Chang" Ciancaglini—August 5, 1993

As a war between Sicilian John Stanfa and young upstart Skinny Joey Merlino was playing out on the streets of Philadelphia, both sides were gearing up to take out the head of the other faction. While walking down a South Philly street, Joey Merlino was shot in the buttocks, but Mickey Chang was hit in the chest and died on the street.

Robert DeCicco and Rudolph Izzi—June 6 and 7, 2007

Gambino soldier Robert DeCicco was shot on a Bay Ridge street while emerging from a pharmacy. He survived. Genovese associate Rudolph "Rudy Cue Ball" Izzi was not so lucky. He took one shot behind his ear. Both hits took place the week before the final episode of *The Sopranos*.

Mafia Lingo

action:
Gambling that is done through a bookie or other illegal means. The Mafia always demands "a piece of the action."

administration:
In the corporate hierarchy, this is the top echelon of a Mafia family. It includes the boss, underboss, and consigliere. Like the top officers in any legitimate corporation, these are the men who make the decisions, though in the underworld, termination has more finality than a pink slip.

agita:
The Italian expression for a tummy ache. It is also used to convey a general state of free-floating anxiety.

airing:
If a Mafioso says this to you he is not inviting you to join him to savor the gentle evening breeze. It means that he is going to kill you.

alkali:
Whiskey, especially of the bootleg variety. It is slang for the word *alcohol*.

alky cooker:
Prohibition language for a still, a makeshift distillery to make moonshine alcohol.

alky racket:
Prohibition expression for the bootleg business. *Alky* is a slang expression for "alcohol" and sometimes for an alcoholic.

American way:
This is not a patriotic slogan; it is the Mafia's phrase for the peaceful coexistence of rival crime families.

amico:
A friend or associate of a crime family who is not a member of the family.

amico nostro:
The Italian phrase for "friend of ours." It is how a member of a crime family introduces a stranger who is also a made man.

Apache Indian job:
Attack by firebomb that kills the victim and destroys the building he was in with such efficiency that identification of the body is difficult.

area man:
An organized crime official who has jurisdiction over a particular area within a crime family's turf.

The Arm:
The name for the Buffalo crime family.

assassin's special:
The preferred weapon of choice for many a Mafia hit man: A .22-caliber handgun with a silencer.

associate:
The Mafia equivalent of an office temp. He works for a crime family but is not a wise guy or a made man.

attaché casing:
Making the rounds and collecting bribes of such volume that they have to be lugged home to the don in a briefcase.

away:
When a Mafioso is doing jail time, he is simply said to be "away." Another euphemism is the ironic "away at college."

babania:
The drug traffic, especially heroin.

baby sitter:
A police or federal bodyguard for a "rat" who is under witness protection.

bag man:
A low-level hood who is sent on errands. He is usually either picking up or delivering money.

banana race:
A horserace that has a "sure thing" winner. In other words, the race has been fixed.

B-and-A racket:
A beer and alcohol racket; it is another expression for Prohibition.

Bangkok Connection:
The path that illegal drugs travel from Southeast Asia to the United States. The narcotics industry, long eschewed by the Mafia, eventually became one of its biggest moneymaking rackets.

barracuda:
A politically incorrect expression for an unattractive woman.

barrel murder:
When a murder victim is stuffed into a barrel and left there to decompose, or sometimes weighted down and dumped in the river or at sea.

beauty doctor:
A steel-tipped club. This particularly nasty weapon is designed to maim and mutilate the victim.

beef:
A disagreement with or grievance against someone.

big earner:
The Mafia equivalent of Salesman of the Year. A member of a crime family whose activities make a lot of money for the team.

big papa:
A slang word for the Thompson machine gun, the weapon of choice for many mobsters in the 1930s.

the books:
The "roll" of the family. When the books are closed, no new members are officially inducted. When there is an opening to join a family, the books are open.

boosters:
Small-time street thieves.

borgata:
Another name for a Mafia crime family.

boss:
Another name for the head of a Mafia family. See also *don*.

Boss of Bosses *(Capo di tutti Capi* in Italian):
The Mafia don who was the de facto head of the Commission. Outsiders assume that the Alpha Mafioso among the heads of the five families is the Boss of Bosses, but internally the term is not used, since the other four family heads would disagree with the fifth don's claim to the title.

broken:
This Mafia term has the same meaning that it has in the military: to be demoted in rank for an offense against "the family."

***brugad*:**
Another name for a crime family. See also *borgata*.

buckwheats:
A particularly nasty murder where the victim is tortured at length before being put out of his misery. This was used in revenge killings of men who had done something especially bad in the eyes of the Mafia.

***buon'anima*:**
This Italian phrase is translated as "rest his soul." It is obviously uttered in reference to one of the dearly departed—or with mordant irony about someone who has just been whacked.

burn:
To blow someone off, disrespect them, or a more serious snub.

bust out:
Bankruptcy the hard way. Not through abusing credit cards, but through theft and corruption by the mob. It was used as a method to destroy an enemy's livelihood.

buttlegging:
It refers to another form of bootlegging—the buying and selling of untaxed cigarettes.

button:
Another name for a Mafioso who has become a made man.

***cafone*:**
A disreputable character, or as Shakespeare would say, "a slight, unmeritable man."

canary:
A "stool pigeon." Someone who "sings" to the law, betraying fellow members of the Mafia.

cane corn:
A type of bootleg alcohol made from corn and cane sugar.

***capo*:**
The Italian word for "captain." A middle-management Mafioso, usually in charge of a crew or two.

***Capo di tutti Capi*:**
The Italian expression meaning "Boss of Bosses."

***caporegime*:**
A lieutenant in a crime family. Unlike the military, where a captain is the superior officer to a lieutenant, the caporegime outranks the capo.

captains of industry:
An early name for the Commission, or National Syndicate. Perhaps used as an ironic term by the Mafia, comparing themselves with the Carnegies, Vanderbilts, and other legitimate businessmen whom the Mafia believed to be, in their own way, as ruthless and corrupt as themselves.

carpet:
Another phrase for a meeting held between two or more Mafia families to settle disputes. Perhaps a variation of the slang expression "called on the carpet."

case:
Checking out a site of a planned robbery or hit, as in "casing the joint."

cement coffin:
This is when a murder victim is stuffed into a tub or barrel that is filled with cement and dumped in whatever body of water is most convenient.

cement overcoat:
Similar to *cement coffin*.

cement shoes:
In this instance, only the feet are encased in cement until it hardens, then the victim is buried at sea, sometimes while still alive.

chairman:
A consultant or adviser to the Commission.

chairman of the board:
Another term for don, boss, or head of a crime family. Also a nickname given to Old Blue Eyes himself, Frank Sinatra.

chased:
To be outcast by the Mafia.

***che bruta*:**
An Italian phrase that means "how ugly you are."

***che peccato*:**
An Italian phrase that means "what a pity, what a shame."

***chiacchierone*:**
An Italian phrase that means "chatterbox."

chief corrupter:
The member of a crime family whose job it is to corrupt police, judges, elected officials, and others.

CI:
Law enforcement term for a confidential informant.

cleaning:
The efforts that a mobster takes to avoid being followed by any enemy or the law. It involves eluding a tail, or someone following the mobster in a car or on foot or by other means.

clip:
To kill someone.

clock:
To monitor someone's activities; keeping an eye on a person. To hit someone in the face.

code of silence:
See *Omerta*.

***Col tempo la foglia di gelso diventa seta*:**
An Italian phrase that means "Time and patience change the mulberry leaf to satin."

comare:
A Mafia girlfriend. A term of endearment.

The Combination:
A 1930s name for the Mafia.

come heavy:
To arrive on the scene carrying a gun. If a Mafioso is told to "come heavy," he knows that there is likely to be gunplay.

come in:
An audience with the don when he requests your presence. This is an invitation you can't refuse.

The Commission:
The Mafia leadership made up of the bosses of the five New York families—Gambino, Genovese, Lucchese, Colombo, and Bonanno.

compare:
A pal, chum, or a buddy in Mafia lingo.

connected:
A person who regularly does business with the Mafia but is not a member of a family.

consigliere:
The counselor or adviser to the don, often but not always an attorney.

contract:
a hit ordered on a specific person, usually accompanied by a monetary award.

Cosa Nostra:
The Italian phrase literally meaning "Our Thing," which is what the Mafia calls itself. The phrase came to national attention during the Valachi hearings.

crew:
A band of Mafia soldiers that reports to a capo. Crews engage in all manner of mischief, including heists and hijacking. Some crews can also report to a soldier, or in some cases a well-connected associate.

cugine:
An ambitious and youthful Mafioso whose goal is to be "made." Though he is valuable, he is also regarded with a wary eye by the elder gangsters, since he may also be a threat sometime down the line. See also *Young Turks*.

CW:
An FBI term that stands for "cooperating witness."

deadbeat:
Someone who does not pay his debts or is habitually late.

deli:
Abbreviated version of the word *delegate*, as in union delegate.

dime:
The slang expression for $1,000.

district man:
A crime family officer whose turf covers a small section of a city or suburban area.

do a piece of work:
To kill someone.

dollar:
Another slang expression for $1,000.

double-decker coffin:
A coffin with a false bottom that accommodates two bodies. The paying customer is in the top tier, and

the victim of a mob hit whom the Mafia would like to secretly bury is hidden below. Joe Bonanno was one of the first mobsters to use this method of disposal.

drop a dime:
To rat someone out, or to call the police on a mobster.

drop man:
A low-level hood who picks up the bets from the numbers runner.

earner:
A moneymaker for a crime family. See also *big earner*.

eat alone:
To be a greedy gangster and keep the loot for yourself, not allowing others to "wet their beaks."

elder statesman:
Another name for the boss of a crime family.

empty suit:
A Mafioso wannabe, a hanger-on who is regarded with contempt by the members of the family due to his incompetence.

enforcer:
A tough guy who uses violence to send a message from his Mafia superiors. See also *muscle*.

envelope:
Money paid for protection or bribery, handed over in an envelope.

executioner:
An unusually direct Mafia phrase meaning "hit man."

***facia bruta*:**
An Italian expression that means "ugly face."

The feds:
The federal government, specifically its law enforcement wing. It has been the longtime bane of the Mafia's existence.

fence:
A person who takes stolen merchandise and is able to sell it without attracting the attention of the authorities. Oftentimes a fence has a storefront or pawnshop to move items.

field man:
A mobster-manager who supervises a group of numbers runners.

fifth estate:
Another name for organized crime.

finger:
To inform on a person and report them to the Mafia. This could be for a lesser offense or for a hit.

The five families:
The Bonanno, Colombo, Gambino, Genovese, and Lucchese crime families located in New York City. These are the most powerful organized crime units in the country.

five times thirty-eight:
To be shot five times with a .38-caliber revolver. Mafia hit men often empty their guns into their target. Better safe than sorry.

forbidden fruit:
This term refers to a "good" Italian girl who attracts the attention of an amorous Mafioso.

***fratellanza*:**
The Italian word for "brotherhood"; another name for the Mafia.

friend of mine:
The expression for someone who is not a member of the crime family but is deemed trustworthy.

friend of ours:
What one "made" man says when introducing another "made" man to the family. It means the other person is a made member and not an associate.

fugazi:
A slang expression for anything that is counterfeit, including counterfeit currency, made famous in the movie *Donnie Brasco.*

G:
Shorthand for the government. FBI agents were called "G-Men" in the Golden Age of Mafia misbehavior.

gaff:
A crooked person and unrepentant con man and thief.

gangbuster:
A law enforcement officer at the federal, state, or local level whose mandate is to battle organized crime. Eliot Ness and Thomas E. Dewey were two famous gangbusters. So was Rudy Giuliani before he became mayor of New York City.

gangland:
A generic name for organized crime. It was also the nickname for Chicago during the Al Capone years.

get a place ready:
A nice way of saying that a place should be prepared to dispose of a person who is soon to be whacked.

gift:
A euphemism for a bribe.

gira diment:
An Italian phrase that means "going crazy."

give a pass:
This is something that a Mafioso would be happy to hear. It means that he has been granted a stay of execution. In other words, he is not going to be whacked.

giveup:
The percentage of a mobster's ill-gotten earnings that he must hand over to his bosses. Just like any business, the bosses in the boardroom make the big money while the working stiffs get the scraps from the table.

godfather:
Another name for don, which entered the vernacular through Mario Puzo's novel and Francis Ford Coppola's trilogy of the same name.

going:
This refers to a person who has been targeted to be murdered.

going south:
When a mobster goes "on the lam" to avoid the feds.

goner:
A person who had been marked for murder by the Mafia.

goodfellas:
Another name for wise guys. Also the title of one of the most realistic Mafia movies.

good people:
The term that mobsters use for someone who is easy to deal with, that is, someone who will not have to be whacked anytime soon.

goombah:
A Sicilian slang word for "buddy."

goon:
Another term for *leg breaker* and *muscle*.

graft:
Money paid to corrupt politicians, policemen, and judges for favors and to look the other way.

guests of the state:
A euphemism for being in jail.

gumod/gumar:
A term of endearment for the girlfriend or mistress of a gangster. Most Mafiosi have a kept woman on the side.

hack:
Mafia slang for a prison guard, not an underpaid free-lance writer.

half-assed wise guy:
A wannabe who seeks entry into a crime family.

ham-and-cheese sandwich:
Graft paid to a union official.

handbook:
The mobster who sponsors a bookie's gambling operation.

head crusher:
Yet another colorful name for *leg breaker, muscle*, and *goon*.

headhunter:
A gun for hire. A contract killer; hit man.

heat:
Pressure and scrutiny from the law.

hijack:
To steal goods and products, usually from a vehicle. Hijacking stuff from airports before it gets to its final destination is a common Mafia enterprise.

hit:
To kill someone.

hit man:
The assassin who does the hit.

hitmobile:
The vehicle the hit man drives, always a nondescript car to avoid attention.

The Honored Society:
A reverential name for the Sicilian Mafia.

hot place:
A location that the Mafia suspects or knows is being targeted by the feds and is probably under surveillance by camera and wiretaps.

ice:
Another of the many synonyms for murder.

ice pick kill:
Just what it sounds like. An ice pick is jammed into the ear and enters the brain of the victim.

independent:
A bookie that is not a Mafioso but pays a tribute to be allowed to stay in business. Kind of like a 7-11 franchise operation.

in the wind:
A person who has disappeared into the Witness Protection Program. They are "gone with the wind."

Italian rope trick:
Not as charming as it sounds. Strangulation by a rope.

jamook:
An insulting expression. A jamook is basically a dope.

joint:
A slang expression for prison.

juice:
The interest charged on a loan from a loan shark, which is invariably higher than your worst credit card company. Anything over 25 percent interest is illegal, which is why some credit card companies stop at 24.99 percent.

kickback:
Payoff given to the law to look the other way and to avoid the inconvenience of raids.

kiss of death:
A mobster kisses another in a public place. This is not an expression of affection. It means that the Mafioso being kissed is in danger of getting whacked if he doesn't play ball.

lammest:
A person who has gone "on the lam," meaning he has gone on the run or into hiding to avoid arrest by the police or the wrath of the Mafia.

large:
Slang expression for $1,000.

LCN:
The acronym for La Cosa Nostra.

Little Joe:
This is an assassination technique reserved for compulsive gamblers in over their heads to the loan shark. They are shot four times in the head in two rows of two shots.

loan shark:
A person who loans money with a higher interest rate than your friendly neighborhood credit card company.

made guy:
A hoodlum who is made an official and trusted member of a crime family. The prerequisite for admission is usually to kill someone.

madonn':
This is an expression of surprise.

mafie:
Sicilian gangs that terrorized the peasants and townsfolk back in the Old Country. This was the genesis of the modern Mafia.

make a marriage:
When two mobsters are brought together for family business.

make one's bones:
Making a killing, quite literally, in order to become a "made" man in the Mafia.

mannagge:
This means going to the mattresses in a mob war.

mattresses, going to:
Term meaning getting prepared for a long and drawn-out gang war.

the meets:
When the Mafia families get together to discuss business.

mercy room:
Mafia slang for the emergency room of a hospital.

message job:
This means to shoot someone in a particular body part to send a message to his buddies as to why he was killed.

mezza morta:
An Italian phrase that means "half dead."

middle:
In gambling parlance, this is a "sure thing." This is a bet you cannot lose.

middling:
Reselling stolen merchandise that "fell off the back of a truck."

mobbed up:
Someone who is either "connected" to the Mafia or involved with them in some shady dealings.

Moe Green Special:
Moe Green was a character in *The Godfather* who was shot in the eye. The character gave the name to this type of Mafia hit.

mortadella:
Another Mafia insult, it literally means an Italian sausage.

motorcade murders:
Drive-by shootings are not a modern phenomenon. During the 1920s there were numerous celebrated drive-bys.

muscle:
Low-level Mafiosi who are the bodyguards, enforcers. Those who are called upon by their superiors to use violence to get the point across.

Mustache Petes:
Name given to an old-fashioned or conservative Mafioso. Though the true Petes were wiped out in gangland wars in the late 1920s and early 1930s, the name still applies to some older mobsters.

nickel:
The Mafia monetary denomination that means $500.

OC:
The acronym for organized crime.

off:
Another synonym for murdering someone.

off the record:
Doing something that is not sanctioned by the family.

The Office:
The nickname for the New England Mafia.

old man:
An affectionate name for the don.

Omerta:
The code of silence that a Mafioso takes when he is initiated into a crime family. Breaking the vow is punishable by death.

on the record:
Doing something that has the approval of the family.

oobatz, u'pazzu: An Italian expression meaning "crazy."

The Outfit:
The name for the Chicago Mafia branch.

parakeet:
A not very politically correct term for a good-looking woman.

Partnership:
Name for the Detroit mafia family.

payola:
Another word for *graft*. Payoffs to corrupt officials to ensure their cooperation.

pazzo:
The Italian word meaning "crazy" or "nuts."

piacere:
An Italian phrase that means "Pleasure to meet you."

piece:
Slang for a gun, as in "packing a piece."

piece of work:
A contract to assassinate a person.

pigeon:
As in stool pigeon, an informant who betrays the Mafia by going to the cops.

pinched:
Meaning to be arrested.

pop:
Another word for murder.

pre-hits:
Ancillary targets in a major hit. It is wise to whack the associates of a bigwig, lest they try to seek vengeance when their don is killed.

problem:
An expression for someone who has caused a problem and is worthy of being whacked.

The Program:
Shorthand for the Witness Protection Program.

put the X on:
To mark for murder. See *finger*.

put to sleep:
The Mafia probably has more euphemisms than any other organization for murder. This is another.

racket:
Any illegal business. There was the bootleg racket, gambling racket, prostitution racket, and so on.

rat:
A mobster who violates the sacred code of Omerta.

respect:
Something demanded by all Mafiosi. The Mafia brand of respect is, of course, based on fear of getting whacked.

RICO:
Passed into law in 1970, the Racketeer Influenced and Corrupt Organizations Act gives prosecutors latitude to get tougher sentences for criminals if it is proven that they are members of an organized crime family.

right arm:
See *underboss*.

rub out:
Another in the lengthy litany of Mafia synonyms for murder.

screw:
Mafia name for a prison guard.

serious headache:
Mafiosi have an ironic penchant for understatement. It means a bullet in the head.

shills:
The characters you see in a gambling situation who are winning and making it look easy. They are plants to lure in unsuspecting gamblers.

shiv:
Prison slang for a knife made of anything available.

shylock:
Another term for loan shark. Shylock is a character in William Shakespeare's play *The Merchant of Venice*.

Sicilian necktie:
Piano wire used to strangle the Mafioso's target.

sit-down:
A meeting among high-level Mafiosi to settle disputes and grievances before violence ensues.

skim:
Taking money off the top, usually from gambling profits, so it is not reported to the IRS as taxable income. One of the Mafia's biggest scams was skimming profits from Vegas casinos.

skipper:
Another name for a capo.

snitch:
Another word for someone who is revealing things he shouldn't. A snitch can be relaying information to the police or to another Mafia family.

soldier:
An infantryman in a Mafia crime family. He is a low-level member of the organization and reports to the capo.

sottocapo:
The Italian name for "underboss," the second in command in the Mafia family.

spring cleaning:
This refers to getting rid of the evidence after a crime has been committed.

stand-up guy:
Someone who is eminently trustworthy and will not "rat out" other mobsters under any circumstances.

stone killer:
An especially sadistic and ruthless professional assassin.

stoolie:
See *pigeon*.

straightened out:
To become a "made man," that is, inducted into a Mafia family.

swag:
Another word for stolen property.

take for a ride:
If you are taken for a ride, chances are you won't be coming back.

tax:
A euphemism for taking a cut of another's Mafioso's booty.

telephone solicitor:
A bookmaker, or bookie, who takes bets over the phone.

through the eye:
As in a bullet in the eye.

through the mouth:
As in a bullet in the mouth. This is a form of execution administered to turncoats and stoolies.

trunk music:
This would not be music to your ears. This is the Mafia euphemism for the decomposing flesh of a murder victim stuffed into the trunk of a car.

underboss:
Second in command in a Mafia family.

underworld:
Not the Hades of Greek mythology. This is a generic expression for the world of organized crime.

usury:
Lending money and collecting interest. It was once banned by the Catholic Church but is a common practice by your credit card company and the corner loan shark. And the interest rate is not all that's different between the two.

va fa napole:
An Italian expression that literally means "go to Naples" but is used to convey the sentiment "go to hell."

vig:
The excessive interest of a loan shark, measured in points.

walking book:
A bookmaker who does not have an office. He makes the rounds to visit his clients.

walk-talk, take a walk:
To have a discussion in a public place, such as a golf course, to avoid the possibility that listening devices might pick up the conversation.

waste management business:
A slang expression for organized crime.

whack:
To commit murder.

wise guys:
Mafiosi who are not "made men," hence not admitted to the inner sanctum.

Young Turks:
Aggressive and ambitious young Mafiosi who are a threat to the older established dons.

zips:
A term used to describe Sicilian Mafiosi operating in America. Originally a put-down, the term morphed into a catch-all term for any Italian mobster made overseas.

Mafia Timeline

1890–1891:	New Orleans police chief David Hennessy is murdered, allegedly by members of the Mafia. The subsequent trial and mob vigilantism makes international headlines.
1920:	The Volstead Act becomes law, beginning Prohibition.
1927–1931:	The Castellammarese War occurs.
1929:	St. Valentine's Day Massacre.
1930:	Bosses in Detroit, New York, Cleveland, and Chicago are murdered.
1931:	Lucky Luciano orchestrates the assassination of Masseria and Maranzano. Al Capone is sentenced to eleven years for income tax evasion.
1933:	Prohibition is repealed.
1935:	Dutch Schultz is killed.
1936:	Lucky Luciano is convicted on prostitution charges and sentenced to thirty to fifty years.
1941:	Abe Reles "falls" to his death from a Coney Island hotel window.
1944:	Louis "Lepke" Buchalter gets the electric chair.
1945:	Lucky Luciano is released from prison and deported to Italy.
1946	The Flamingo Hotel opens in Las Vegas.
1947:	Bugsy Siegel is murdered.
1950:	The Kefauver Commission takes its mob busting hearings on the road, exposing organized crime to the public.
1956:	Meetings between American and Sicilian mobsters regarding control of heroin traffic.

1957:	Frank Costello survives a botched hit. The raid on the Mafia conference on Apalachin, New York, gives the gangsters unwanted publicity. Carlo Gambino becomes the Boss of Bosses.
1959:	Fidel Castro takes control of Cuba, kicking out the American mobsters and closing their casinos.
1961:	Height of the Gallo-Profaci war in New York City
1962:	Lucky Luciano, Joe Profaci, and Philly boss Sal Sabella die.
1963:	McClellan Committee starts hearings into organized crime.
1966:	Mafia meeting at La Stella restaurant in Queens, dubbed "Little Apalachin." Bonanno family internal war.
1969:	Thomas Lucchese and Vito Genovese die.
1971:	Joe Colombo is shot at the Italian-American Unity Day he organized. He lingers in a vegetative state for years before dying.
1973:	Frank Costello dies.
1975:	Jimmy Hoffa disappears. Sam Giancana murdered.
1976:	Carlo Gambino dies and is succeeded by Paul Castellano.
1977–1978:	Intrafamily mob war in Kansas City.
1980:	Beginning of bloody Philly mob war.
1982:	Meyer Lansky dies.
1984:	Las Vegas skimming case nets Kansas City, Milwaukee, and Chicago mobsters. Beginning of end of mob control in Vegas.
1985:	Paul Castellano is killed; John Gotti takes over. The Commission case takes down the heads of the five families.
1987:	Santo Trafficante Jr. dies.
1992:	John Gotti is sentenced to life for racketeering and murder.
1995–1998:	The Mafia moves into stock scams on Wall Street, netting tens of millions.
2002:	John Gotti dies in prison. Joe Bonanno dies at age ninety-seven.
2007:	Leadership of Chicago Outfit convicted for gangland killings in Operation Family Secrets trial.
2008:	The feds arrest more than sixty members and associates of the Gambino family.

Index

THE EVERYTHING SERIES!

BUSINESS & PERSONAL FINANCE

Everything® Accounting Book
Everything® Budgeting Book, 2nd Ed.
Everything® Business Planning Book
Everything® Coaching and Mentoring Book, 2nd Ed.
Everything® Fundraising Book
Everything® Get Out of Debt Book
Everything® Grant Writing Book, 2nd Ed.
Everything® Guide to Buying Foreclosures
Everything® Guide to Fundraising, $15.95
Everything® Guide to Mortgages
Everything® Guide to Personal Finance for Single Mothers
Everything® Home-Based Business Book, 2nd Ed.
Everything® Homebuying Book, 3rd Ed., $15.95
Everything® Homeselling Book, 2nd Ed.
Everything® Human Resource Management Book
Everything® Improve Your Credit Book
Everything® Investing Book, 2nd Ed.
Everything® Landlording Book
Everything® Leadership Book, 2nd Ed.
Everything® Managing People Book, 2nd Ed.
Everything® Negotiating Book
Everything® Online Auctions Book
Everything® Online Business Book
Everything® Personal Finance Book
Everything® Personal Finance in Your 20s & 30s Book, 2nd Ed.
Everything® Personal Finance in Your 40s & 50s Book, $15.95
Everything® Project Management Book, 2nd Ed.
Everything® Real Estate Investing Book
Everything® Retirement Planning Book
Everything® Robert's Rules Book, $7.95
Everything® Selling Book
Everything® Start Your Own Business Book, 2nd Ed.
Everything® Wills & Estate Planning Book

COOKING

Everything® Barbecue Cookbook
Everything® Bartender's Book, 2nd Ed., $9.95
Everything® Calorie Counting Cookbook
Everything® Cheese Book
Everything® Chinese Cookbook
Everything® Classic Recipes Book
Everything® Cocktail Parties & Drinks Book
Everything® College Cookbook
Everything® Cooking for Baby and Toddler Book
Everything® Diabetes Cookbook
Everything® Easy Gourmet Cookbook
Everything® Fondue Cookbook
Everything® Food Allergy Cookbook, $15.95
Everything® Fondue Party Book
Everything® Gluten-Free Cookbook
Everything® Glycemic Index Cookbook
Everything® Grilling Cookbook
Everything® Healthy Cooking for Parties Book, $15.95
Everything® Holiday Cookbook
Everything® Indian Cookbook
Everything® Lactose-Free Cookbook
Everything® Low-Cholesterol Cookbook

Everything® Low-Fat High-Flavor Cookbook, 2nd Ed., $15.95
Everything® Low-Salt Cookbook
Everything® Meals for a Month Cookbook
Everything® Meals on a Budget Cookbook
Everything® Mediterranean Cookbook
Everything® Mexican Cookbook
Everything® No Trans Fat Cookbook
Everything® One-Pot Cookbook, 2nd Ed., $15.95
Everything® Organic Cooking for Baby & Toddler Book, $15.95
Everything® Pizza Cookbook
Everything® Quick Meals Cookbook, 2nd Ed., $15.95
Everything® Slow Cooker Cookbook
Everything® Slow Cooking for a Crowd Cookbook
Everything® Soup Cookbook
Everything® Stir-Fry Cookbook
Everything® Sugar-Free Cookbook
Everything® Tapas and Small Plates Cookbook
Everything® Tex-Mex Cookbook
Everything® Thai Cookbook
Everything® Vegetarian Cookbook
Everything® Whole-Grain, High-Fiber Cookbook
Everything® Wild Game Cookbook
Everything® Wine Book, 2nd Ed.

GAMES

Everything® 15-Minute Sudoku Book, $9.95
Everything® 30-Minute Sudoku Book, $9.95
Everything® Bible Crosswords Book, $9.95
Everything® Blackjack Strategy Book
Everything® Brain Strain Book, $9.95
Everything® Bridge Book
Everything® Card Games Book
Everything® Card Tricks Book, $9.95
Everything® Casino Gambling Book, 2nd Ed.
Everything® Chess Basics Book
Everything® Christmas Crosswords Book, $9.95
Everything® Craps Strategy Book
Everything® Crossword and Puzzle Book
Everything® Crosswords and Puzzles for Quote Lovers Book, $9.95
Everything® Crossword Challenge Book
Everything® Crosswords for the Beach Book, $9.95
Everything® Cryptic Crosswords Book, $9.95
Everything® Cryptograms Book, $9.95
Everything® Easy Crosswords Book
Everything® Easy Kakuro Book, $9.95
Everything® Easy Large-Print Crosswords Book
Everything® Games Book, 2nd Ed.
Everything® Giant Book of Crosswords
Everything® Giant Sudoku Book, $9.95
Everything® Giant Word Search Book
Everything® Kakuro Challenge Book, $9.95
Everything® Large-Print Crossword Challenge Book
Everything® Large-Print Crosswords Book
Everything® Large-Print Travel Crosswords Book
Everything® Lateral Thinking Puzzles Book, $9.95
Everything® Literary Crosswords Book, $9.95
Everything® Mazes Book
Everything® Memory Booster Puzzles Book, $9.95

Everything® Movie Crosswords Book, $9.95
Everything® Music Crosswords Book, $9.95
Everything® Online Poker Book
Everything® Pencil Puzzles Book, $9.95
Everything® Poker Strategy Book
Everything® Pool & Billiards Book
Everything® Puzzles for Commuters Book, $9.95
Everything® Puzzles for Dog Lovers Book, $9.95
Everything® Sports Crosswords Book, $9.95
Everything® Test Your IQ Book, $9.95
Everything® Texas Hold 'Em Book, $9.95
Everything® Travel Crosswords Book, $9.95
Everything® Travel Mazes Book, $9.95
Everything® Travel Word Search Book, $9.95
Everything® TV Crosswords Book, $9.95
Everything® Word Games Challenge Book
Everything® Word Scramble Book
Everything® Word Search Book

HEALTH

Everything® Alzheimer's Book
Everything® Diabetes Book
Everything® First Aid Book, $9.95
Everything® Green Living Book
Everything® Health Guide to Addiction and Recovery
Everything® Health Guide to Adult Bipolar Disorder
Everything® Health Guide to Arthritis
Everything® Health Guide to Controlling Anxiety
Everything® Health Guide to Depression
Everything® Health Guide to Diabetes, 2nd Ed.
Everything® Health Guide to Fibromyalgia
Everything® Health Guide to Menopause, 2nd Ed.
Everything® Health Guide to Migraines
Everything® Health Guide to Multiple Sclerosis
Everything® Health Guide to OCD
Everything® Health Guide to PMS
Everything® Health Guide to Postpartum Care
Everything® Health Guide to Thyroid Disease
Everything® Hypnosis Book
Everything® Low Cholesterol Book
Everything® Menopause Book
Everything® Nutrition Book
Everything® Reflexology Book
Everything® Stress Management Book
Everything® Superfoods Book, $15.95

HISTORY

Everything® American Government Book
Everything® American History Book, 2nd Ed.
Everything® American Revolution Book, $15.95
Everything® Civil War Book
Everything® Freemasons Book
Everything® Irish History & Heritage Book
Everything® World War II Book, 2nd Ed.

HOBBIES

Everything® Candlemaking Book
Everything® Cartooning Book
Everything® Coin Collecting Book
Everything® Digital Photography Book, 2nd Ed.

Everything® Drawing Book
Everything® Family Tree Book, 2nd Ed.
Everything® Guide to Online Genealogy, $15.95
Everything® Knitting Book
Everything® Knots Book
Everything® Photography Book
Everything® Quilting Book
Everything® Sewing Book
Everything® Soapmaking Book, 2nd Ed.
Everything® Woodworking Book

HOME IMPROVEMENT

Everything® Feng Shui Book
Everything® Feng Shui Decluttering Book, $9.95
Everything® Fix-It Book
Everything® Green Living Book
Everything® Home Decorating Book
Everything® Home Storage Solutions Book
Everything® Homebuilding Book
Everything® Organize Your Home Book, 2nd Ed.

KIDS' BOOKS

All titles are $7.95

Everything® Fairy Tales Book, $14.95
Everything® Kids' Animal Puzzle & Activity Book
Everything® Kids' Astronomy Book
Everything® Kids' Baseball Book, 5th Ed.
Everything® Kids' Bible Trivia Book
Everything® Kids' Bugs Book
Everything® Kids' Cars and Trucks Puzzle and Activity Book
Everything® Kids' Christmas Puzzle & Activity Book
Everything® Kids' Connect the Dots
    Puzzle and Activity Book
Everything® Kids' Cookbook, 2nd Ed.
Everything® Kids' Crazy Puzzles Book
Everything® Kids' Dinosaurs Book
Everything® Kids' Dragons Puzzle and Activity Book
Everything® Kids' Environment Book $7.95
Everything® Kids' Fairies Puzzle and Activity Book
Everything® Kids' First Spanish Puzzle and Activity Book
Everything® Kids' Football Book
Everything® Kids' Geography Book
Everything® Kids' Gross Cookbook
Everything® Kids' Gross Hidden Pictures Book
Everything® Kids' Gross Jokes Book
Everything® Kids' Gross Mazes Book
Everything® Kids' Gross Puzzle & Activity Book
Everything® Kids' Halloween Puzzle & Activity Book
Everything® Kids' Hanukkah Puzzle and Activity Book
Everything® Kids' Hidden Pictures Book
Everything® Kids' Horses Book
Everything® Kids' Joke Book
Everything® Kids' Knock Knock Book
Everything® Kids' Learning French Book
Everything® Kids' Learning Spanish Book
Everything® Kids' Magical Science Experiments Book
Everything® Kids' Math Puzzles Book
Everything® Kids' Mazes Book
Everything® Kids' Money Book, 2nd Ed.
Everything® Kids' Mummies, Pharaoh's, and Pyramids
    Puzzle and Activity Book
Everything® Kids' Nature Book
Everything® Kids' Pirates Puzzle and Activity Book
Everything® Kids' Presidents Book
Everything® Kids' Princess Puzzle and Activity Book
Everything® Kids' Puzzle Book

Everything® Kids' Racecars Puzzle and Activity Book
Everything® Kids' Riddles & Brain Teasers Book
Everything® Kids' Science Experiments Book
Everything® Kids' Sharks Book
Everything® Kids' Soccer Book
Everything® Kids' Spelling Book
Everything® Kids' Spies Puzzle and Activity Book
Everything® Kids' States Book
Everything® Kids' Travel Activity Book
Everything® Kids' Word Search Puzzle and Activity Book

LANGUAGE

Everything® Conversational Japanese Book with CD, $19.95
Everything® French Grammar Book
Everything® French Phrase Book, $9.95
Everything® French Verb Book, $9.95
Everything® German Phrase Book, $9.95
Everything® German Practice Book with CD, $19.95
Everything® Inglés Book
Everything® Intermediate Spanish Book with CD, $19.95
Everything® Italian Phrase Book, $9.95
Everything® Italian Practice Book with CD, $19.95
Everything® Learning Brazilian Portuguese Book with CD, $19.95
Everything® Learning French Book with CD, 2nd Ed., $19.95
Everything® Learning German Book
Everything® Learning Italian Book
Everything® Learning Latin Book
Everything® Learning Russian Book with CD, $19.95
Everything® Learning Spanish Book
Everything® Learning Spanish Book with CD, 2nd Ed., $19.95
Everything® Russian Practice Book with CD, $19.95
Everything® Sign Language Book, $15.95
Everything® Spanish Grammar Book
Everything® Spanish Phrase Book, $9.95
Everything® Spanish Practice Book with CD, $19.95
Everything® Spanish Verb Book, $9.95
Everything® Speaking Mandarin Chinese Book with CD, $19.95

MUSIC

Everything® Bass Guitar Book with CD, $19.95
Everything® Drums Book with CD, $19.95
Everything® Guitar Book with CD, 2nd Ed., $19.95
Everything® Guitar Chords Book with CD, $19.95
Everything® Guitar Scales Book with CD, $19.95
Everything® Harmonica Book with CD, $15.95
Everything® Home Recording Book
Everything® Music Theory Book with CD, $19.95
Everything® Reading Music Book with CD, $19.95
Everything® Rock & Blues Guitar Book with CD, $19.95
Everything® Rock & Blues Piano Book with CD, $19.95
Everything® Rock Drums Book with CD, $19.95
Everything® Singing Book with CD, $19.95
Everything® Songwriting Book

NEW AGE

Everything® Astrology Book, 2nd Ed.
Everything® Birthday Personology Book
Everything® Celtic Wisdom Book, $15.95
Everything® Dreams Book, 2nd Ed.
Everything® Law of Attraction Book, $15.95
Everything® Love Signs Book, $9.95
Everything® Love Spells Book, $9.95
Everything® Palmistry Book
Everything® Psychic Book
Everything® Reiki Book

Everything® Sex Signs Book, $9.95
Everything® Spells & Charms Book, 2nd Ed.
Everything® Tarot Book, 2nd Ed.
Everything® Toltec Wisdom Book
Everything® Wicca & Witchcraft Book, 2nd Ed.

PARENTING

Everything® Baby Names Book, 2nd Ed.
Everything® Baby Shower Book, 2nd Ed.
Everything® Baby Sign Language Book with DVD
Everything® Baby's First Year Book
Everything® Birthing Book
Everything® Breastfeeding Book
Everything® Father-to-Be Book
Everything® Father's First Year Book
Everything® Get Ready for Baby Book, 2nd Ed.
Everything® Get Your Baby to Sleep Book, $9.95
Everything® Getting Pregnant Book
Everything® Guide to Pregnancy Over 35
Everything® Guide to Raising a One-Year-Old
Everything® Guide to Raising a Two-Year-Old
Everything® Guide to Raising Adolescent Boys
Everything® Guide to Raising Adolescent Girls
Everything® Mother's First Year Book
Everything® Parent's Guide to Childhood Illnesses
Everything® Parent's Guide to Children and Divorce
Everything® Parent's Guide to Children with ADD/ADHD
Everything® Parent's Guide to Children with Asperger's
    Syndrome
Everything® Parent's Guide to Children with Anxiety
Everything® Parent's Guide to Children with Asthma
Everything® Parent's Guide to Children with Autism
Everything® Parent's Guide to Children with Bipolar Disorder
Everything® Parent's Guide to Children with Depression
Everything® Parent's Guide to Children with Dyslexia
Everything® Parent's Guide to Children with Juvenile Diabetes
Everything® Parent's Guide to Children with OCD
Everything® Parent's Guide to Positive Discipline
Everything® Parent's Guide to Raising Boys
Everything® Parent's Guide to Raising Girls
Everything® Parent's Guide to Raising Siblings
Everything® Parent's Guide to Raising Your
    Adopted Child
Everything® Parent's Guide to Sensory Integration Disorder
Everything® Parent's Guide to Tantrums
Everything® Parent's Guide to the Strong-Willed Child
Everything® Parenting a Teenager Book
Everything® Potty Training Book, $9.95
Everything® Pregnancy Book, 3rd Ed.
Everything® Pregnancy Fitness Book
Everything® Pregnancy Nutrition Book
Everything® Pregnancy Organizer, 2nd Ed., $16.95
Everything® Toddler Activities Book
Everything® Toddler Book
Everything® Tween Book
Everything® Twins, Triplets, and More Book

PETS

Everything® Aquarium Book
Everything® Boxer Book
Everything® Cat Book, 2nd Ed.
Everything® Chihuahua Book
Everything® Cooking for Dogs Book
Everything® Dachshund Book
Everything® Dog Book, 2nd Ed.
Everything® Dog Grooming Book

Everything® Dog Obedience Book
Everything® Dog Owner's Organizer, $16.95
Everything® Dog Training and Tricks Book
Everything® German Shepherd Book
Everything® Golden Retriever Book
Everything® Horse Book, 2nd Ed., $15.95
Everything® Horse Care Book
Everything® Horseback Riding Book
Everything® Labrador Retriever Book
Everything® Poodle Book
Everything® Pug Book
Everything® Puppy Book
Everything® Small Dogs Book
Everything® Tropical Fish Book
Everything® Yorkshire Terrier Book

REFERENCE

Everything® American Presidents Book
Everything® Blogging Book
Everything® Build Your Vocabulary Book, $9.95
Everything® Car Care Book
Everything® Classical Mythology Book
Everything® Da Vinci Book
Everything® Einstein Book
Everything® Enneagram Book
Everything® Etiquette Book, 2nd Ed.
Everything® Family Christmas Book, $15.95
Everything® Guide to C. S. Lewis & Narnia
Everything® Guide to Divorce, 2nd Ed., $15.95
Everything® Guide to Edgar Allan Poe
Everything® Guide to Understanding Philosophy
Everything® Inventions and Patents Book
Everything® Jacqueline Kennedy Onassis Book
Everything® John F. Kennedy Book
Everything® Mafia Book
Everything® Martin Luther King Jr. Book
Everything® Pirates Book
Everything® Private Investigation Book
Everything® Psychology Book
Everything® Public Speaking Book, $9.95
Everything® Shakespeare Book, 2nd Ed.

RELIGION

Everything® Angels Book
Everything® Bible Book
Everything® Bible Study Book with CD, $19.95
Everything® Buddhism Book
Everything® Catholicism Book
Everything® Christianity Book
Everything® Gnostic Gospels Book
Everything® Hinduism Book, $15.95
Everything® History of the Bible Book
Everything® Jesus Book
Everything® Jewish History & Heritage Book
Everything® Judaism Book
Everything® Kabbalah Book
Everything® Koran Book
Everything® Mary Book
Everything® Mary Magdalene Book
Everything® Prayer Book

Everything® Saints Book, 2nd Ed.
Everything® Torah Book
Everything® Understanding Islam Book
Everything® Women of the Bible Book
Everything® World's Religions Book

SCHOOL & CAREERS

Everything® Career Tests Book
Everything® College Major Test Book
Everything® College Survival Book, 2nd Ed.
Everything® Cover Letter Book, 2nd Ed.
Everything® Filmmaking Book
Everything® Get-a-Job Book, 2nd Ed.
Everything® Guide to Being a Paralegal
Everything® Guide to Being a Personal Trainer
Everything® Guide to Being a Real Estate Agent
Everything® Guide to Being a Sales Rep
Everything® Guide to Being an Event Planner
Everything® Guide to Careers in Health Care
Everything® Guide to Careers in Law Enforcement
Everything® Guide to Government Jobs
Everything® Guide to Starting and Running a Catering Business
Everything® Guide to Starting and Running a Restaurant
Everything® Guide to Starting and Running a Retail Store
Everything® Job Interview Book, 2nd Ed.
Everything® New Nurse Book
Everything® New Teacher Book
Everything® Paying for College Book
Everything® Practice Interview Book
Everything® Resume Book, 3rd Ed.
Everything® Study Book

SELF-HELP

Everything® Body Language Book
Everything® Dating Book, 2nd Ed.
Everything® Great Sex Book
Everything® Guide to Caring for Aging Parents, $15.95
Everything® Self-Esteem Book
Everything® Self-Hypnosis Book, $9.95
Everything® Tantric Sex Book

SPORTS & FITNESS

Everything® Easy Fitness Book
Everything® Fishing Book
Everything® Guide to Weight Training, $15.95
Everything® Krav Maga for Fitness Book
Everything® Running Book, 2nd Ed.
Everything® Triathlon Training Book, $15.95

TRAVEL

Everything® Family Guide to Coastal Florida
Everything® Family Guide to Cruise Vacations
Everything® Family Guide to Hawaii
Everything® Family Guide to Las Vegas, 2nd Ed.
Everything® Family Guide to Mexico
Everything® Family Guide to New England, 2nd Ed.

Everything® Family Guide to New York City, 3rd Ed.
Everything® Family Guide to Northern California and Lake Tahoe
Everything® Family Guide to RV Travel & Campgrounds
Everything® Family Guide to the Caribbean
Everything® Family Guide to the Disneyland® Resort, California Adventure®, Universal Studios®, and the Anaheim Area, 2nd Ed.
Everything® Family Guide to the Walt Disney World Resort®, Universal Studios®, and Greater Orlando, 5th Ed.
Everything® Family Guide to Timeshares
Everything® Family Guide to Washington D.C., 2nd Ed.

WEDDINGS

Everything® Bachelorette Party Book, $9.95
Everything® Bridesmaid Book, $9.95
Everything® Destination Wedding Book
Everything® Father of the Bride Book, $9.95
Everything® Green Wedding Book, $15.95
Everything® Groom Book, $9.95
Everything® Jewish Wedding Book, 2nd Ed., $15.95
Everything® Mother of the Bride Book, $9.95
Everything® Outdoor Wedding Book
Everything® Wedding Book, 3rd Ed.
Everything® Wedding Checklist, $9.95
Everything® Wedding Etiquette Book, $9.95
Everything® Wedding Organizer, 2nd Ed., $16.95
Everything® Wedding Shower Book, $9.95
Everything® Wedding Vows Book, 3rd Ed., $9.95
Everything® Wedding Workout Book
Everything® Weddings on a Budget Book, 2nd Ed., $9.95

WRITING

Everything® Creative Writing Book
Everything® Get Published Book, 2nd Ed.
Everything® Grammar and Style Book, 2nd Ed.
Everything® Guide to Magazine Writing
Everything® Guide to Writing a Book Proposal
Everything® Guide to Writing a Novel
Everything® Guide to Writing Children's Books
Everything® Guide to Writing Copy
Everything® Guide to Writing Graphic Novels
Everything® Guide to Writing Research Papers
Everything® Guide to Writing a Romance Novel, $15.95
Everything® Improve Your Writing Book, 2nd Ed.
Everything® Writing Poetry Book